THE BIBLE ON LOCATION

This book was published with
the generous support of IGT
Israel and Ayelet Tours.

THE BIBLE

UNIVERSITY OF NEBRASKA PRESS | LINCOLN

Julie Baretz

ON LOCATION

OFF THE BEATEN PATH IN
ANCIENT AND MODERN ISRAEL

THE JEWISH PUBLICATION SOCIETY | PHILADELPHIA

All rights reserved. Published by the University of Nebraska
Press as a Jewish Publication Society book.
Manufactured in Korea. ⊗

Bible texts are reprinted from *JPS Tanakh: The Holy
Scriptures* by permission of the publisher. Copyright © 1985
by the Jewish Publication Society, Philadelphia.

Photos are by the author, unless otherwise stated.
Maps by Soffer Mapping.

Library of Congress Cataloging-in-Publication Data
Baretz, Julie.
The Bible on location: off the beaten path in ancient and
modern Israel / Julie Baretz.
pages   cm
Includes bibliographical references.
ISBN 978-0-8276-1222-8 (pbk.: alk. paper)
ISBN 978-0-8276-1190-0 (epub)
ISBN 978-0-8276-1191-7 (mobi)
ISBN 978-0-8276-1189-4 (pdf)
1. Bible stories, English—Old Testament.
2. Bible—Geography. 3. Palestine—Description
and travel. 4. Israel—Description and travel. I. Title.
BS550.3.B37 2015
221.9'1—dc23
2014035524

Set in Lyon Text by Lindsey Auten.
Designed by A. Shahan.

For my parents,
Carol Baretz and Roger Baretz (z"l)

CONTENTS

ILLUSTRATIONS

MAPS

ACKNOWLEDGMENTS

Many thanks are in order for the support and encouragement I received throughout the stages of this book's conception:

To Rabbi Peretz Rodman for inspiration in the genesis of this project;

To Rabbi Barry Schwartz of the Jewish Publication Society for his vote of confidence and gentle guidance, and to Carol Hupping, also at JPS, for her reassuring hand on my back;

To Rabbi Susan Rheins and Rabbi Norman Cohen for their enthusiasm and encouragement at a critical juncture;

To Benny Sivan, Diane Rubtchinsky, Jeff Rubtchinsky, Seffie Epstein, and Maranatha Tours, Phoenix, for their generosity in helping me fulfill the book's greater potential;

To Professor Yaira Amit, the scientific advisor for this project, for her wisdom and friendship. Her exacting standards enabled me to refine the manuscript to a level I could never have reached on my own. It was a joy and privilege to learn with her;

To Rutie Yudkowitz, Laura Nelson-Levy, Sara Cohen, Dan Schoenfeld, Naomi Rockowitz, Randy Myers, Linda Myers, Frances Oppenheimer, Steve Langfur, Diana Lipton, and Gali Fleischer for their insights, suggestions, advice, and cheerleading;

To Danny Chamowitz and Miriam Feinberg for their august advice on the world of publishing;

To the libraries at Hebrew Union College, the National Library, Hebrew University, Yad Ben Zvi, and the Israel Museum;

To the Jewish Publication Society for permission to use its English translation of the Bible;

To my husband, Benny, for all the kinds of support ever invented.

Do you know anyone named Debbie? Josh? David? Everyone recognizes those names from the Bible, but how much do we really know about the characters from one of the greatest works of literature ever written? The Hebrew Bible is an anthology of thirty-nine texts. While most people are familiar with the Genesis stories and the Exodus narrative, the books that chronicle the Israelites after they arrive in the promised land are often far less familiar and infrequently read. Yet they contain a captivating array of complex characters faced with social, ethical, and spiritual dilemmas.

This is an unconventional guidebook. Rather than point you toward recognizable landmarks, it leads you in the footsteps of fascinating literary characters. In Israel little remains of monumental buildings and cities from the time of the Hebrew Bible, but the landscape is virtually unaltered.

The stories in this guidebook come from the biblical books of Joshua, Judges, Ruth, 1 Samuel, 2 Samuel, 1 Kings, 2 Kings, Ezra, and Nehemiah. In contrast to the Torah (Genesis, Exodus, Leviticus, Numbers, and Deuteronomy), which we read cyclically in the Jewish tradition every year, the books that follow chronologically are often ignored, apart from selected readings as the *haftarot*. These nine biblical books form the outline of this guidebook because all their action takes place in the land of Israel, and almost all the locations mentioned in the narrative have been identified.

Did the events of the Bible really happen? The development of biblical scholarship as an academic discipline has enabled us to dig deeply into the text in search of linguistic clues, cultural patterns, and nuance. The modern science of archaeology has enriched our knowledge of the biblical period immensely—sometimes correlating, sometimes illuminating, and sometimes challenging the historical authenticity of the stories.

Yet despite the wealth of knowledge accrued in the modern age, the Bible still remains something of an enigma. It is written in an ancient Hebrew dialect no longer spoken. Letters and words are missing throughout the Hebrew text. The interpretation of a word can change the meaning of an entire sentence. The abbreviated storytelling style can be puzzling. All this means that the text is interpretable by anyone who chooses to read it.

But oddly enough, many Jews don't read the Bible. Classic Jewish scholarship concentrates on the Talmud, the rabbinic literature that interprets the biblical laws. Zionism reserves a place of honor for the Bible in the Israeli educational curriculum, but nonreligious Jews educated in the diaspora rarely crack the good book's spine in a methodical, studious fashion. I am a classic example. My Jewish upbringing was buttressed by membership in a Conservative synagogue, bat mitzvah, Camp Ramah, and the Zionist youth movement Young Judaea. The Jewish bookshelf in my home included tomes such as *The Joys of Yiddish*, *My Life* by Golda Meir, and *The War against the Jews* by Lucy Dawidowicz. The Bible wasn't anywhere on the shelf—it wasn't even on the radar.

The impetus for my Bible studies was embarrassment. Close to 70 percent of the tourists who visit Israel are Christians—bread and butter for Jewish tour guides. Early on in my guiding career, I found myself standing before groups of evangelical Christians who knew the Hebrew Bible inside and out. Most had read the Bible in its entirety several times, many were members of church Bible study groups, many could recite text passages by heart, and they all wanted to visit the places where the events of the Bible had transpired. In order to get up to speed (and not look like an idiot), I spent hours poring over texts and marking up my travel-sized Bible. Ultimately I was able to whip out passages on site and refer to people and places with ease. Eventually I began reading these stories with Jewish groups too, who always clamored for more

However, I soon felt I was shortchanging people by simply reading the stories and not commenting on them. In order to expound I had to study the texts methodically, a challenge I embraced eagerly as a BA in English literature and an MA in creative writing. Jerusalem is probably the easiest place in the world to find a Bible teacher, so I got myself a rabbi, and together we began to read, comment, analyze, and deconstruct the historical books whose events took place in the land of Israel. I was intrigued by the complexity of the characters, the ethical dilemmas they often faced, and the uncanny parallels between them and many contemporary leaders. Early in the study process I already knew that I wanted to share what I had learned by writing a book.

Ultimately, I chose twenty compelling stories from the post-Torah books that frame the events and the geography of ancient Israel from the conquest of the promised land until the return from exile. I have approached the Bible first and foremost as a work of literature, and not from a faith perspective. The commentary on the stories reflects my fascination, wonder, and frustration as I attempt to find meaning and relevance in this often perplexing tome. My subjective understanding, however, comes from a place of deep love and respect for the Bible and for Israel.

My role as tour guide is not spiritual; it's up to the pastors and rabbis to provide guidance and commentary on issues of faith. When I read a Bible story on site, my task is to provide the context and make the story come alive using history, archaeology, modern scholarship, and literary analysis. In my commentary I have relied heavily on the academic literature written by modern Bible scholars in an attempt to find the middle ground between those who read the Bible as an uncontested factual document and those who read it as a dubious historical account. However, I have also drawn frequently from midrash, the rabbinic folk literature, to help illuminate the texts. These commentaries range from the colorful to the outlandish, and while not historically based they have been used for centuries to teach the Bible and have deeply influenced our traditional understanding of biblical narratives.

So where do we start? The Bible attempts to portray an ancient historical reality. However, a wealth of evidence from textual analysis, extrabiblical sources, and archaeology indicate that it is not an objective historical document. In fact, it is unabashedly subjective, compiled by writers and editors spanning centuries of revision who had a clear message to impart. They interpreted the events described through the prism of their theological worldview, which, in its simplest form, was based on the idea that the people of Israel signed a covenant with God and were bound to abide by it.

From a literary point of view, this is a perfect set-up for imminent conflict, the heart of any good story. The authors, however, were determined to tell it on their terms. One of the most intriguing challenges in reading the Bible is attempting to figure out what the writers *haven't* told us. Readers have been trying to crack this nut for centuries, and anyone can give it a shot, regardless of religion, spiritual inclination, or experience.

This guidebook sets out to accomplish two goals:

The first is to put you in the landscape where it is told the action transpired. Reading a Bible story on location imbues it with a new dimension, and this book leads you to the sites where the stories unfolded, most of which are off the beaten track. In the appendix you will find detailed instructions for walking or driving to all the sites visited in this book. Sites located in rural areas can be found either by setting your GPS to the key location words or by using a map. Sites in and around the Old City of Jerusalem are more easily reached by taxi, public transportation, or on foot. Shade is often hard to find, so be sure to set out equipped with hats and water. Remember that reading out loud takes far longer than reading silently. Allow yourself plenty of time on site if you plan to share the commentary out loud with others. You may wish to familiarize yourself with a story by reading it the night before your visit.

Israel is brimming with exciting sites that span the timeline. In the sections titled "Make It a Day," you will find suggestions for additional locations of historical, cultural, and geographic interest in the vicinities of the Bible sites.

The second goal is actually attainable from the comfort of your living-room couch, without ever visiting Israel. While each of the twenty stories discussed in the guidebook stands on its own and may be read independently of one another, together they trace the chronology and the narrative arc of the biblical action. This trajectory begins with the Israelites' arrival in the land (following the exodus from Egypt and the forty years of wandering) and continues over more than six hundred years, until the Babylonian destruction of the temple and the eventual return of the exiles to the land. By reading the guidebook from beginning to end, one chapter at a time, a rich, complex picture of the post-Torah biblical period and its most prominent characters and events emerges.

Each chapter is preceded by a short historical introduction that explains the context of the events, so even if it's the first Bible story you've ever read you will grasp the bigger picture. The backstory is followed by the text. These stories were meant to be told orally, so don't be ashamed to read them out loud. People won't think you're loony—they'll probably come closer because they'll want to hear the story too (and they might even offer a few comments of their own). The text is followed by a short commentary that attempts to decipher what's between the lines of the narrative and to suggest food for thought. (References to biblical and extrabiblical sources are noted in the text; see the key to abbreviations at the beginning of the book.)

Behind this adventure is an attempt to rediscover perhaps the most influential work of literature ever written. Once a story becomes accessible, its layers of relevance begin to reveal themselves.

Many years of experience in guiding have convinced me that stories are gifts. While information is often quickly forgotten, tales of human endeavor reach and rest in a deeper place in the mind. When you lace up your walking shoes, decipher the map, and settle onto the cool rocks in the shade of tree to read a story, it becomes yours forever.

ABBREVIATIONS

b. *Babylonian version of Talmudic tractates*
1 Chron. 1 Chronicles
2 Chron. 2 Chronicles
Deut. Deuteronomy
Exod. Exodus
Ezek. Ezekiel
Gen. Genesis
Hag. Haggai
Isa. Isaiah
Jer. Jeremiah
Josh. Joshua
Judg. Judges
Lev. Leviticus
Mal. Malachi
Neh. Nehemiah
Num. Numbers
Ps(s). Psalms
1 Sam. 1 Samuel
2 Sam. 2 Samuel
Sif. *Sifre*
TJ *Targum Jonathan*
v. verse
YD Yoreh Deah
Zech. Zechariah

TIME LINE

	1240	1200	1020
Joshua	JOSHUA		
Deborah, Gideon, Samson, Ruth, the Levite and His Concubine		JUDGES	
Saul, David			1 SAMUEL
David, Bathsheba, Amnon, Tamar, Absalom			
Solomon, Jereboam, Elijah, Ahab, Jezebel, Naboth			
Elijah, Elisha, Hezekiah, Zedekiah			
Ezra, Nehemiah			

MAIN CHARACTERS

BOOK OF THE BIBLE

Cross-references from extrabiblical sources have made it possible

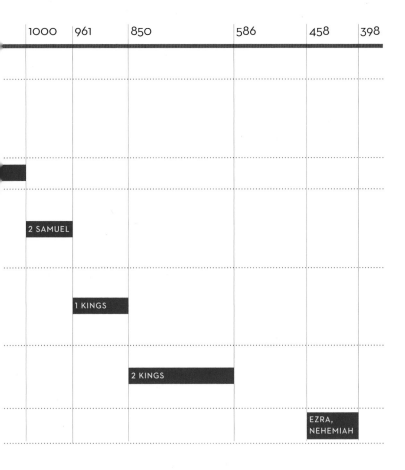

1000	961	850	586	458	398

2 SAMUEL

1 KINGS

2 KINGS

EZRA,
NEHEMIAH

to pinpoint dates from the monarchy onward. All dates are approximate.

Map 1. Sites visited in *The Bible on Location*

Rahab at Jericho

Joshua 2:1–23; 6:21–25

A Canaanite prostitute aids and encourages the Israelite spies

See page 311 for visitor information.

WHERE ARE WE?

Vered Yericho lies in the Jordan Valley area of the West Bank. It is a secular cooperative village founded in 1980 with a population of about fifty families. Most are engaged in tourism, agriculture, and small businesses.

SETTING THE SCENE

Looking eastward, in the distance you can see the mountains of Moab, today Jordan. Although difficult to pinpoint from here, one of those mountains is Nebo, whose summit was Moses's lookout into the promised land after the forty-year sojourn in the wilderness (Deut. 34:1–5). The Jordan River lies just below; we will descend to the banks of the river at the next stop.

Looking northward to the left, you can see the present-day city of Jericho sprawled below. An oasis, Jericho's lush surroundings are fed by the spring of Elisha (Ein es-Sultan), a freshwater spring with an average capacity of fifty gallons of water per second. The abundant water source, rich alluvial soil, and its strategic location on the ancient trade routes have made Jericho a desirable place to settle since antiquity.

Fig. 1. The Jordan River at Qasr el Yehud baptism site

Home to the remains of the oldest city on the world (ten thousand years old), today Jericho is a Palestinian municipality numbering over twenty thousand inhabitants. Tel Jericho, the site of the ancient settlement, is the small brown mound to the right of the foot of the hill.

THE CONTEXT

The book of Joshua is part of a larger unit within the biblical anthology known as the Deuteronomistic history, which was inspired by the ideas of the book of Deuteronomy and was probably penned in the seventh–sixth centuries BCE. The objective of the authors and editors was to tell the story of the people of Israel from the moment they stood poised to enter the promised land after forty years of wandering in the wilderness, until they were banished into exile over six hundred years later.

The Deuteronomistic history kicks off with Deuteronomy, when Moses, in his final act as leader, delivers his last long speech to the people of Israel. He reviews their experiences together, reiterates the laws by which they have agreed to abide, and exhorts them to remain faithful to their God. The central idea of Deuteronomy, at the heart of its history, is the importance of the covenant between the Israelites and God. The books that follow—Joshua, Judges, 1 and 2 Samuel, 1 and 2 Kings—recount the ups and downs in this unique relationship as the Israelites take possession of the land, adapt to an agricultural lifestyle, fend off their enemies, establish a monarchy, and violate the covenant again and again. The story culminates with the destruction of Solomon's temple and Jerusalem and the forced exile of the Jewish people from the land.

An important theme in this context is the threat inherent in contact with the indigenous Canaanite population, which worshipped foreign gods. It was clear from the get-go that the Israelites would have a hard time resisting the temptation to mingle with their gentile neighbors. As they prepared to take possession of the land, Moses specifically commanded them to have no pity on the locals and to destroy all the peoples there in a sweeping injunction known in Hebrew as a *herem* (e.g., Deut. 7:1–2).

After Moses completed his instructive orations, he climbed up to the summit of Mount Nebo to view the promised land from afar as his last act. Following his death, the baton of leadership passed to Joshua, son of Nun, whose task was to lead the people of Israel on the next leg of their odyssey (Josh. 1:1–9). In the beginning of the book of Joshua, we meet the Israelites as they make ready to cross over the Jordan River and enter the land (Josh. 1–5).

In an unmistakable echo of the Exodus story, just as Moses led the Israelites through the parted waters of the

Red Sea forty years earlier (Exod.14), Joshua leads them across the waters of the Jordan River (Josh. 3–4). Just as Moses sent a squadron of men to spy in the land (Num. 13), Joshua dispatches two scouts to gather intelligence on the region of Jericho, the first city they will encounter after they cross the river. However, while Moses's spies spent forty days hiking the width and breadth of the land, closely examining the terrain, Joshua's spies embark on a completely different experience.

The first place they land is in a brothel.

- -

Joshua 2

[1]Joshua son of Nun secretly sent two spies from Shittim, saying, "Go, reconnoiter the region of Jericho." So they set out, and they came to the house of a harlot named Rahab and lodged there. [2]The king of Jericho was told, "Some men have come here tonight, Israelites, to spy out the country." [3]The king of Jericho thereupon sent orders to Rahab: "Produce the men who came to you and entered your house, for they have come to spy out the whole country." [4]The woman, however, had taken the two men and hidden them. "It is true," she said, "the men did come to me, but I didn't know where they were from. [5]And at dark, when the gate was about to be closed, the men left; and I don't know where the men went. Quick, go after them, for you can overtake them."—[6]Now she had taken them up to the roof and hidden them under some stalks of flax which she had lying on the roof.—[7]So the men pursued them in the direction of the Jordan down to the fords; and no sooner had the pursuers gone out than the gate was shut behind them.

[8]The spies had not yet gone to sleep when she came up to them on the roof. [9]She said to the men, "I know that the LORD has given the country to you, because dread of you

has fallen upon us, and all the inhabitants of the land are quaking before you. ¹⁰For we have heard how the LORD dried up the waters of the Sea of Reeds for you when you left Egypt, and what you did to Sihon and Og, the two Amorite kings across the Jordan, whom you doomed. ¹¹When we heard about it, we lost heart, and no man had any more spirit left because of you; for the LORD your God is the only God in heaven above and on earth below. ¹²Now, since I have shown loyalty to you, swear to me by the LORD that you in turn will show loyalty to my family. Provide me with a reliable sign ¹³that you will spare the lives of my father and mother, my brothers and sisters, and all who belong to them, and save us from death." ¹⁴The men answered her, "Our persons are pledged for yours, even to death! If you do not disclose this mission of ours, we will show you true loyalty when the LORD gives us the land."

¹⁵She let them down by a rope through the window—for her dwelling was at the outer side of the city wall and she lived in the actual wall. ¹⁶She said to them, "Make for the hills, so that the pursuers may not come upon you. Stay there in hiding three days, until the pursuers return; then go your way."

¹⁷But the men warned her, "We will be released from this oath which you have made us take ¹⁸[unless,] when we invade the country, you tie this length of crimson cord to the window through which you let us down. Bring your father, your mother, your brothers, and all your family together in your house; ¹⁹and if anyone ventures outside the doors of your house, his blood will be on his head, and we shall be clear. But if a hand is laid on anyone who remains in the house with you, his blood shall be on our heads. ²⁰And if you disclose this mission of ours, we shall likewise be released from the oath which you made us take." ²¹She replied, "Let it be as you say."

She sent them on their way, and they left; and she tied the crimson cord to the window.

²²They went straight to the hills and stayed there three days, until the pursuers turned back. And so the pursuers, searching all along the road, did not find them.

²³Then the two men came down again from the hills and crossed over. They came to Joshua son of Nun and reported to him all that had happened to them. ²⁴They said to Joshua, "The LORD has delivered the whole land into our power; in fact, all the inhabitants of the land are quaking before us."

6

²¹They exterminated everything in the city with the sword: man and woman, young and old, ox and sheep and ass. ²²But Joshua bade the two men who had spied out the land, "Go into the harlot's house and bring out the woman and all that belong to her, as you swore to her." ²³So the young spies went in and brought out Rahab, her father and her mother, her brothers and all that belonged to her—they brought out her whole family and left them outside the camp of Israel.

²⁴They burned down the city and everything in it. But the silver and gold and the objects of copper and iron were deposited in the treasury of the House of the LORD. ²⁵Only Rahab the harlot and her father's family were spared by Joshua, along with all that belonged to her, and she dwelt among the Israelites—as is still the case. For she had hidden the messengers that Joshua sent to spy out Jericho.

PRETTY WOMAN

The account of the battle of Jericho comes shortly before this story in chapter 6, when the walls of the city come famously tumbling down. The archaeological excavations at Jericho have not, as yet, yielded evidence to support the biblical account of the city's destruction. It seems that Jericho was deserted at the time of the Israelite conquest and probably had been abandoned more than four hundred years earlier. At most, a small settlement existed there, patched together from the salvageable ruins and probably ruled over by an insignificant king. However, in our story Jericho, the first city conquered by the Israelites, has enormous symbolic significance as proof of the guiding power of the Israelite God. Likewise, Rahab the Canaanite also has great symbolic importance; ultimately, she and her family will be adopted into the nation of Israel.

It's hard not to wonder how this harlot found her way into the narrative. Why would the honorable biblical editors choose to introduce a prostitute, the quintessential prototype of a depraved native, right at the beginning of the glorious story of the holy conquest?

The ancient rabbis clearly felt uncomfortable with the term "prostitute," and in early translations of the Bible into the vernacular Aramaic they referred to Rahab as a "supplier of provisions." When used in the feminine, and with a wink, the euphemism was understood by everyone. (When the Rahab text is taught today in Israeli elementary schools, Rahab is still called a supplier of provisions, but without the wink.)

Still, the problematic character of Rahab the hussy was nonetheless warmly embraced in the rabbinic literature because of her contribution to the Israelite victory. Her aiding and encouragement of the Israelite spies was a vote of confidence in God from a previously unenlightened foreigner. When she declared her faith in the Israelite deity, she transformed herself from the lowliest idolater to the ideal proselyte, a fallen woman who has seen the light.

Liberated by Rahab's complete moral makeover, in the midrash, the rabbinic folk literature, the sages really let loose in their discussion of the formerly licentious woman. First, they slam her: she became a harlot at age ten and worked until she was fifty years old (*Zevahim* 116b). She had an entrance to her establishment outside the walls for the convenience of her clients, which included thieves (*Pesikta Rabbati* p. 40:3) She had relations with every prince and ruler, and her talents were bought by everyone. Her name was a byword for lewdness (*b. Zevahim* 116b). Shhh . . . they even admit that simply to mention Rahab's name was to risk having an involuntary seminal emission! (*b. Megillah* 15a).

After rollicking in the mud bath of Rahab's earlier depravity, the sages clean her up very nicely. They note that the former lady of ill repute was one of the most beautiful women in the world (*Megillah* 15a). She was a model convert and even a kind of prophetess (*Deuteronomy Rabbah* 2:26–27). Two hundred of Rahab's relatives survived the Jericho onslaught thanks to her, and her family and her descendants are the subject of in-depth discussion. She eventually married Joshua (don't miss the movie, starring Richard Gere and Julia Roberts), and among her progeny were eight prophet/priests, including Jeremiah and Hulda (*Sifrei* on Numbers 78 et al.). The midrash notes that the Divine Spirit rested on Rahab when she stood up for Israel (*Ruth Rabbah* m1,1), and that rather than being called by God, she choose the faith of Israel by her own free will (*Exodus Rabbah* 27:2, p. 48b). Her transformation from harlot to shining moral example was complete.

CHOOSE YOUR ENEMIES

If Rahab experienced a religious epiphany, then it is easy to understand why she cooperated with the spies. However, if we attempt to deconstruct her as a real-life character acting within the reality of her time and circumstances, then we have to wonder about her motives. Why would a local Canaanite woman sell out her people to an invading enemy? Why would she cut a deal to save her family, but no one else? Two hypotheses emerge.

News of the exploits of the Israelites and their God had reached Canaan by wandering nomads before the twelve tribes' arrival. As Rahab described it, the Canaanites were quaking in their boots just thinking about what would happen to them once the actual invasion began. Rahab may have coldly calculated that militarily, the locals had no chance against the Israelite army. She may have decided to help the spies after plainly considering the options and concluding, if you can't beat 'em, join 'em.

Another possible explanation for Rahab's betrayal of her own people may lie in the feudal nature of ancient Canaanite society. City-states like Jericho typically comprised two sectors: the royalty and the upper class, who owned all the land, and the peasantry, who worked it. We may assume that there was no love lost between the two. In fact, there was often deep animosity between the privileged class and the poor. When the invading Israelites appeared on the scene, the local Canaanites were forced to choose their loyalties. While the kings of the city-states naturally resisted the invaders, many of the people of the lower class may have opted to throw their lot in with the Israelites. It is certainly possible that Rahab, a woman who lived on the margins of society, felt she had nothing to lose by turning her back on the local aristocracy and joining forces with the foreign attackers.

WE ARE FAMILY

Yet other considerations quietly surface when we contemplate Rahab's social role. Let's remember that the Bible was written from a male perspective, for a male audience; anything relating to sexual matters was to be understood from the male point of view. In ancient times prostitution was considered a necessary evil. The laws against fornication, or extramarital relations, applied mainly to married women, who were considered the exclusive sexual property of their husbands. Since the unmarried ladies who plied the trade profaned no man's honor, technically they weren't doing anything illegal. The professional gals enabled the men of ancient patriarchal society to jealously guard their women's chastity, and at the same time get a few thrills on the side whenever the need arose. References to prostitutes are scattered throughout the biblical text (Jephthah's mom was one [Judg.11:1]; Samson visited one in Gaza [Judg.16:1]), indicating that they were a tolerated part of the landscape, albeit strongly stigmatized. (In an echo of the biblical toleration of prostitution as a necessary evil, modern Israel has adopted a fairly lenient attitude toward women who choose to sell their bodies. Prostitution is not a criminal offense, but brothels, pimping, and advertising sexual services are all illegal.)

For a prostitute Rahab receives fairly positive treatment from the biblical author. While we know what she does for a living, we're given to understand that she is a smart, resourceful woman who acts coolly and confidently in a time of crisis. She knows where to hide the intruders, she lies artfully to the king, and she cunningly plans the spies' getaway. From the Israelite perspective, she's the classic whore with a heart of gold, and we're led to believe that beneath her coarse exterior lies one tough cookie.

Rahab's gumption notwithstanding, it's reasonable to assume that, like most women forced to sell their bodies, she did not choose to be a prostitute. The midrash mentions that Rahab went out into the streets at age ten. While this is not a reliable historical source, it's reasonable to surmise that under any circumstances, Rahab most probably did not grow up in a loving, supportive family.

Modern research on women who practice the oldest profession in the world reveals that the overwhelming majority of young women who go into prostitution have been sexually, physically, and emotionally abused by family members. They flee the home environment with low self-esteem, a negative self-image, and a sense of deep isolation. Most of them have never experienced parental love or affection.

It seems highly unlikely that smart and sassy Rahab bore no scars from her troubled personal history. Yet when she named her conditions to the Israelite spies, she bargained not only for her own life but for the safety of all the members of her family—father and mother, brothers and sisters, and all who belonged to them. When we pause to consider what a damaged human being Rahab probably was, it's easier to understand her motivation for the betrayal of her fellow Canaanites. A woman who has been ostracized her whole life suddenly is presented with an opportunity to become the savior of her family. By joining forces with the Israelites, Rahab transformed herself from a despised, degraded woman into a heroine.

Indeed, the story of the conquest of Jericho relates that Rahab and her family were the only living creatures allowed to leave the city before the Israelites obliterated it. However, despite Rahab's important contribution to the victory, she and her Canaanite family were not warmly welcomed into the Israelite circle at first. Instead, they were left on the edge of the camp and treated like outsiders (Josh. 6:23). As they encountered the exclusionary treatment on the part of the Israelites, Rahab and her clan—we may assume—stuck to their guns. They explained, again and again, the unshaking belief of their matriarch in the God of Israel and the role she played in the Israelite victory until, despite their pagan roots, within a short time they were assimilated into Israelite society (Josh. 6:25), and the story of Rahab the prostitute became part of the larger history of the people of Israel.

2

Joshua in the Valley of Aijalon

Joshua 10:1–15

The solar system is manipulated at a critical moment in battle

See page 316 for visitor information.

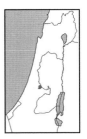

WHERE ARE WE?

We are standing on a hilltop overlooking the Valley of Aijalon (pronounced Ayalone). This hilltop was the site of a Crusader fortress called Le toron des chevaliers (the Castle of the Knights), locally known as Latrun. Built during the twelfth century CE, its ruins are visible all around us. During and after Israel's War of Independence in 1948, this hill served the Jordanian army as a lookout point over the strategic Aijalon Valley until the Six-Day War in 1967. Its guard post and trenches are still extant all over the hilltop. The Latrun monastery below was established by Trappist monks in 1890. Many of the vineyards visible in the Aijalon Valley belong to the monastery, and the wine it produces is for sale at the small shop at the entrance.

Below you lies the picturesque expanse of the Valley of Aijalon. On the far left (south) is Neve Shalom, a village founded together by Jews and Arabs to serve as a model for coexistence. The village directly in front of us and toward the right is Kfar Bin Nun, a moshav founded in 1952 by Romanian immigrants and named for the military operation (inspired by Joshua son of Nun) that attempted to break through the road to Jerusalem in May 1948. In the distance you can see the two towers of the Nesher cement factory and the adjacent towns of Ramle and Lod. Beyond them further west are the high rises of Tel Aviv. Further to the right, slightly out of view, are Mini Israel and the Museum of the Israel Defense Forces (IDF) Armored Corps.

SETTING THE SCENE

The Valley of Aijalon lies in the geographic area of Israel known as the Shphelah, or lowlands. This area sits between the coastal plain and its ancient highway to the west, and the Judaean hills to the east. In the past the Valley of Aijalon was a strategic passageway for invaders seeking to access the Israelite villages in the highlands. After the Israelite settlement it became the dividing line between the southern tribes of Judah and Simon and the northern tribes of Benjamin, Ephraim, Manasseh, and the others.

THE CONTEXT

The Bible tells us that Joshua and the Israelite tribes crossed the Jordan River, invading the land of Canaan from the east. They established the camp of Gilgal near Jericho, a city with an abundant water source that they wisely pinpointed as their bridgehead. From Jericho they penetrated westward to the city of Ai, into the hills (Josh. 1–8:29). Their goal was to reach the spine of the central highlands, a natural stronghold and key to the control of the territory of Canaan.

As related in Joshua 9:1–3, news of the trouncing defeat at Jericho and Ai spread quickly throughout Canaan. The Israelites were soon approached by a delegation claiming to hail from a far-off country requesting a treaty. Joshua and the men of Israel agreed, but after signing the pact they found that they had been duped. The petitioners who had craftily disguised themselves as dusty travelers com-

Fig. 2. The Valley of Aijalon

ing from afar, with moldy bread and ragged sacks, were actually Gibeonites, the residents of four cities in the central highlands (Josh. 9:3–10:15).

The artful Gibeonites were, as it turns out, well informed regarding the *herem*, the Israelites' merciless intention to eradicate the land of its indigenous inhabitants (Deut. 20:10–18). Masquerading as foreigners enabled them to seek protection, albeit duplicitously, from the invincible invaders. Although the Israelites were incensed at the deception, they could not revoke the treaty—in the world of the Bible, an oath was an oath.

When the five Amorite kings, also from the central highland area, heard that their formidable neighbors the Gibeonites had defected to the enemy, they launched an attack on the city of Gibeon. The Gibeonites relayed a frantic message to Joshua imploring him to come to their rescue. The Israelite army was camped at Gilgal, on the western edge of the Jordan River, about thirty kilometers (eighteen and a half miles) from Gibeon. The Israelite forces set out immediately, marching all through the night under cover of darkness. They probably ascended via the canyon of Wadi Kelt, replete with natural springs, until they reached the besieged city, nestled in a valley surrounded by hills.

- -

Joshua 10

¹When King Adoni-zedek of Jerusalem learned that Joshua had captured Ai and proscribed it, treating Ai and its king as he had treated Jericho and its king, and that, moreover, the people of Gibeon had come to terms with Israel and remained among them, ²he was very frightened. For Gibeon was a large city, like one of the royal cities—in fact, larger than Ai—and all its men were warriors. ³So King Adoni-zedek of Jerusalem sent this message to King Hoham of Hebron, King Piram of Jarmuth, King Japhia of Lachish, and King Debir of Eglon: ⁴"Come up and help me defeat Gibeon; for it has come to terms with Joshua and the Israelites."

⁵The five Amorite kings—the king of Jerusalem, the king of Hebron, the king of Jarmuth, the king of Lachish, and the king of Eglon, with all their armies—joined forces and marched on Gibeon, and encamped against it and attacked it. ⁶The people of Gibeon thereupon sent this message to Joshua in the camp at Gilgal: "Do not fail your servants; come up quickly and aid us and deliver us, for all the Amorite kings of the hill country have gathered against us." ⁷So Joshua marched up from Gilgal with his whole fighting force, all the trained warriors.

⁸The LORD said to Joshua, "Do not be afraid of them, for I will deliver them into your hands; not one of them shall

withstand you." [9]Joshua took them by surprise, marching all night from Gilgal. [10]The LORD threw them into a panic before Israel: [Joshua] inflicted a crushing defeat on them at Gibeon, pursued them in the direction of the Beth-horon ascent, and harried them all the way to Azekah and Makkedah. [11]While they were fleeing before Israel down the descent from Beth-horon, the LORD hurled huge stones on them from the sky, all the way to Azekah, and they perished; more perished from the hailstones than were killed by the Israelite weapons.

[12]On that occasion, when the LORD routed the Amorites before the Israelites, Joshua addressed the LORD; he said in the presence of the Israelites:

"Stand still, O sun, at Gibeon,

O moon, in the Valley of Aijalon!"

[13]And the sun stood still

And the moon halted,

While a nation wreaked judgment on its foes

—as is written in the Book of Jashar. Thus the sun halted in midheaven, and did not press on to set, for a whole day; [14]for the LORD fought for Israel. Neither before nor since has there ever been such a day, when the LORD acted on words spoken by a man. [15]Then Joshua together with all Israel returned to the camp at Gilgal.

WONDERS AND MIRACLES

David Ben Gurion once purportedly quipped, "Anyone who doesn't believe in miracles is not a realist." Miracles may occur every day—an imminent accident averted, a grave illness healed, a doomed army victorious in battle. Some folks choose to understand these events as fortuitous, and some as moments of divine intervention. For the authors and editors of the Bible, miracles were an important way to demonstrate the power of God and to emphasize, again and again, that the Israelites' destiny was guided by a heavenly hand. Nonetheless, curious readers have sought and offered fascinating explanations for miracles related in the Bible. For example, the ten plagues may have resulted from a colossal volcanic eruption that brought about dramatic changes in regional weather. The sudden death of 185,000 Assyrian soldiers who besieged Jerusalem might have been caused by the bubonic plague. The crossing of the River Jordan by the Israelites was probably enabled by an earthquake that loosed rock and debris to temporarily dam up the water.

So how do we explain the two miracles in Joshua 10: the barrage of heaven-sent projectiles and Joshua's interference in the rotations of the sun and the moon? These conundrums have intrigued people of faith and science alike, and the possible explanations are myriad.

The rabbinic sages posited that the stones raining down on the Amorites, picking them off like targets in a video game, were actually hailstones (*Berakhot* 54b). (God threw them around generously; see Ps. 147:17; Job 38:22–23; Isa. 30:30.) However, based on similar circumstances in the past, military historians theorize that the townspeople of Gibeon, buoyed by their allies' victory, hurried to the edge of the city to watch the enemy's defeat and hurled a shower of stones on them as they retreated in panic. The problem inherent in this explanation is that it's too handy; if the Gibeonites successfully ganged up on their fleeing enemies with an arsenal of stones, then who needs God to intervene?

The Gibeonite esprit de corps notwithstanding, the midrash prefers to spin this event as a wondrous continuation of Jewish history by posing that the hailstones that fell on the fleeing Amorites were the very same ones from the seventh plague that rained down on Pharaoh in Egypt. When Moses granted Pharaoh's request and stopped the hailstones, God pressed the pause button, freezing them in midair, enabling them to resume their trajectory only at the battle of Gibeon (*b. Berakhot* 54b). (This subtle reminder of the Exodus story also quietly emphasizes the link between Moses's and Joshua's leadership and the mighty hand of God behind them.)

THE BENEFITS OF EARLY RISING

And how do we explain Joshua's manipulation of the heavenly bodies? Meteorologists have suggested a freak weather phenomenon—perhaps a midsummer cloudburst or an intense winter cold causing refraction of light. Astronomers have put forward a lunar eclipse, or a meteorite shower causing the persistence of diffused light. However, a closer reading of the text reveals that Joshua actually had no hand in any manipulation; his directives to the sun and the moon were addressed to God, in the knowledge that it was God who controlled the forces of nature. The miracle pointedly acknowledged in the text is that "Neither before nor since has there ever been such a day, when the LORD acted on words spoken by a man" (Josh. 10:14).

So what exactly happened out there on the battlefield between Gibeon in the east and the Valley of Aijalon in the west? We may never know, but here is one hypothesis: the Israelite army had hiked uphill from the Jordan to Gibeon by night, no doubt powered by a tremendous surge of adrenaline, and launched its attack at dawn. By the time the Israelites routed the Amorites and chased them down the Bet Horon road, the sun had risen. Joshua no doubt understood that at this point his exhilarated but exhausted troops were on the brink of collapse and were in desperate need of a second wind.

A careful observer who regularly visits the Valley of Aijalon at daybreak will note that during the last week of each lunar month, the moon remains visible in the sky after sunrise. By looking east toward Gibeon and west toward the Valley of Aijalon, you can see the sun and the moon in the sky simultaneously.

The soldiers' sense of time was probably distorted by sleep deprivation and the confusion of battle. Joshua beseeched God to come to their assistance by halting the very visible sun and moon in their paths so that the Israelite army could complete its humiliating defeat of the enemy. When Joshua bellowed a war whoop, imploring God to halt the sun and the moon, it seemed like they stood still.

THIS LAND IS OUR LAND

Although we can brainstorm some fairly satisfying explanations for this story, in fact the presentation of historical events in Joshua is extremely problematic. The land of Canaan is painted as a vast territory with numerous inhabitants, yet only a few battles are actually recounted. The account of the Israelites crossing the Jordan sounds suspiciously like the crossing of the Red Sea, suggesting that certain literary templates were used by the authors. The depiction of the conquest in Joshua 1–12 as a one-time event carried out by a united army of all twelve tribes under the leadership of Joshua is blatantly contradicted in 13:1–6 and toward the end of the book in Josh. 23:1–7, when Joshua, in his old age, summons the Israelite leadership and reminds them that God has given them the territory of the nations that remain in the land and warns them not to mingle with them. What's more, the first chapter of Judges, the next book in the chronology, clearly states that the Israelites were unable to drive out many of the Canaanite inhabitants of the land and were forced to live alongside them (Judg. 1:19, 21, 27–36). (This means humanists can relax. Not only was the conquest an unlikely one-time event, but the brutal ethnic cleansing of the local Canaanites as required by the *herem* evidently never took place.)

Most importantly, the archaeological evidence unearthed thus far does not support the conquest narrative related in Joshua 1–12. There is little, if any indication that Canaan was vanquished in a swift, sudden campaign by outsiders. Rather, the Israelite takeover appears to have been gradual and intermittent, and many scholars believe that there wasn't even a bona fide invasion. At this time, in the thirteenth century BCE, the Middle East was in the throes of a great upheaval. Egypt, which had long ruled Canaan, was severely weakened by wars with its enemies. Its territory was now invaded from the west by the Sea Peoples, among them the Philistines, wreaking havoc along the coastal plain. Some scholars explain that the instability brought on by the Egyptian crisis and the invasion of the Philistines from the west prompted an internal migration of local populations from the plains to the highlands. The tribal, seminomadic people who settled in the hills probably evolved socially and culturally into a unique cohesive group that emerged from within Canaanite society. Another theory suggests that climatic changes and famine in widespread areas of the eastern Mediterranean in the thirteenth–eleventh centuries BCE caused the mass migration of numerous ethnic groups that ultimately arrived in Canaan. So if a lightning conquest never actually took place, why is the book of Joshua written in such militaristic, cataclysmic terms?

The Joshua narrative, like many of the books that make up the biblical anthology, was written and edited over time by authors who had a clear theological message to impart to the readers of the Bible. The concepts of God-given land and covenant so central to Joshua were of particular importance at the end of the eighth century BCE after the fall of the northern kingdom of Israel and during the Assyrian occupation, during the time of King Josiah's far-reaching religious reform, and especially after the destruction of Judah in 586 BCE and during the Babylonian exile. The ancient folk tales retold in Joshua emphasized to the people of the surviving kingdom of Judah that God would never fail them if they were faithful. The stories of the conquest reminded them that the tribal lands of Israel that had been wrested away by the Assyrians were rightfully theirs.

Later on, in the second half of the sixth century BCE, Cyrus the Persian king conquered Babylon and invited the people of Judah living in exile to return to their homeland. The cultivation of an Israelite identity based on invasion by outsiders served to reinforce the returnees' sense of purpose as they embarked on the long and difficult enterprise of the return to Zion.

Yet the Joshua narrative continues to be reinterpreted. The rise of the Zionist movement, Israel's War of Independence in 1948, and then the new reality created in 1967 by the Israeli conquest of the West Bank (the biblical lands of Judaea and Samaria), inspired many to reexamine the story of the Israelite conquest of the land in Joshua. Some read it as a model for the gradual settlement of the land by waves of Jewish immigration to Palestine in the seventy years of Zionist renewal leading up to the establishment of the state. Others construed it as justification for the eviction of the local Arab population during the War of Independence. Still others understood it as a divine stamp of approval for the Jewish settlement of the lands of Judaea and Samaria, despite their location beyond the borders of the State of Israel determined by the War of Independence.

Over the ages Judaism has evolved from a biblical faith to a rabbinic one. For example, when the text says, "an eye for an eye and a tooth for a tooth" (Exod. 21:23–25), we consciously choose to read the passage interpretively, and not literally, understanding that money may be substituted for an eye or a tooth. For centuries our greatest minds have been discussing, deconstructing, and searching for meaning in the words and stories of the Bible and raising questions such as: What is historical? What is allegorical? Should we read Joshua as an inspirational folktale or a manifesto for modern Zionism? As the tribal elders say, the Torah has seventy faces. Yet sandwiched beneath the layers of interpretation throughout the ages is a profound understanding of the centrality of the land of Israel to the identity of the Jewish people.

3

Deborah and Jael at Mount Tabor

Judges 4 (see also 5)

Two unusual women lead the Israelites to military victory

See page 323 for visitor information.

WHERE ARE WE?

Mount Tabor can be beautifully observed from the mountain spur known locally as the Hill of the Precipice. The Gospel of Luke tells how Jesus was rejected by the residents of his hometown, Nazareth, after reading from the book of Isaiah in the synagogue and stating that he was the fulfillment of its messianic prophecy. The angry throng chased him out of town to the brow of a hill, threatening to push him over the edge. Ultimately, Jesus walked back through the crowd unharmed. Tradition identifies this hill as the site, although scholars believe the actual location was probably closer to the center of modern Nazareth. (For the complete story, see Luke 4:14–30.)

SETTING THE SCENE

To the west (right) lies Nazareth, the cultural and political capital of Israel's northern Arab communities. While the Nazareth of Jesus's time was probably a tiny hamlet with just a few dozen families, modern Nazareth is Israel's largest Arab metropolis, with about eighty thousand Christian and Muslim inhabitants. The city was chosen to host an outdoor mass by Pope Benedict XVI in 2009,

Fig. 3. The view of Mount Tabor from the Hill of the Precipice

and the large amphitheater built into the side of the Hill of the Precipice was constructed specially for the occasion.

To the south (straight ahead) lies the magnificent expanse of the Jezreel Valley. Shaped like an isosceles triangle at 24 x 24 x 32 kilometers (15 x 15 x 20 miles), its verdant patchwork is a veritable breadbasket, one of the most fertile areas in Israel, with a pastoral tranquility. However, the Song of Deborah alludes to torrential downpours and dangerous rushing rivers in the valley, whose low basin makes it particularly susceptible to flash flooding during heavy rains. The creek beds that traverse it must be constantly maintained to ensure that they are not obstructed. For centuries following the biblical period, the valley was neglected and degenerated into a malarial swamp. The land was purchased by the American Zionist Commonwealth in the early twentieth century, and the swamp was drained by the legendary pioneers of the Labor Zionist movement, who went on to found many of the veteran Jezreel Valley communities such as the town of Afula, Moshav Tel Adashim, and Kibbutz Mizra, which you can see here below. To the east (left) at the foot of the Nazareth hills lies the Muslim Arab village of Iksal.

In the distance the rounded summit of Mount Tabor rises from the valley. Soft and wooded, it marked the meeting point of the tribal lands of Naphtali, Zebulun, and Issachar. At 575 meters high (1,886 feet), this hill controlled an extremely strategic juncture of the ancient trade routes that passed through the Jezreel Valley. Tabor's altitude provided a protected gathering place where the Israelite forces could prepare for battle beyond reach of the Canaanite chariots. Although technologically sophisticated, the chariots were incapable of negotiating hilly terrain, and as they moved toward the Israelite camp on Mount Tabor, the Canaanite forces had to wait for the Israelites to come down the hill and engage them.

THE CONTEXT

The book of Judges takes place during a difficult transition period for the Israelites. After the tumultuous exodus from Egypt, receiving the Ten Commandments at Mount Sinai, and forty years of wandering in the desert, they had finally arrived in the promised land. The tribes were allotted regions in which to settle down permanently, and they dispersed in all directions. The end of the long journey in the wilderness and the fulfillment of God's promise by conquering the land would seem to have propelled the Israelites forward into a glorious new age. As it turns out, forty years in the desert were a picnic compared to the challenges they faced once they had settled down in the land.

To begin with, they suffered from an acute lack of strong centralized leadership. Moses and Joshua, the powerful, charismatic personalities who had led the Israelites faithfully through all their tribulations, had passed. No man of their stature rose up to fill their shoes. Instead, each tribe was ruled by a council of its elders and fought its own wars. The twelve tribes had no guiding hand, no inspirational role model, and no authority figure at the helm. Whereas under Moses and Joshua they had functioned as a cohesive collective, now they devolved into a loose confederation of tribes preoccupied with their own interests.

At this time a new model of leader was emerging. Judges, or chieftains, were unlikely heroes imbued with God-given charisma who rose from anonymity to authority in times of trouble. And troubles were aplenty. The Israelites found themselves constantly fending off aggressions and invasions by a myriad of hostile neighbors, often outnumbered or at a technological disadvantage. The Israelite tribes were on the receiving end of wave after wave of devastating attacks.

Moreover, after forty years in the desert, a period described by the prophet Jeremiah as a honeymoon (Jer. 2:1), the Israelites had to make the difficult shift from nomadic shepherds to farmers. They now had to grow their own food, a tricky undertaking in a land with such complex weather conditions. Crops often failed, and in their desperation the Israelites sometimes turned to their Canaanite neighbors, who were experts in local farming techniques and probably amenable to offering some good advice. The amicable Canaanites' well-developed agricultural and urban culture enabled them to wield considerable influence over the Israelites, and they soon introduced them to Baal and Asherah, the Canaanite gods who provided rain and fertility. Many Israelites incorporated the local deities into their worship system. The first and second commandments about one God and no idols, which had seemed so nonnegotiable during the halcyon days of the wilderness, somehow got swept under the rug. The Israelites mixed freely with their gentile neighbors, intermarried with them, and worshipped their gods. In short, it seems that for many, the covenant went out the window.

The crisis created by all of these conditions resulted in an absence of traditional male dynastic leadership in Israel. This vacuum was filled by two unusual women.

Judges 4

[1]The Israelites again did what was offensive to the LORD—Ehud now being dead. [2]And the LORD surrendered them to King Jabin of Canaan, who reigned in Hazor. His army commander was Sisera, whose base was Harosheth-goiim. [3]The Israelites cried out to the LORD; for he had nine hundred iron chariots, and he had oppressed Israel ruthlessly for twenty years.

[4]Deborah, wife of Lappidoth, was a prophetess; she led Israel at that time. [5]She used to sit under the Palm of Deborah, between Ramah and Bethel in the hill country of Ephraim, and the Israelites would come to her for decisions.

[6]She summoned Barak son of Abinoam, of Kedesh in Naphtali, and said to him, "The LORD, the God of Israel, has commanded: Go, march up to Mount Tabor, and take with you ten thousand men of Naphtali and Zebulun. [7]And I will draw Sisera, Jabin's army commander, with his chariots and his troops, toward you up to the Wadi Kishon; and I will deliver him into your hands." [8]But Barak said to her, "If you will go with me, I will go; if not, I will not go." [9]"Very well, I will go with you," she answered. "However, there will be

no glory for you in the course you are taking, for then the LORD will deliver Sisera into the hands of a woman." So Deborah went with Barak to Kedesh. 10Barak then mustered Zebulun and Naphtali at Kedesh; ten thousand men marched up after him; and Deborah also went up with him.

11Now Heber the Kenite had separated from the other Kenites, descendants of Hobab, father-in-law of Moses, and had pitched his tent at Elon-bezaanannim, which is near Kedesh.

12Sisera was informed that Barak son of Abinoam had gone up to Mount Tabor. 13So Sisera ordered all his chariots—nine hundred iron chariots—and all the troops he had to move from Harosheth-goiim to the Wadi Kishon. 14Then Deborah said to Barak, "Up! This is the day on which the LORD will deliver Sisera into your hands: the LORD is marching before you." Barak charged down Mount Tabor, followed by the ten thousand men, 15and the LORD threw Sisera and all his chariots and army into a panic before the onslaught of Barak. Sisera leaped from his chariot and fled on foot 16as Barak pursued the chariots and the soldiers as far as Harosheth-goiim. All of Sisera's soldiers fell by the sword; not a man was left.

17Sisera, meanwhile, had fled on foot to the tent of Jael, wife of Heber the Kenite; for there was friendship between King Jabin of Hazor and the family of Heber the Kenite. 18Jael came out to greet Sisera and said to him, "Come in, my lord, come in here, do not be afraid." So he entered her tent, and she covered him with a blanket. 19He said to her, "Please let me have some water; I am thirsty." She opened a skin of milk and gave him some to drink; and she covered him again. 20He said to her, "Stand at the entrance of the tent. If anybody comes and asks you if there is anybody here, say 'No.'" 21Then Jael wife of Heber took a tent pin and grasped the mallet. When he was fast asleep from exhaustion, she approached him stealthily and drove the pin through his temple till it went down to the ground. Thus he died.

²²Now Barak appeared in pursuit of Sisera. Jael went out to greet him and said, "Come, I will show you the man you are looking for." He went inside with her, and there Sisera was lying dead, with the pin in his temple.

²³On that day God subdued King Jabin of Canaan before the Israelites. ²⁴The hand of the Israelites bore harder and harder on King Jabin of Canaan, until they destroyed King Jabin of Canaan.

THE BATTLE

Deborah, who was a prophetess, informed Barak ben Avinoam that he had been chosen by God to lead the people of Israel into battle, but the man who was supposed to save the day refused to accept the job unless she went along with him. Was she surprised? Incensed? Frustrated? We will never know what Deborah uttered under her breath, but objectively it would not have been hard to sympathize with Barak. Sisera had nine hundred chariots with sophisticated iron fittings, while the Israelite army was disorganized and poorly equipped. Would anyone in Israel take Barak seriously when he announced he was preparing to fight the far-superior enemy? The only chance he had to muster an army of dedicated, faithful soldiers was with Deborah at his side, vouching for him and the mission.

Barak still seemed somewhat reluctant as Deborah practically shoved him down Mount Tabor into battle, saying "Up! . . . the LORD is marching before you" But just as she had promised, victory was swift, and almost no Canaanite soldiers survived the Israelite onslaught, no doubt leaving the motley army that Barak had managed to patch together in awe.

How did it happen? The Song of Deborah in Judges 5, another version of the same event, provides clues to what actually transpired:

The torrent Kishon swept them away,
The raging torrent, the torrent Kishon. (v. 21)

Divine intervention in the form of a freak rainstorm turned the Jezreel Valley into a mucky, miry mud bath, rendering the fancy Canaanite chariots useless and forcing the enemy soldiers to jump out of them and flee. Many were vanquished by the sword, and many, no doubt, were swept away by sudden flash floods, whose fury even in modern times can claim lives.

JAEL, MOST BLESSED OF WOMEN

The only survivor was Sisera, who fled on foot to the tent camp of the Kenites. The word *qeni* in Aramaic means "smith," which may mean that Heber the Kenite was a metalworker, and that he had moved his tent closer to the battlefield in order to service the Canaanite weapons. If he was employed by Jabin, then the fugitive general Sisera would have had good reason to take refuge with Jael, Heber's wife. She had to be trustworthy—her husband was on the payroll. In fact, the text specifies that Sisera went to Jael's tent.

Hmm. Straight to her tent? That sounds suspicious. Could Jael and Sisera have been carrying on behind our backs during the earlier verses of Judges 4, and if so, could their illicit dalliance have been part of the divine plan? The sages have a very sexual reading of the whole encounter. The midrash tells us:

When Jael saw Sisera approach, she went to meet him arrayed in rich garments and jewels. She was unusually beautiful, and her voice was the most seductive a woman ever possessed. (Pseudo-Philo, 34:31.3)

Wait. It gets better:

When Sisera, on stepping into her tent saw the bed strewn with roses which Jael had prepared for him, he resolved to take her home to his mother as his wife, as soon as his safety should be assured. (Pseudo-Philo, 34–35; 31:3–7)

The Babylonian Talmud purports that Jael played the romantic game with Sisera because it was the only means she had of ensnaring him (*Yevamot* 103a–103b). In an eyebrow-raising interpretive passage, one text asserts that Yael gave Sisera to drink "the milk of her breast" (*Tosefta Shabbat* 8:24).

Whoa! Jael, "most blessed of woman," actually a kinky, conniving femme fatale? What were those old Jewish sages thinking? Well, it depends on what you're reading. According to the story, Jael extends the warmest hospitality to Sisera by slaking his thirst and covering him with a cozy blanket, reassuring him that he is safe in her tent. Sisera is convinced enough to fall deeply asleep, and as soon as he starts to snore Jael hammers a tent peg through his head, thus fulfilling Deborah's prophecy that the Lord would hand Sisera over to a woman.

Jael's victory over Sisera as recounted in Judges 4 is for the family hour. The R-rated version is in the Song of Deborah in Judges 5, a second version of the story in poetry form (which probably predates the prose version). It offers hints to a much racier denouement, privy to those who read the Bible in the original Hebrew. Verse 27 describes Sisera's position at the moment Jael lanced him with the tent peg. Your translation probably says, "At her feet he sank," whereas the Hebrew reads, *bein ragleyha*—"between her legs." If you didn't understand the subtlety, the Talmudic commentary on this verse leaves no room for doubt. Freely translated, it reads:

> That profligate (i.e., the shameless, immoral Sisera) had seven sexual connections on that day (i.e., he had intercourse with Jael seven times), for it is said, Between her feet he sunk, he fell, he lay; at her feet he sunk, he fell; where he sunk there he fell down dead. (*b. Yevamot* 103a)

Let your imagination run wild. Then go argue that one with your religious schoolteacher. Can you blame the sages for getting a little carried away?

For a man in Bible times, there was no more humiliating way to die than at the hand of a woman. The disgrace of Sisera reverberates several chapters forward, all the way to the end of Judges 9. An astute woman drops a millstone from a tower on one Abimelech, scoring a direct hit and fracturing his skull. In verse 54 we read, "He immediately cried out to his attendant, his arms bearer, "Draw your dagger and finish me off, so that they may not say of me, 'A woman killed him.'" Ah, men.

How disappointing too then, must it have been for the reluctant hero Barak. Appointed by a woman, his victory in battle credited to the handiwork of the Lord, now his last chance to shine was to cut down Sisera with a final flourish. He raced up to the tent camp fresh from the fight, swashbuckling, buoyed by the great victory over the Canaanite soldiers and found his arch enemy already slain and attached to the floor by . . . a woman? Ouch.

ALL IN A NAME

Deborah is described in Judges as a prophetess and a judge. However, she is also referred to as *eshet lapidot*, and how we choose to translate this title can provide the key to understanding Deborah's role in this story. *Eshet* can mean "the wife of." *Lapidot* can mean "flames" but here may be understood to be a man's name. In most English versions of the Hebrew Bible, *eshet lapidot* is translated as "the wife of Lappidoth," clearly defining Deborah by her husband, which is how she would have been identified in her day. The sages seem to concur; in the *midrash*, they tell us that Deborah made candles and her husband carried them to the sanctuary, thus earning himself the nickname "Flames" (*b. Megillah* 14a). However, although she was clearly recognized as a judge, she had to receive her petitioners under a palm tree in the open air so as not to be behind closed doors alone with the men folk (*Exodus Rabbah* 10:48–49). To ensure her lesser status we're told by the sages that "pride is unbecoming to women; the prophetesses Deborah (Bee) and Hulda (Rat) were proud women and both bore ugly names" (*b. Megillah* 14b).

They leave no room for doubt about their opinion when they write, "Woe unto the generation whose leader (judge) is a woman" (Zohar III, 19:2). The rabbinic commentators clearly felt that the Israelites had hit rock bottom if a member of the female persuasion was running the show.

Would it be fair to say that the great Jewish sages were a bunch of prejudiced, narrow-minded chauvinists? Yer darn tootin'. In their wildest dreams they probably could not have imagined that one day learned Jewish women would provide brilliant new insights about our sacred texts from their unique and previously unvoiced perspective. In the men-only world of ancient Jewish scholarship, you could bash women forward and backward, and no one would complain. It was the ultimate good old boys club.

But modern egalitarians, take heart. While the sages viewed Deborah through their social filters as an embarrassing episode in gender role reversal, the laws of nature ensured that there were plenty of smart, courageous women like Deborah and Jael around in ancient times. Regardless of their talents, the social conventions of the day forbade them to venture beyond the hearth. Nonetheless, Jael proved herself a true heroine by neatly disposing of Sisera from the limited confines of her woman's tent. Marvel Comics couldn't have done it better.

This brings us to the alternative translation of Deborah's title, *eshet lapidot*. *Eshet* also means "woman of," and *lapidot*, "torches." A twenty-first century sensibility enables us to read this description of Deborah as the Torch Lady, an exemplary individual who bore the light of faith, leadership, and justice higher than any Israelite of her time, man or woman. She overcame the prejudices of her own people to lead Israel unwaveringly through difficult times. What a woman.

4

Gideon at En Harod

Judges 6; 7; 8:22–28 (additional reading: 8:1–21)

An unwitting hero rises to the occasion

See page 324 for visitor information.

WHERE ARE WE?

The spring of Harod lies at the foot of Mount Gilboa, the southern border of the Jezreel Valley. This valley, which is actually a composition of three smaller valleys, crosses Israel almost completely from east to west, making it an important passageway for the ancient highways of the Middle East. Dozens of battles have been fought in the Jezreel Valley throughout history because of its strategic location.

SETTING THE SCENE

The freshwater spring of Harod emerges from a natural cavern known as Gideon's Cave. Although close to the Hill of Moreh to the north, the spring's location, nestled in a small hollow, concealed it from enemy eyes.

THE CONTEXT

A clear pattern has already developed in the book of Judges that is about to repeat itself. In this predictable loop of betrayal the Israelites succumb to the enticements of their gentile neighbors by worshipping their pagan gods. Each time they stray from the path of the covenant, God punishes them by dispatching a cruel oppressor to rule over

Fig. 4. The spring of Harod

them. In their wretchedness the Israelites cry out to God (probably after they've exhausted all the other idolatrous options), begging for deliverance from the merciless enemy.

Full of compassion for his errant people, God steps in and transforms an anonymous Israelite tribesman into a judge (really a chieftain) imbued with divine charisma and great military prowess who proceeds to vanquish the oppressor. The Israelites are inspired to return to the spiritual path from which they've strayed, and a period of several years of peace and faithfulness ensues. Usually when the judge dies, the cycle begins again.

In the book of Judges thus far we have met Othniel, raised up to defeat the evil king of Aram-naharaim far in the north (Judg. 3:7–11); Ehud son of Gera, who thrust a sword through the tubby paunch of the powerful Eglon, king of Moab, while he was in his cool upper chamber on the toilet (Judg. 3:12–30); and Deborah, a prophetess and advisor of field marshal Barak, who marched into battle at Mount Tabor to trounce the Canaanite army of King Jabin and his military leader Sisera (Judg. 4–5).

After Deborah and Barak's glorious victory, the Israelites were able to move down into the richly fertile Valley of Jezreel to settle and plant their crops. However, the troubled relationship between Israel and God soon resumed its old course, and the cycle began anew. This time the affliction was the Midianites, a nomadic tribe that came up from the deserts bordering on Israelite territory, probably in the wake of a prolonged drought that forced them to seek grazing pastures beyond the boundaries of the lands they usually wandered. The recent widespread utilization of the camel for transport enabled them to traverse long distances and to penetrate deeply into settled areas, which they raided and then quickly escaped, devastating the farming communities.

Since at this time the Israelites lacked a central governing authority, they were incapable of organizing a defense system to secure the borders from invasion. The Midianites terrorized them, looting and pillaging relentlessly. Not surprisingly, the Israelites beseeched their God to rescue them, but at this juncture the pattern deviates significantly. Instead of choosing a fresh judge, God first sent a prophet, who announced that it was time to call in the Israelites' bets. No more automatic redemption. You want to be saved? Let's get out that contract you signed and refresh our memories. If you want God to help, you will have to hold up your end of the bargain. Deliverance will come, but only if you change your idolatrous ways.

Soon afterward we meet Gideon.

Judges 6

¹Then the Israelites did what was offensive to the LORD, and the LORD delivered them into the hands of the Midianites for seven years. ²The hand of the Midianites prevailed over Israel; and because of Midian, the Israelites provided themselves with refuges in the caves and strongholds of the mountains. ³After the Israelites had done their sowing, Midian, Amalek, and the Kedemites would come up and raid them; ⁴they would attack them, destroy the produce of the land all the way to Gaza, and leave no means of sustenance in Israel, not a sheep or an ox or an ass. ⁵For they would come up with their livestock and their tents, swarming as thick as locusts; they and their camels were innumerable. Thus they would invade the land and ravage it. ⁶Israel was reduced to utter misery by the Midianites, and the Israelites cried out to the LORD.

⁷When the Israelites cried to the LORD on account of Midian, ⁸the LORD sent a prophet to the Israelites who said to them, "Thus said the LORD, the God of Israel: I brought you up out of Egypt and freed you from the house of bondage. ⁹I rescued you from the Egyptians and from all your oppressors; I drove them out before you, and gave you their land. ¹⁰And I said to you, 'I the LORD am your God. You must not worship the gods of the Amorites in whose land you dwell.' But you did not obey Me."

¹¹An angel of the LORD came and sat under the terebinth at Ophrah, which belonged to Joash the Abiezrite. His son Gideon was then beating out wheat inside a winepress in order to keep it safe from the Midianites. ¹²The angel of the LORD appeared to him and said to him, "The LORD is with you, valiant warrior!" ¹³Gideon said to him, "Please, my lord, if the LORD is with us, why has all this befallen us? Where are all His wondrous deeds about which our fathers

told us, saying, 'Truly the LORD brought us up from Egypt'? Now the LORD has abandoned us and delivered us into the hands of Midian!" ¹⁴The LORD turned to him and said, "Go in this strength of yours and deliver Israel from the Midianites. I herewith make you My messenger." ¹⁵He said to Him, "Please, my lord, how can I deliver Israel? Why, my clan is the humblest in Manasseh, and I am the youngest in my father's household." ¹⁶The LORD replied, "I will be with you, and you shall defeat Midian to a man." ¹⁷And he said to Him, "If I have gained Your favor, give me a sign that it is You who are speaking to me: ¹⁸do not leave this place until I come back to You and bring out my offering and place it before You." And He answered, "I will stay until you return."

¹⁹So Gideon went in and prepared a kid, and [baked] unleavened bread from an ephah of flour. He put the meat in a basket and poured the broth into a pot, and he brought them out to Him under the terebinth. As he presented them, ²⁰the angel of God said to him, "Take the meat and the unleavened bread, put them on yonder rock, and spill out the broth." He did so. ²¹The angel of the LORD held out the staff that he carried, and touched the meat and the unleavened bread with its tip. A fire sprang up from the rock and consumed the meat and the unleavened bread. And the angel of the LORD vanished from his sight. ²²Then Gideon realized that it was an angel of the LORD; and Gideon said, "Alas, O Lord GOD! For I have seen an angel of the LORD face to face."

²³But the LORD said to him, "All is well; have no fear, you shall not die." ²⁴So Gideon built there an altar to the LORD and called it Adonaishalom. To this day it stands in Ophrah of the Abiezrites.

²⁵That night the LORD said to him: "Take the young bull belonging to your father and another bull seven years old; pull down the altar of Baal which belongs to your

father, and cut down the sacred post which is beside it. ²⁶Then build an altar to the LORD your God, on the level ground—on top of this stronghold. Take the other bull and offer it as a burnt offering, using the wood of the sacred post that you have cut down." ²⁷So Gideon took ten of his servants and did as the LORD had told him; but as he was afraid to do it by day, on account of his father's household and the townspeople, he did it by night. ²⁸Early the next morning, the townspeople found that the altar of Baal had been torn down and the sacred post beside it had been cut down, and that the second bull had been offered on the newly built altar. ²⁹They said to one another, "Who did this thing?" Upon inquiry and investigation, they were told, "Gideon son of Joash did this thing!" ³⁰The townspeople said to Joash, "Bring out your son, for he must die: he has torn down the altar of Baal and cut down the sacred post beside it!" ³¹But Joash said to all who had risen against him, "Do you have to contend for Baal? Do you have to vindicate him? Whoever fights his battles shall be dead by morning! If he is a god, let him fight his own battles, since it is his altar that has been torn down!" ³²That day they named him Jerubbaal, meaning "Let Baal contend with him, since he tore down his altar."

³³All Midian, Amalek, and the Kedemites joined forces; they crossed over and encamped in the Valley of Jezreel. ³⁴The spirit of the LORD enveloped Gideon; he sounded the horn, and the Abiezrites rallied behind him. ³⁵And he sent messengers throughout Manasseh, and they too rallied behind him. He then sent messengers through Asher, Zebulun, and Naphtali, and they came up to meet the Manassites.

³⁶And Gideon said to God, "If You really intend to deliver Israel through me as You have said—³⁷here I place a fleece of wool on the threshing floor. If dew falls only on

the fleece and all the ground remains dry, I shall know that You will deliver Israel through me, as You have said." 38And that is what happened. Early the next day, he squeezed the fleece and wrung out the dew from the fleece, a bowlful of water. 39Then Gideon said to God, "Do not be angry with me if I speak just once more. Let me make just one more test with the fleece: let the fleece alone be dry, while there is dew all over the ground." 40God did so that night: only the fleece was dry, while there was dew all over the ground.

7

1Early next day, Jerubbaal—that is, Gideon—and all the troops with him encamped above En-harod, while the camp of Midian was in the plain to the north of him, at Gibeath-moreh. 2The LORD said to Gideon, "You have too many troops with you for Me to deliver Midian into their hands; Israel might claim for themselves the glory due to Me, thinking, 'Our own hand has brought us victory.' 3Therefore, announce to the men, 'Let anybody who is timid and fearful turn back, as a bird flies from Mount Gilead.'" Thereupon, 22,000 of the troops turned back and 10,000 remained.

4"There are still too many troops," the LORD said to Gideon. "Take them down to the water and I will sift them for you there. Anyone of whom I tell you, 'This one is to go with you,' that one shall go with you; and anyone of whom I tell you, 'This one is not to go with you,' that one shall not go." 5So he took the troops down to the water. Then the LORD said to Gideon, "Set apart all those who lap up the water with their tongues like dogs from all those who get down on their knees to drink." 6Now those who "lapped" the water into their mouths by hand numbered three hundred; all the rest of the troops got down on their knees to drink. ⁷Then the LORD said to Gideon, "I will deliver you and I will put Midian into your hands through the three hundred 'lappers'; let the rest of the troops go home." ⁸So [the lappers] took the provisions and horns that the other men had with them, and he sent the rest of the men of Israel back to their homes, retaining only the three hundred men.

The Midianite camp was below him, in the plain. ⁹That night the LORD said to him, "Come, attack the camp, for I have delivered it into your hands. ¹⁰And if you are afraid to attack, first go down to the camp with your attendant Purah ¹¹and listen to what they say; after that you will have the courage to attack the camp." So he went down with his attendant Purah to the outposts of the warriors who were in the camp.—¹²Now Midian, Amalek, and all the Kedemites were spread over the plain, as thick as locusts; and their camels were countless, as numerous as the sands on the seashore.—¹³Gideon came there just as one man was narrating a dream to another. "Listen," he was saying, "I had this dream: There was a commotion—a loaf of barley bread was whirling through the Midianite camp. It came to a tent and struck it, and it fell; it turned it upside down, and the tent collapsed." ¹⁴To this the other responded, "That can only mean the sword of the Israelite Gideon son of Joash. God is delivering Midian and the entire camp into his hands."

¹⁵When Gideon heard the dream told and interpreted, he bowed low. Returning to the camp of Israel, he shouted, "Come on! The LORD has delivered the Midianite camp into your hands!" ¹⁶He divided the three hundred men into three columns and equipped every man with a ram's horn and an empty jar, with a torch in each jar. ¹⁷"Watch me," he said, "and do the same. When I get to the outposts of the camp, do exactly as I do. ¹⁸When I and all those with me

blow our horns, you too, all around the camp, will blow your horns and shout, 'For the LORD and for Gideon!'"

¹⁹Gideon and the hundred men with him arrived at the outposts of the camp, at the beginning of the middle watch, just after the sentries were posted. They sounded the horns and smashed the jars that they had with them, ²⁰and the three columns blew their horns and broke their jars. Holding the torches in their left hands and the horns for blowing in their right hands, they shouted, "A sword for the LORD and for Gideon!" ²¹They remained standing where they were, surrounding the camp; but the entire camp ran about yelling, and took to flight. ²²For when the three hundred horns were sounded, the LORD turned every man's sword against his fellow, throughout the camp, and the entire host fled as far as Beth-shittah and on to Zererah—as far as the outskirts of Abel-meholah near Tabbath.

²³And now the men of Israel from Naphtali and Asher and from all of Manasseh rallied for the pursuit of the Midianites. ²⁴Gideon also sent messengers all through the hill country of Ephraim with this order: "Go down ahead of the Midianites and seize their access to the water all along the Jordan down to Beth-barah." So all the men of Ephraim rallied and seized the waterside down to Beth-barah by the Jordan. ²⁵They pursued the Midianites and captured Midian's two generals, Oreb and Zeeb. They killed Oreb at the Rock of Oreb and they killed Zeeb at the Winepress of Zeeb; and they brought the heads of Oreb and Zeeb from the other side of the Jordan to Gideon.

8

²²Then the men of Israel said to Gideon, "Rule over us— you, your son, and your grandson as well; for you have saved us from the Midianites." ²³But Gideon replied, "I will

not rule over you myself, nor shall my son rule over you; the LORD alone shall rule over you." 24And Gideon said to them, "I have a request to make of you: Each of you give me the earring he received as booty." (They had golden earrings, for they were Ishmaelites.) 25"Certainly!" they replied. And they spread out a cloth, and everyone threw onto it the earring he had received as booty. 26The weight of the golden earrings that he had requested came to 1,700 shekels of gold; this was in addition to the crescents and the pendants and the purple robes worn by the kings of Midian and in addition to the collars on the necks of their camels. 27Gideon made an ephod of this gold and set it up in his own town of Ophrah. There all Israel went astray after it, and it became a snare to Gideon and his household.

28Thus Midian submitted to the Israelites and did not raise its head again; and the land was tranquil for forty years in Gideon's time.

THE IDEAL HERO

Just as in the other stories from Judges, the biblical redactors made sure to emphasize that Gideon's victory over the Midianites was the result of divine intervention. Nevertheless, Gideon the commando has been the object of much admiration from generations of Bible readers partial to war heroes. Organizations inspired by him called the Gideons include a secret youth group in Ottoman-controlled Palestine, the special night squads trained by Orde Wingate in British mandatory Palestine, the radio communications unit of the Hagana, a revenge gang of Dachau survivors active in Germany after World War II, and a special forces unit of the Israeli police. Gideon is often understood as a humble man, a great warrior, and a paragon of heroism.

Despite his complete lack of experience in matters of war, military analysts have declared Gideon a strategist par excellence. By carefully observing the enemy's immense encampments, he understood that the wildly inexperienced Israelite forces had no chance of success in a conventional attack during daylight hours. Although the Midianites' large tent camps were extremely intimidating, he astutely discerned that they were actually the enemy's weakest point. Noisy and full of women and children, they would be easy to surprise under cover of darkness.

Another challenge faced by the Israelites was the Midianite camels, powerful animals that enabled the enemy to charge and advance rapidly. Gideon concluded that the camels could only be neutralized by a surprise attack at night, when the animals were riderless and tethered. Accordingly, he planned his assault for the middle watch, in the wee hours of the morning, when the Midianites would be fast asleep. Under these conditions confusion and panic would spread like wildfire.

To choose his fighters, he brought the men down to the spring of Harod and observed them as they knelt to drink in close proximity to the enemy camp. Gideon then wisely split his forces into three small, crack units of one hundred warriors, confident and stealthy, to take the offensive and sow pandemonium in the enemy camp with a thunderbolt rush under cover of darkness.

Based on his own reconnaissance he determined the enemy's exact location, security arrangements, and morale. When the time came to attack, rather than taking on the Midianite soldiers, Gideon's men surrounded their camp and generated the noise and commotion of a huge invading army. Taken unawares and disoriented, the Midianites fled in alarm, straight into the trap of the large Israelite forces waiting to pursue them.

Beyond God's guiding hand, to military analysts the blueprint for Gideon's success was a bold, rapid initiative deep into the enemy camp using the element of surprise and psychological effects such as light and noise to compensate for his force's weaknesses.

Yet if we dig a little more deeply into the story, some serious questions about Gideon arise. First, we cannot help but raise an eyebrow over the minimal but significant biographical information the text supplies on the three judges who preceded Gideon. Othniel is described as the younger brother of Caleb the spy, but also as a Kenizzite (Judg. 3:9), quite possibly the descendent of a foreign tribe that mixed with the Judaeans a few generations earlier. We learn that Ehud ben Gera was left handed (Judg. 3:15), a circumstance considered a birth defect until the mid-twentieth century. Deborah was a woman. So the great leaders of Israel raised from obscurity by divine intervention thus far have been a half-breed, a physically handicapped man, and a woman. (If we skip ahead a few chapters, we will also meet Jepthah, son of a prostitute [Judg. 11–12:7], and Samson, a Philistine skirt-chaser [Judg. 13].)

Gideon does not break the mold, but takes his place in the motley crew of Israelite leadership. His most obvious flaw was his bothersome lack of self-confidence, even after he had met God face-to-face. He had the gall to demand proof of God's power three times because he could not believe that the angel was actually God's messenger. God, with the patience of a saint, played along.

As a result Gideon is depicted as a coward. His first task was to put his (that is, Israel's) money where his mouth was and tear down his father's altar to Baal, but Gideon wasn't exactly enthusiastic about challenging the townspeople. Gideon was so fearful and lacking in conviction that he destroyed the altar in the dead of night, accompanied by ten of his servants, when no one was looking. When his handiwork was discovered the next day, he lay low and left the mess for his father to clean up.

Somehow, this milquetoast demonstration of character seems to have been enough for God, and after receiving the requisite signs Gideon prepared to go out to battle. However, a note of icy resentment rings through the scene at the spring of Harod (Judg. 7:2). God suspected the Israelites could not be relied on to give him due credit when they defeated the Midianites; hence, the battle would be fought and won not with the thousands of troops who came down after Gideon but with a mere three hundred men. The description of who laps like a dog with their tongues and who kneels and laps with their hands is confusing. Although the winnowing process is unclear, this passage has traditionally been interpreted to understand that the three hundred chosen were the best men. The first-century Jewish historian Josephus Flavius challenges this reading, taking the opposite tack in his retelling of the story. He asserts that God actually chose the most cowardly, inept men of the lot (*Jewish Antiquities* 5.210). When a group of bumbling idiots is sent out to battle and returns triumphant, there can be no doubt about God's role in the victory.

However, after understanding the meaning of the Midianite soldier's dream (7:9–15a) and after experiencing God's support in the battle (7:15b–22), Gideon the doubtful underwent a metamorphosis. The reluctant warrior was empowered by the incredible victory and finally understood: God has his, and Israel's, back. In an impressive demonstration of leadership and self-confidence, Gideon then called up all the fighting men from the tribes of Manasseh, Asher, Zebulun, and Naphtali to hurry down and pursue the Midianites (Judg. 6:35; 7:23); he also diffused a tense situation with the tribe of Ephraim and prevented the outbreak of a civil war (Judg. 7:24–8:1–3). After they trounced the enemy, the army urged him to establish a monarchy, but Gideon wisely declined, understanding that as long as all twelve tribes were not united, the time for kingship was not yet ripe. The coward we met at the beginning of the story has now been transformed into a warrior, a leader, and a politician.

HAPPY END?

Despite Gideon's admirable transformation, the denouement of this story is disturbing. After the enemy was defeated, Gideon called everyone together and took up a collection of gold earrings. He melted them down and formed an ephod, in this context probably a statue representing Israel's deliverance. Regardless of his intention, within a short time the Israelites were prostrating themselves before it. When Gideon died, they renewed their apostasy (Judg. 8:33–35).

So Gideon joins the lineup of very flawed leaders known as judges. Like those that came before him, Gideon was given a mission of defeating the enemy and the means to fulfill it through divine intervention. Let there be no misunderstanding—not a single one of these "judges" was capable of victory without God's support. However, in the Gideon story for the first time the Israelites were required to take affirmative steps toward mending their idolatrous ways. Their refusal is a hint to readers that an end to Israel's misery was nowhere in sight. It's only a matter of time before the cycle was renewed and the people of Israel tumbled deeper into the black hole that would eventually lead them to violate the covenant yet again by worshipping other gods.

One evening in 1898 two strangers were asked to room together in a crowded hotel in Boscobel, Wisconsin. Upon discovering that they were both evangelical Christians, they prayed together and later decided to form an association of traveling Christian businessmen. They named it after Gideon, whose faith, obedience, and humility they wished to emulate. The goal of the association was to provide fellowship, support, and encouragement for its members. One way they devised to assist their associates was to ensure that every hotel room in the United States had a copy of the Bible. Since the first tome was placed in a Montana hotel in 1908, they have distributed over 1.6 billion Bibles in ninety languages in 190 countries all over the world. The Gideons' logo shows the two-handled jug and torch used by Gideon's men in the battle against the Midianites.

5

Samson at Zorah

Judges 13–16

A strong man battles the enemy without and within

See page 317 for visitor information.

WHERE ARE WE?

We are standing on top of Tel Bet Shemesh, which looks out on the scene of the Samson stories. The ancient city, an area comprising seven acres on the hilltop, sat at the crossroads of three cultures: Philistine, Canaanite, and Israelite. Named for the Canaanite sun god, it was home to the Israelites when the ark of the covenant, captured by the Philistines in battle, was returned to them (check out the full story in 1 Samuel 6). Archaeological excavations from the period of Judges indicate a large village with Canaanite-style architecture and pottery. The animal bones found here suggest the inhabitants did not eat pork, a food eschewed by both Canaanites and Israelites. Neighborly relations seem to have been cordial.

During the tenth–eighth centuries BCE Bet Shemesh expanded into a large administrative center with complex fortifications, an iron workshop, and an impressive underground reservoir hewn from the rock. The Israelite city was ultimately destroyed by the Assyrians in 701 BCE. The reservoir was eventually blocked with 150 tons of landfill to prevent Judaeans from returning to resettle

Fig. 5. Tel Bet Shemesh

the city. Bet Shemesh ultimately lost its prominence; it is mentioned once in the Talmudic literature as a very small town (*j. Ta'anit* 4).

Remains of a fifth-century CE Byzantine monastery are visible here.

SETTING THE SCENE

Behind you, to the east of the tel, is the modern city of Bet Shemesh. Straight ahead, westward, is Yishi, a moshav founded by Yemenite immigrants in 1950. To the right, northwest, is Kibbutz Zorah, named for the biblical town of Zorah, which was located nearby. You passed Eshtaol as you came here on Route 38, and Timnah, also not visible from here, would have been located several miles northwest of Bet Shemesh. All these towns are mentioned in the Samson stories.

The Samson cycle of stories in Judges 13–16 takes place on the home turf of Israel's most formidable enemy, the Philistines. The tribe of Dan, Samson's tribe, set out to claim its inheritance in the area between the foothills of Judaea and the coastal plain, a rich swath of agricultural land controlling an important segment of the ancient trade route. However, this area had already been claimed by an invader arriving in ancient Canaan from the west, about the same time the children of Israel were arriving from the east and settling in the promised land. The Philistines were one of the Sea Peoples who left their homelands in the Aegean Sea following a violent upheaval at the beginning of the twelfth century BCE. They arrived in the land of Israel from the sea, violently displacing the local Canaanites who lived there and taking control of the coastal plain and inner lowlands.

The Philistines are portrayed in the Bible as strong and organized, but they are repeatedly referred to as "uncircumcised," evidently their most distinguishing characteristic in a region where Israelites, many Canaanite peoples, and Egyptians practiced circumcision. This ethnic and cultural marker set them apart from the locals and the readers who identified with them. Today "Philistine" is a byword for a person lacking in culture and indifferent to aesthetic values (regardless of what's under his overalls). This misguided stereotype is a minor victory for the authors of the Bible, who clearly wished us to remember the Philistines in a negative light.

However, the archaeological evidence teaches us that the Philistines were a highly sophisticated society. The technological innovations they brought with them to Canaan deeply enriched the local culture and sparked a long-lasting developmental trend in the eastern Mediter-ranean. The Sea Peoples invented the prototype of the ship widely used for commerce in the region for hundreds of years, as well as important innovations such as advanced rigging, the crow's nest, and the composite anchor. Their round-bottomed jars safely fitted into round holes in the hold enabled the safe transport of liquids such as wine and oil over the high seas, and their introduction of square-cut building stones became a standard of local architecture. They had a unique style of pottery and a well-organized administrative system.

Perhaps most importantly the Philistines held a distinct advantage over the tribes of Israel in two realms: military prowess and metallurgy. The Israelite army was made up of volunteers, often reluctant tribesmen who had to be convinced to take up arms. The Philistine army was well organized, consisting of multitudes of conscripted troops ready to operate on very short notice. They took control of the fertile coastal plain and the valleys of the lowlands, threatening to move eastward into the Israelite enclaves.

The second significant advantage of the Philistines over the Israelites was their monopoly of metal technology and raw materials. The seafaring Philistines were able to access the international markets for tin and copper, the two components of bronze. Tin was unavailable at this time in ancient Israel. They also arrived in Canaan already equipped with the technology and the means to transform iron into steel, enabling them to outfit their army with swords, spears, and fittings for chariots. (For an abbreviated catalog of some of these items, read the description of Goliath as he goes out to battle in 1 Sam. 17:4–7.) The Philistines ensured that the Israelites would remain militarily inferior by preventing their access to bronze and iron. They allowed their Israelite neighbors to patronize Philistine blacksmiths in order to service their agricultural implements (1 Sam. 13:19–22), but the Israelites had no means of producing or procuring bronze and iron weapons, putting them at a distinct disadvantage vis-à-vis their Philistine adversaries.

Judges 13

[1]The Israelites again did what was offensive to the LORD, and the LORD delivered them into the hands of the Philistines for forty years.

[2]There was a certain man from Zorah, of the stock of Dan, whose name was Manoah. His wife was barren and had borne no children. [3]An angel of the LORD appeared to the woman and said to her, "You are barren and have borne no children; but you shall conceive and bear a son. [4]Now be careful not to drink wine or other intoxicant, or to eat anything unclean. [5]For you are going to conceive and bear a son; let no razor touch his head, for the boy is to be a nazirite to God from the womb on. He shall be the first to deliver Israel from the Philistines."

[6]The woman went and told her husband, "A man of God came to me; he looked like an angel of God, very frightening. I did not ask him where he was from, nor did he tell me his name. [7]He said to me, 'You are going to conceive and bear a son. Drink no wine or other intoxicant, and eat nothing unclean, for the boy is to be a nazirite to God from the womb to the day of his death!'"

[8]Manoah pleaded with the LORD. "Oh, my Lord!" he said, "please let the man of God that You sent come to us again, and let him instruct us how to act with the child that is to be born." [9]God heeded Manoah's plea, and the angel of God came to the woman again. She was sitting in the field and her husband Manoah was not with her. [10]The woman

ran in haste to tell her husband. She said to him, "The man who came to me before has just appeared to me." [11]Manoah promptly followed his wife. He came to the man and asked him: "Are you the man who spoke to my wife?" "Yes," he answered. [12]Then Manoah said, "May your words soon come true! What rules shall be observed for the boy?" [13]The angel of the LORD said to Manoah, "The woman must abstain from all the things against which I warned her. [14]She must not eat anything that comes from the grapevine, or drink wine or other intoxicant, or eat anything unclean. She must observe all that I commanded her."

[15]Manoah said to the angel of the LORD, "Let us detain you and prepare a kid for you." [16]But the angel of the LORD said to Manoah, "If you detain me, I shall not eat your food; and if you present a burnt offering, offer it to LORD."—For Manoah did not know that he was an angel of the LORD. [17]So Manoah said to the angel of the LORD, "What is your name? We should like to honor you when your words come true." [18]The angel said to him, "You must not ask for my name; it is unknowable!"

[19]Manoah took the kid and the meal offering and offered them up on the rock to the LORD; and a marvelous thing happened while Manoah and his wife looked on. [20]As the flames leaped up from the altar toward the sky, the angel of the LORD ascended in the flames of the altar, while Manoah and his wife looked on; and they flung themselves on their faces to the ground.—[21]The angel of the LORD never appeared again to Manoah and his wife.—Manoah then realized that it had been an angel of the LORD. [22]And Manoah said to his wife, "We shall surely die, for we have seen a divine being." [23]But his wife said to him, "Had the LORD meant to take our lives, He would not have accepted a burnt offering and meal offering from us, nor let us see all these things; and He would not have made such an announcement to us."

²⁴The woman bore a son, and she named him Samson. The boy grew up, and the LORD blessed him. ²⁵The spirit of the LORD first moved him in the encampment of Dan, between Zorah and Eshtaol.

14

¹Once Samson went down to Timnah; and while in Timnah, he noticed a girl among the Philistine women. ²On his return, he told his father and mother, "I noticed one of the Philistine women in Timnah; please get her for me as a wife." ³His father and mother said to him, "Is there no one among the daughters of your own kinsmen and among all our people, that you must go and take a wife from the uncircumcised Philistines?" But Samson answered his father, "Get me that one, for she is the one that pleases me." ⁴His father and mother did not realize that this was the LORD's doing: He was seeking a pretext against the Philistines, for the Philistines were ruling over Israel at that time. ⁵So Samson and his father and mother went down to Timnah.

When he came to the vineyards of Timnah [for the first time], a full-grown lion came roaring at him. ⁶The spirit of the LORD gripped him, and he tore him asunder with his bare hands as one might tear a kid asunder; but he did not tell his father and mother what he had done. ⁷Then he went down and spoke to the woman, and she pleased Samson.

⁸Returning the following year to marry her, he turned aside to look at the remains of the lion; and in the lion's skeleton he found a swarm of bees, and honey. ⁹He scooped it into his palms and ate it as he went along. When he rejoined his father and mother, he gave them some and they ate it; but he did not tell them that he had scooped the honey out of a lion's skeleton.

¹⁰So his father came down to the woman, and Samson made a feast there, as young men used to do. ¹¹When they saw him, they designated thirty companions to be with him. ¹²Then Samson said to them, "Let me propound a riddle to you. If you can give me the right answer during the seven days of the feast, I shall give you thirty linen tunics and thirty sets of clothing; ¹³but if you are not able to tell it to me, you must give me thirty linen tunics and thirty sets of clothing." And they said to him, "Ask your riddle and we will listen." ¹⁴So he said to them:

"Out of the eater came something to eat,
Out of the strong came something sweet."

For three days they could not answer the riddle.

¹⁵On the seventh day, they said to Samson's wife, "Coax your husband to provide us with the answer to the riddle; else we shall put you and your father's household to the fire; have you invited us here in order to impoverish us?" ¹⁶Then Samson's wife harassed him with tears, and she said, "You really hate me, you don't love me. You asked my countrymen a riddle, and you didn't tell me the answer." He replied, "I haven't even told my father and mother; shall I tell you?" ¹⁷During the rest of the seven days of the feast she continued to harass him with her tears, and on the seventh day he told her, because she nagged him so. And she explained the riddle to her countrymen. ¹⁸On the seventh day, before the sunset, the townsmen said to him:

"What is sweeter than honey,
And what is stronger than a lion?"

He responded:

"Had you not plowed with my heifer,
You would not have guessed my riddle!"

¹⁹The spirit of the LORD gripped him. He went down to Ashkelon and killed thirty of its men. He stripped them and

gave the sets of clothing to those who had answered the riddle. And he left in a rage for his father's house.

²⁰Samson's wife then married one of those who had been his wedding companions.

15

¹Some time later, in the season of the wheat harvest, Samson came to visit his wife, bringing a kid as a gift. He said, "Let me go into the chamber to my wife." But her father would not let him go in. ²"I was sure," said her father, "that you had taken a dislike to her, so I gave her to your wedding companion. But her younger sister is more beautiful than she; let her become your wife instead." ³Thereupon Samson declared, "Now the Philistines can have no claim against me for the harm I shall do them."

⁴Samson went and caught three hundred foxes. He took torches and, turning [the foxes] tail to tail, he placed a torch between each pair of tails. ⁵He lit the torches and turned [the foxes] loose among the standing grain of the Philistines, setting fire to stacked grain, standing grain, vineyards, [and] olive trees.

⁶The Philistines asked, "Who did this?" And they were told, "It was Samson, the son-in-law of the Timnite, who took Samson's wife and gave her to his wedding companion." Thereupon the Philistines came up and put her and her father to the fire. ⁷Samson said to them, "If that is how you act, I will not rest until I have taken revenge on you." ⁸He gave them a sound and thorough thrashing. Then he went down and stayed in the cave of the rock of Etam.

⁹The Philistines came up, pitched camp in Judah and spread out over Lehi. ¹⁰The men of Judah asked, "Why have you come up against us?" They answered, "We have come

to take Samson prisoner, and to do to him as he did to us." ¹¹Thereupon three thousand men of Judah went down to the cave of the rock of Etam, and they said to Samson, "You knew that the Philistines rule over us; why have you done this to us?" He replied, "As they did to me, so I did to them." ¹²"We have come down," they told him, "to take you prisoner and to hand you over to the Philistines." "But swear to me," said Samson to them, "that you yourselves will not attack me." ¹³"We won't," they replied. "We will only take you prisoner and hand you over to them; we will not slay you." So they bound him with two new ropes and brought him up from the rock.

¹⁴When he reached Lehi, the Philistines came shouting to meet him. Thereupon the spirit of the LORD gripped him, and the ropes on his arms became like flax that catches fire; the bonds melted off his hands. ¹⁵He came upon a fresh jawbone of an ass and he picked it up; and with it he killed a thousand men. ¹⁶Then Samson said:

"With the jaw of an ass,

Mass upon mass!

With the jaw of an ass

I have slain a thousand men."

¹⁷As he finished speaking, he threw the jawbone away; hence that place was called Ramath-lehi.

¹⁸He was very thirsty and he called to the LORD, "You Yourself have granted this great victory through Your servant; and must I now die of thirst and fall into the hands of the uncircumcised?" ¹⁹So God split open the hollow which is at Lehi, and the water gushed out of it; he drank, regained his strength, and revived. That is why it is called to this day "En-hakkore of Lehi."

²⁰He led Israel in the days of the Philistines for twenty years.

16

¹Once Samson went to Gaza; there he met a whore and slept with her. ²The Gazites [learned] that Samson had come there, so they gathered and lay in ambush for him in the town gate the whole night; and all night long they kept whispering to each other, "When daylight comes, we'll kill him." ³But Samson lay in bed only till midnight. At midnight he got up, grasped the doors of the town gate together with the two gateposts, and pulled them out along with the bar. He placed them on his shoulders and carried them off to the top of the hill that is near Hebron.

⁴After that, he fell in love with a woman in the Wadi Sorek, named Delilah. ⁵The lords of the Philistines went up to her and said, "Coax him and find out what makes him so strong, and how we can overpower him, tie him up, and make him helpless; and we'll each give you eleven hundred shekels of silver."

⁶So Delilah said to Samson, "Tell me, what makes you so strong? And how could you be tied up and made helpless?" ⁷Samson replied, "If I were to be tied with seven fresh tendons that had not been dried, I should become as weak as an ordinary man." ⁸So the lords of the Philistines brought up to her seven fresh tendons that had not been dried. She bound him with them, ⁹while an ambush was waiting in her room. Then she called out to him, "Samson, the Philistines are upon you!" Whereat he pulled the tendons apart, as a strand of tow comes apart at the touch of fire. So the secret of his strength remained unknown.

¹⁰Then Delilah said to Samson, "Oh, you deceived me; you lied to me! Do tell me now how you could be tied up." ¹¹He said, "If I were to be bound with new ropes that had never been used, I would become as weak as an ordinary man." ¹²So Delilah took new ropes and bound him with

them, while an ambush was waiting in a room. And she cried, "Samson, the Philistines are upon you!" But he tore them off his arms like a thread. ¹³Then Delilah said to Samson, "You have been deceiving me all along; you have been lying to me! Tell me, how could you be tied up?" He answered her, "If you weave seven locks of my head into the web." ¹⁴And she pinned it with a peg and cried to him, "Samson, the Philistines are upon you!" Awaking from his sleep, he pulled out the peg, the loom, and the web.

¹⁵Then she said to him, "How can you say you love me, when you don't confide in me? This makes three times that you've deceived me and haven't told me what makes you so strong." ¹⁶Finally, after she had nagged him and pressed him constantly, he was wearied to death ¹⁷and he confided everything to her. He said to her, "No razor has ever touched my head, for I have been a nazirite to God since I was in my mother's womb. If my hair were cut, my strength would leave me and I should become as weak as an ordinary man."

¹⁸Sensing that he had confided everything to her, Delilah sent for the lords of the Philistines, with this message: "Come up once more, for he has confided everything to me." And the lords of the Philistines came up and brought the money with them. ¹⁹She lulled him to sleep on her lap. Then she called in a man, and she had him cut off the seven locks of his head; thus she weakened him and made him helpless: his strength slipped away from him. ²⁰She cried, "Samson, the Philistines are upon you!" And he awoke from his sleep, thinking he would break loose and shake himself free as he had the other times. For he did not know that the LORD had departed from him. ²¹The Philistines seized him and gouged out his eyes. They brought him down to Gaza and shackled him in bronze fetters, and he became a mill slave in the prison. ²²After his hair was cut off, it began to grow back.

²³Now the lords of the Philistines gathered to offer a great sacrifice to their god Dagon and to make merry. They chanted,

"Our god has delivered into our hands
Our enemy Samson."

²⁴When the people saw him, they sang praises to their god, chanting,

"Our god has delivered into our hands
The enemy who devastated our land,
And who slew so many of us."

²⁵As their spirits rose, they said, "Call Samson here and let him dance for us." Samson was fetched from the prison, and he danced for them. Then they put him between the pillars. ²⁶And Samson said to the boy who was leading him by the hand, "Let go of me and let me feel the pillars that the temple rests upon, that I may lean on them." ²⁷Now the temple was full of men and women; all the lords of the Philistines were there, and there were some three thousand men and women on the roof watching Samson dance. ²⁸Then Samson called to the LORD, "O Lord GOD! Please remember me, and give me strength just this once, O God, to take revenge of the Philistines, if only for one of my two eyes." ²⁹He embraced the two middle pillars that the temple rested upon, one with his right arm and one with his left, and leaned against them; ³⁰Samson cried, "Let me die with the Philistines!" and he pulled with all his might. The temple came crashing down on the lords and on all the people in it. Those who were slain by him as he died outnumbered those who had been slain by him when he lived.

³¹His brothers and all his father's household came down and carried him up and buried him in the tomb of his father Manoah, between Zorah and Eshtaol. He had led Israel for twenty years.

Judges 13 begins with the standard opener we have come to expect in the stories of the settlement period in the book of Judges: the undisciplined Israelites had strayed from the path of faith yet again, and God had punished them by delivering them into the hands of the enemy. This time it was the Philistines, and the Israelite tribes of Dan and Judah had suffered under them for forty years. Presumably, God was ready to give them a break and dispatched an angel to inform the barren wife of Manoah the Danite that she would conceive a son. This child would be dedicated to the Lord, and "he shall be the first to deliver Israel from the Philistines" (13:5).

Right away we know this story is not going to end well. The phrase "he shall be the first" implies that the liberation of Israel from the Philistines will be a long, tortuous process that will not be completed by Samson (but eventually by David). He will have impressive successes, but he will not vanquish the enemy; rather, they will vanquish him. The people of Israel have not yet proven their commitment to the covenant they made with God. Therefore, they are not deserving of complete deliverance. Instead, they get a problematic hero. This is a setup.

For starters Samson's pedigree is somewhat questionable. His mother is never mentioned by name, remaining largely anonymous throughout the story. His father, Manoah, is depicted as a doofus; he is not privy to the announcement of Samson's conception and is left trailing after his wife in search of information from the messenger angel (Judg.13:11). Much has been written in the rabbinic literature about his bumbling nature and dubious intelligence. Not the sharpest tool in the shed. Curiously, an intimate union between Manoah and his wife is never reported. In fact, some commentators have suggested that Manoah's absence when the angel spoke to his wife the first time is a hint to the identity of Samson's real father. She was out there by herself in a field when the angel appeared, no witnesses. Who knows what really happened, and anyway, would you blame her?

Young Samson was blessed by God and gradually grew aware of his special gifts. As a kind of BamBam Flintstone, innocent and naive, he no doubt surprised those around him and himself with his feats of superhuman strength. Although he may have been frightened by the realization that he was a freak of nature, perhaps he took comfort in knowing he was destined for great things. Then he hit puberty, and all hell broke loose.

SAMSON'S WOMEN

Samson the hero struggled to build normative relationships with women. When we next meet him, he is hopelessly infatuated with a Philistine girl he had caught sight of on a jaunt to Timnah, a city of the uncircumcised. He demanded that his parents arrange a marriage to her at once, and they responded with that timeless "Jewish" guilt trip: couldn't you find someone from the tribe to marry? Unbeknown to all of them, the hand of God was behind Samson's hots for the Philistine maiden (Judg. 14:4), but it seems that even in ancient Israel gentile girls wielded a magnetic power over men of the Mosaic faith. What was it about them? Did they have cute, upturned noses? Narrow hips? Blonde highlights from frolics in the crow's nest? Opposite these bewitching women, Samson couldn't think straight.

The first showdown came at the wedding when Samson's Philistine guests at the bachelor party were frustratingly stumped by his riddle. Clearly unwilling to concede gentlemanly defeat, they threatened to ice the bride and her family if she didn't come up with the answer. An intelligent woman would have appealed rationally to her new husband: "Darling, the townies' honor is at stake. If you make them look bad, they will kill me. Please find a way to let them win and boost their self-esteem so that you and I can conclude the celebrations and live together happily ever after."

However, the Philistine bride (who, interestingly, also remained nameless) instead chose the newlywed tack: she accused Samson of withholding information because he didn't really love her. She then proceeded to lock herself in the equivalent of the bathroom and to cry for the entire weeklong wedding party. She nagged her new husband so relentlessly that he finally gave in and revealed the answer to the riddle. Not only did Samson go home furious after being bested by the wedding guests, but the reader is left wondering how the hero of Israel gave in to a whining, vapid Philistine "princess." He vented his anger by slaughtering thirty Philistines in Ashkelon. As the Samson story unfolds, every failed relationship with a Philistine girl will be followed by an act of terrorism.

After three experiences with Philistine women, hundreds of dead Philistines, and untold damage caused by Samson, the story climaxes with Delilah the infamous temptress. Her origins are never mentioned; she may have been a Judaean girl (according to the rabbinic commentators her Hebrew name means "she who weakened") or the ultimate shiksa. She is the only woman in Samson's life whose name is revealed to us, and we are told that Samson loved her, although she was unaware of his nazarite vows and the significance of his long hair. We never learn whether she loved him, but if she was willing to entrap him in exchange for money it's possible that his love for her was unrequited. Samson must have known this, but he played along at her game, coyly offering false explanations for the secret of his strength. She tied him up every which way and made him jump while her handlers waited for results. He sent her running for fresh thongs, new ropes, pins with a loom—anything to keep her busy and out of reach of his secret. But Delilah too pulled the emotional card. "How can you say you love me, when you don't confide in me?" (16:15). And he fell for it. Samson, the great Jewish hero, was humiliatingly defeated because he couldn't resist the power of a nagging girlfriend. He succumbed knowing full well that the consequences would be horrendous, preferring death to her relentless hectoring.

AN IMPERFECT HERO

The most vexing question about these stories is the glaring contradiction between Samson's designation as a superhero without an army and his potential to defeat the Philistines, and his undoing to a very tragic end thanks to his great weakness in the face of a woman. Despite the unique circumstances of his birth and God's blessing over him, Samson's destiny was ultimately to be defeated by his own character flaws. How could God have chosen such a problematic individual to be the redeemer of Israel? What was God thinking when he devised this bizarre strategy to deliver his people?

If we reread the verses about Samson's birth story and the prediction that he would *begin* the conquest of the Philistines, we can't say we weren't warned that the Philistines would prevail over him. Samson was not the ideal hero, but he was probably the best the Israelites had to offer in the search for leadership potential. The fact that he couldn't deliver the goods was indicative of the sorry state the people of Israel had reached at this point. Scattered, incohesive, in constant violation of the special covenant they had taken on, the tribes of Israel were a mess. God, in his mercy, tried to help out, and Samson was the best material he had to work with. He was a reflection of the rut into which the Israelites had fallen and were now stuck, spinning their wheels wildly in an attempt to extricate themselves. In revealing the disappointing results of Samson's gifts, the book of Judges is leading us toward an inevitable conclusion: the answer to Israel's tribulations is not charismatic chieftains but rather a stable monarchy.

So, should we urge our kids to eat their spinach so they can be strong like Samson? The rabbinic sages concluded that Samson was not a great role model, insisting that physical strength is meaningless as long as it is not matched by strong character and integrity. The Mishna declares, "Who is strong? He who can control his desire" (*Avot* iv,1), thus effectively framing Samson in a negative light.

Yet, Samson's might has left an indelible impression nonetheless. The Danite strongman is a bona fide brand name in modern Israel; the name "Samson" has been adopted by a diverse collection of groups such as units of the Israel Defense Forces, special force squads of the police, and a chain of body-building gyms. With the birth of the Zionist movement, the idea of the new Jew—physically strong, independent, and resolute—was nourished by the Samson character, who, rediscovered and reinvented, symbolized strength, self-reliance, and victory in his modern Zionist remaking.

Ruth the Moabitess at Bethlehem

Ruth 1–4

6

A gentile woman leaves her life behind
and joins the nation of Israel

See page 320 for visitor information.

WHERE ARE WE?

The Bell Position, overlooking Bethlehem and in between Kibbutz Ramat Rachel and the village of Tsur Baher, was the southern border of west Jerusalem between 1948 and 1967. This spot, our lookout point, was a Jordanian military complex of bunkers and caves surrounded by mines and stretching over three hundred *dunams* (seventy-five acres). Its shape on the ground resembles a bell, hence its name. The position was captured from the Jordanians by the Israel Defense Forces during the Six-Day War of 1967. Little remains of the original trenches and bunkers; on the central bunker stands a memorial to the six soldiers killed here, made of bell clappers.

SETTING THE SCENE

Standing on the platform looking east (to the left), we can see the residential buildings of the Har Homa neighborhood, established in 1997 during Benjamin Netanyahu's first term as prime minister. The construction caused a controversy because it was initiated during a period in which Yitzhak Rabin, before he was assassinated, had

Fig. 6. The city of Bethlehem, 2013

agreed with Yasser Arafat to maintain the status quo in Jerusalem until the city's borders came up for final status negotiations. While the neighborhood is officially over the Green Line, some Israelis view it as a legitimate expansion of Jewish Jerusalem. Others may view it as a settlement.

Looking west (to the right) you can see the square bell tower of Mar Elias, erected by the Byzantines in the sixth century CE and today a Greek Orthodox monastery. Mar Elias is Aramaic for Saint or Lord Elijah, who, according to tradition, stopped here to rest as he escaped from Jezebel's wrath after slaughtering the prophets at Mount Carmel. Further beyond Mar Elias to the west are the high rises of the Gilo neighborhood of Jerusalem, one of the new Jerusalem neighborhoods built after 1967.

Directly ahead of us, off in the distance to the south, is the sprawling metropolis of Bethlehem. Inside the area under the jurisdiction of the Palestinian Authority, Bethlehem is one of the eight largest cities in the West Bank; its population, together with the adjacent villages of Bet Sahour and Bet Jalla, numbers about 61,000, half Christian and half Muslim. The greater Bethlehem district numbers 140,000 and includes the populations of cities, villages, farms, and refugee camps as well as Bedouins.

In trying to imagine the Bethlehem of Ruth's time, it's helpful to study the landscape just over the fence to the south. Rocky and uninhabited, this hilly terrain is typical of the Judaean Highlands and is probably what we would have seen all around us had we stood here over three thousand years ago. Ruth and Naomi's Bethlehem was a small village, its rooftops perhaps just visible from this distance. The mountains of Moab lie to the east, in modern-day Jordan. If we could drive there directly, it would take little more than an hour to get from Jerusalem to Amman; at night the headlights of the cars winding through the hills on the other side are easily visible from here. Although the journey to Moab included a steep descent into the rift valley of the Dead Sea area and then an arduous climb out, it probably would have taken Elimelech and his family just two or three days to get there from Bethlehem.

THE CONTEXT

The book of Ruth is an exquisitely crafted gem that stands on its own in relation to the biblical history. Although Ruth's first verse announces that the story takes place "in the days when the chieftains ruled," in the Hebrew Bible Ruth is not part of the book of Judges. Instead, it is included in the Kethuvim, or Writings, a diverse collection of works in the third and final section of the Tanakh, all of which were written long after the Torah. Ruth has been included here at this point in the chronology thanks to its historical hint, even though the language and textual references clearly indicate it is a later work. (In contrast, in Christian Bibles Ruth follows Judges.)

The period of the judges was a time of social upheaval, foreign invasions, lawlessness, and anarchy. Yet the events in Ruth transpire in a parallel universe of pastoral tranquility, just as a long period of famine gives way to a bountiful harvest. An important source of background information for this story is midrash, the rabbinic folk literature.

The midrash is about as reliable a historical record as the story of George Washington chopping down the cherry tree. Both are probably based on a kernel of truth but were embellished and expanded over the ages for educational purposes. If we imagine the elders of Israel in ancient times crouching around the tribal campfire and regaling the folk with tales of their ancestors, this is how they might have introduced the story of Ruth the Moabitess:

A very long time ago, in the days when the chieftains ruled, the Israelites sinned. They had no respect for the chieftains God sent to govern them, they did not honor the messengers of God, and they disobeyed the laws of the covenant. Since the Israelites were unrepentant, God punished them with a famine.

Elimelech was a wealthy aristocrat from Bethlehem in Judah. His wife was Naomi, and their sons were called Mahlon ,which means sickness, and Chilion, consumptive, symbolic names that surely hinted at their fate. As an upstanding citizen, during the famine Elimelech could have demonstrated leadership by organizing the townspeople and assisting the poor. Unfortunately, his only concern was that the needy would come knocking at his door and bankrupt him. Instead of using his position and wealth to help, he took his family, left Bethlehem, and moved to Moab, abandoning the needy.

As members of a rich family of high birth, Elimelech and his sons were welcomed by the Moabites and appointed as officers in their army. The sons, Mahlon and Chilion, prospered and were married to Ruth and Orpah, the daughters of the Moabite king Eglon, after Elimelech died.

However, the sons' wives were unable to conceive, and both couples remained childless. After they had been married for some time, the husbands both died. Their mother, Naomi, widowed and now childless, decided to return home to her kinsmen in Bethlehem.

Note: This description is based on the midrashic source compilation in Louis Ginzberg's *The Legends of the Jews*.

- -

Ruth 1

¹In the days when the chieftains ruled, there was a famine in the land; and a man of Bethlehem in Judah, with his wife and two sons, went to reside in the country of Moab. ²The man's name was Elimelech, his wife's name was Naomi, and his two sons were named Mahlon and Chilion—Ephrathites of Bethlehem in Judah. They came to the country of Moab and remained there.

³Elimelech, Naomi's husband, died; and she was left with her two sons. ⁴They married Moabite women, one named Orpah and the other Ruth, and they lived there about ten years. ⁵Then those two—Mahlon and Chilion—also died; so the woman was left without her two sons and without her husband.

⁶She started out with her daughters-in-law to return from the country of Moab; for in the country of Moab she had heard that the LORD had taken note of His people and given them food. ⁷Accompanied by her two daughters-in-

law, she left the place where she had been living; and they set out on the road back to the land of Judah.

⁸But Naomi said to her two daughters-in-law, "Turn back, each of you to her mother's house. May the LORD deal kindly with you, as you have dealt with the dead and with me! ⁹May the LORD grant that each of you find security in the house of a husband!" And she kissed them farewell. They broke into weeping ¹⁰and said to her, "No, we will return with you to your people."

¹¹But Naomi replied, "Turn back, my daughters! Why should you go with me? Have I any more sons in my body who might be husbands for you? ¹²Turn back, my daughters, for I am too old to be married. Even if I thought there was hope for me, even if I were married tonight and I also bore sons, ¹³should you wait for them to grow up? Should you on their account debar yourselves from marriage? Oh no, my daughters! My lot is far more bitter than yours, for the hand of the LORD has struck out against me."

¹⁴They broke into weeping again, and Orpah kissed her mother-in-law farewell. But Ruth clung to her. ¹⁵So she said, "See, your sister-in-law has returned to her people and her gods. Go follow your sister-in-law." ¹⁶But Ruth replied, "Do not urge me to leave you, to turn back and not follow you. For wherever you go, I will go; wherever you lodge, I will lodge; your people shall be my people, and your God my God. ¹⁷Where you die, I will die, and there I will be buried. Thus and more may the LORD do to me if anything but death parts me from you." ¹⁸When [Naomi] saw how determined she was to go with her, she ceased to argue with her; ¹⁹and the two went on until they reached Bethlehem.

When they arrived in Bethlehem, the whole city buzzed with excitement over them. The women said, "Can this be Naomi?" ²⁰"Do not call me Naomi," she replied. "Call me

Mara, for Shaddai has made my lot very bitter. ²¹I went away full, and the LORD has brought me back empty. How can you call me Naomi, when the LORD has dealt harshly with me, when Shaddai has brought misfortune upon me!"

²²Thus Naomi returned from the country of Moab; she returned with her daughter-in-law Ruth the Moabite. They arrived in Bethlehem at the beginning of the barley harvest.

2

¹Now Naomi had a kinsman on her husband's side, a man of substance, of the family of Elimelech, whose name was Boaz.

²Ruth the Moabite said to Naomi, "I would like to go to the fields and glean among the ears of grain, behind someone who may show me kindness." "Yes, daughter, go," she replied; ³and off she went. She came and gleaned in a field, behind the reapers; and, as luck would have it, it was the piece of land belonging to Boaz, who was of Elimelech's family.

⁴Presently Boaz arrived from Bethlehem. He greeted the reapers, "The LORD be with you!" And they responded, "The LORD bless you!" ⁵Boaz said to the servant who was in charge of the reapers, "Whose girl is that?" ⁶The servant in charge of the reapers replied, "She is a Moabite girl who came back with Naomi from the country of Moab. ⁷She said, 'Please let me glean and gather among the sheaves behind the reapers.' She has been on her feet ever since she came this morning. She has rested but little in the hut."

⁸Boaz said to Ruth, "Listen to me, daughter. Don't go to glean in another field. Don't go elsewhere, but stay here close to my girls. ⁹Keep your eyes on the field they are reaping, and follow them. I have ordered the men not to

molest you. And when you are thirsty, go to the jars and drink some of [the water] that the men have drawn."

[10]She prostrated herself with her face to the ground, and said to him, "Why are you so kind as to single me out, when I am a foreigner?"

[11]Boaz said in reply, "I have been told of all that you did for your mother-in-law after the death of your husband, how you left your father and mother and the land of your birth and came to a people you had not known before. [12]May the LORD reward your deeds. May you have a full recompense from the LORD, the God of Israel, under whose wings you have sought refuge!"

[13]She answered, "You are most kind, my lord, to comfort me and to speak gently to your maidservant—though I am not so much as one of your maidservants."

[14]At mealtime, Boaz said to her, "Come over here and partake of the meal, and dip your morsel in the vinegar." So she sat down beside the reapers. He handed her roasted grain, and she ate her fill and had some left over.

[15]When she got up again to glean, Boaz gave orders to his workers, "You are not only to let her glean among the sheaves, without interference, [16]but you must also pull some [stalks] out of the heaps and leave them for her to glean, and not scold her."

[17]She gleaned in the field until evening. Then she beat out what she had gleaned—it was about an 'ephah of barley—[18]and carried it back with her to the town. When her mother-in-law saw what she had gleaned, and when she also took out and gave her what she had left over after eating her fill, [19]her mother-in-law asked her, "Where did you glean today? Where did you work? Blessed be he who took such generous notice of you!" So she told her mother-in-law whom she had worked with, saying, "The name of the man with whom I worked today is Boaz."

20Naomi said to her daughter-in-law, "Blessed be he of the LORD, who has not failed in His kindness to the living or to the dead! For," Naomi explained to her daughter-in-law, "the man is related to us; he is one of our redeeming kinsmen." 21Ruth the Moabite said, "He even told me, 'Stay close by my workers until all my harvest is finished.'" 22And Naomi answered her daughter-in-law Ruth, "It is best, daughter, that you go out with his girls, and not be annoyed in some other field." 23So she stayed close to the maidservants of Boaz, and gleaned until the barley harvest and the wheat harvest were finished. Then she stayed at home with her mother-in-law.

3

1Naomi, her mother-in-law, said to her, "Daughter, I must seek a home for you, where you may be happy. 2Now there is our kinsman Boaz, whose girls you were close to. He will be winnowing barley on the threshing floor tonight. 3So bathe, anoint yourself, dress up, and go down to the threshing floor. But do not disclose yourself to the man until he has finished eating and drinking. 4When he lies down, note the place where he lies down, and go over and uncover his feet and lie down. He will tell you what you are to do." 5She replied, "I will do everything you tell me."

6She went down to the threshing floor and did just as her mother-in-law had instructed her. 7Boaz ate and drank, and in a cheerful mood went to lie down beside the grainpile. Then she went over stealthily and uncovered his feet and lay down. 8In the middle of the night, the man gave a start and pulled back—there was a woman lying at his feet!

9"Who are you?" he asked. And she replied, "I am your handmaid Ruth. Spread your robe over your handmaid, for you are a redeeming kinsman."

¹⁰He exclaimed, "Be blessed of the LORD, daughter! Your latest deed of loyalty is greater than the first, in that you have not turned to younger men, whether poor or rich. ¹¹And now, daughter, have no fear. I will do in your behalf whatever you ask, for all the elders of my town know what a fine woman you are. ¹²But while it is true I am a redeeming kinsman, there is another redeemer closer than I. ¹³Stay for the night. Then in the morning, if he will act as a redeemer, good! let him redeem. But if he does not want to act as redeemer for you, I will do so myself, as the LORD lives! Lie down until morning."

¹⁴So she lay at his feet until dawn. She rose before one person could distinguish another, for he thought, "Let it not be known that the woman came to the threshing floor." ¹⁵And he said, "Hold out the shawl you are wearing." She held it while he measured out six measures of barley, and he put it on her back.

When she got back to the town, ¹⁶she came to her mother-in-law, who asked, "How is it with you, daughter?" She told her all that the man had done for her; ¹⁷and she added, "He gave me these six measures of barley, saying to me, 'Do not go back to your mother-in-law empty-handed.'" ¹⁸And Naomi said, "Stay here, daughter, till you learn how the matter turns out. For the man will not rest, but will settle the matter today."

4

¹Meanwhile, Boaz had gone to the gate and sat down there. And now the redeemer whom Boaz had mentioned passed by. He called, "Come over and sit down here, So-and-so!" And he came over and sat down. ²Then [Boaz] took ten elders of the town and said, "Be seated here"; and they sat down.

³He said to the redeemer, "Naomi, now returned from the country of Moab, must sell the piece of land which belonged to our kinsman Elimelech. ⁴I thought I should disclose the matter to you and say: Acquire it in the presence of those seated here and in the presence of the elders of my people. If you are willing to redeem it, redeem! But if you will not redeem, tell me, that I may know. For there is no one to redeem but you, and I come after you." "I am willing to redeem it," he replied. ⁵Boaz continued, "When you acquire the property from Naomi and from Ruth the Moabite, you must also acquire the wife of the deceased, so as to perpetuate the name of the deceased upon his estate." ⁶The redeemer replied, "Then I cannot redeem it for myself, lest I impair my own estate. You take over my right of redemption, for I am unable to exercise it."

⁷Now this was formerly done in Israel in cases of redemption or exchange: to validate any transaction, one man would take off his sandal and hand it to the other. Such was the practice in Israel. ⁸So when the redeemer said to Boaz, "Acquire for yourself," he drew off his sandal. ⁹And Boaz said to the elders and to the rest of the people, "You are witnesses today that I am acquiring from Naomi all that belonged to Elimelech and all that belonged to Chilion and Mahlon. ¹⁰I am also acquiring Ruth the Moabite, the wife of Mahlon, as my wife, so as to perpetuate the name of the deceased upon his estate, that the name of the deceased may not disappear from among his kinsmen and from the gate of his home town. You are witnesses today."

¹¹All the people at the gate and the elders answered, "We are. May the LORD make the woman who is coming into your house like Rachel and Leah, both of whom built up the House of Israel! Prosper in Ephrathah and perpetuate your name in Bethlehem! ¹²And may your house

be like the house of Perez whom Tamar bore to Judah—through the offspring which the LORD will give you by this young woman."

¹³So Boaz married Ruth; she became his wife, and he cohabited with her. The LORD let her conceive, and she bore a son. ¹⁴And the women said to Naomi, "Blessed be the LORD, who has not withheld a redeemer from you today! May his name be perpetuated in Israel! ¹⁵He will renew your life and sustain your old age; for he is born of your daughter-in-law, who loves you and is better to you than seven sons."

¹⁶Naomi took the child and held it to her bosom. She became its foster mother, ¹⁷and the women neighbors gave him a name, saying, "A son is born to Naomi!" They named him Obed; he was the father of Jesse, father of David.

¹⁸This is the line of Perez: Perez begot Hezron, ¹⁹Hezron begot Ram, Ram begot Amminadab, ²⁰Amminadab begot Nahshon, Nahshon begot Salmon, ²¹Salmon begot Boaz, Boaz begot Obed, ²²Obed begot Jesse, and Jesse begot David.

DO THE RIGHT THING

The book of Ruth has often been described as an idyllic love story, but to read it solely from this perspective is to do it great injustice. Written in the artful style of biblical storytelling, this tale flows with deep undercurrents of the classic themes of the biblical narrative. In an unusual departure from the ideas of nationhood and obedience to law so central to many of the biblical stories, at the heart of Ruth's happy ending is *hesed*—acts of loving kindness.

The first role model for outstanding human behavior is, of course, Ruth. Her foreign husband dead, she is expected to return to her parents' house. While Ruth is not required by law to remain with her mother-in-law, a childless widow who has no one dear to her left on earth, her conscience obligates her to care for Naomi. She knows that as a Moabitess she will remain an outsider in Naomi's world but chooses, nonetheless, to cleave to her and to accept and internalize the culture of the Israelites. (Do you know anyone who would do that for her mother-in-law?) All of Ruth's actions emanate not only from her love for Naomi but also from her commitment to Elimelech's clan, as she takes on Naomi's role by giving birth to a child who will belong first to the family.

The second archetype of noble behavior is Boaz, a relative of Naomi's from the same clan. The Deuteronomic laws of levirate marriage required that a widow be taken as wife by the deceased's brother, in order to perpetuate the name of the dead man and to keep his property in the family (Deut. 25:5–10). As a distant kinsman, Boaz was duty-bound to purchase Naomi's land, but he was not required by law to marry Ruth, especially since she was a foreigner.

Yet from the first time he encountered Ruth in his barley field, Boaz treated her graciously, despite the fact that he was not expected to give her the time of day (Ruth 2). Boaz ensured that the neediest members of the community could glean in his fields, according to the welfare laws of biblical society. His loving kindness crescendoed on the night Ruth came to visit him at the threshing floor (Ruth 3). Much has been written about the sexual connotations in this scene and the actual meaning of the term "uncovered his feet." Some scholars understand this to mean that Ruth actually exposed Boaz's genitals and offered herself to him sexually. However, others read it literally—she uncovered just his feet, and nothing else.

By reinterpreting the original Hebrew text, it is also possible to understand that Ruth actually uncovered herself, that is, she lay down next to Boaz and beseeched him to spread his garment (also translated as "wing") over her, thereby accepting responsibility for her and Naomi by pledging to marry her. This kind of initiative by women is rare in the Bible, and it was not looked upon kindly by the sages. In both interpretations Ruth took an enormous risk by making herself vulnerable to Boaz, but he recognized her altruism immediately. In the extremely unconventional manner of her request, Ruth asked Boaz to take care of the weakest members of the family. Both Ruth and Boaz were individuals who looked beyond the letter of the law to the spirit of the law. They did the right thing, and for this they have been revered as paragons of *hesed* for generations.

AN ISRAELITE BY CHOICE

A second important theme in Ruth concerns the question of conversion: what kind of outsider is worthy to join the people of Israel? According to the biblical text, Moabites were undesirable, due to their despicable origins as the offspring of the incestuous union between Lot and his daughter (Gen. 19:30–38). Later, they lured the Israelites into idolatry (Num. 25:1–3). They were specifically disqualified in Deuteronomy because they were inhospitable to the Israelites after the exodus from Egypt. The Moabites even hired someone to pronounce a curse on them (Deut. 23:4–7).

Ruth was a Moabitess by birth, and she could not change her ethnicity. (In an attempt to "kosher" Ruth despite her Moabite origins, the rabbinic sages claim, in a hairsplitting interpretation of the text, that the biblical prohibition in Deut. 23:4 applies only to Moabites, and not Moabitesses [*b. Yevamot* 76b].) The ancient world had no procedure for religious conversion or adopting a new citizenship, ideas that simply did not exist in the cultural lexicon of the time. In this sense Ruth revolutionized the concept of identity by professing her ability to choose the people to whom she would belong. Her choice was about values, not nationality; by adopting the laws of Israel as her own and setting a personal example in her actions, Ruth determined the gold standard for conversion to Judaism. Boaz beautifully encapsulated this concept when he blessed her by saying, "May you have a full recompense from the Lord, the God of Israel, under whose wings you have sought refuge" (2:12).

Traditionally, Judaism has not encouraged conversion, taking the skeptical stance that the responsibilities and risks inherent in a Jewish identity are too much to expect most folks to take on by choice. For centuries the rabbinic tradition advocated the rejection of a prospective convert three times, in the spirit of Naomi's initial rejection of Ruth, in order to ascertain if his or her motivations were serious.

In later times clear regulations for conversion were formulated. For those who choose the path of the Mosaic faith, men must be circumcised, a token of the covenant between Abraham, and all the Jewish people, with God. In addition, both men and women must undergo full immersion in a ritual bath, the *mikveh*. The act of being completely submerged in water, weightless, symbolizes a spiritual cleansing, a separation from the former life and a rebirth into a new path. Converts to Judaism choose their Hebrew names, followed by *ben Avraham v'Sarah* for a man and *bat Avraham v'Sarah* for a woman. Jewish law dictates that converts are full-fledged members of the Jewish people and are not to be identified as converts.

YOU GO, GIRL

Another thread woven through the Ruth story concerns the role of women. At the beginning of the story Ruth and Naomi are two defenseless females traveling alone, without the protection of any men, and as such are portrayed as the most vulnerable members of society. Ruth's choice to tie her destiny to Naomi's is yet another revolutionary concept in a world where the patriarchal family structure encouraged rivalry between women.

The book of Ruth concludes with a family tree that connects Ruth the Moabitess to King David (Ruth 4:17–22). In the Christian tradition Ruth is prominently listed as a forbearer of Jesus in the genealogy that opens the book of Matthew (Matt. 1:1–3). This recounting of the forty-two generations between Abraham and Jesus includes only four women—Ruth, Tamar, Rahab the harlot, and Bathsheba, the wife of Uriah. Christian scholars have speculated that these names represent the importance of women in Jesus's ministry, gentiles in Jesus's family tree, saints and sinners in his history, and smart, strong women who played a role in God's plan.

(Ruth's counterpart, Orpah, receives a more dubious write-up. In the rabbinic literature Ruth and Orpah were sisters, but Orpah's claim to fame was as a super-slut and the mother of four Philistine giants, one of whom was Goliath. To sully her sufficiently the sages state that her son Goliath was the result of polyspermy—an egg fertilized by more than one sperm, owing to the well over one hundred men that Orpah slept with [*Ruth Rabbah* 1:14]. According to this midrash, David and Goliath were cousins!)

By the end of the book, Ruth is transformed into a heroine because she has given birth to a son and saved the family. In this notion we find a fascinating link in the story to another woman who acted similarly. The last verses of the text list the genealogy of King David, for whom Ruth was a great-grandmother. The line begins with Perez, who was born under highly unusual circumstances. His mother, Tamar, tricked her father-in-law Judah into sleeping with her after her husbands (his sons) died and he refused to take responsibility for her (Gen. 38). Tamar and Ruth are soul sisters because they both cast aside conventions and endangered themselves in order to rescue the family from obliteration. The subtle link to Tamar poses a clear statement of quiet female empowerment: a woman is not merely a womb. Without courageous, exceptional women, all the males listed in the genealogy and David, the father of the Messiah, would never have been born.

Which brings us to the subject of David, whose mention at the end of the story, three generations before his birth, is clearly no accident. Why has he been elegantly slipped into the narrative? The answer may lie in the cultural mind-set of the Israelites, who were probably deeply disturbed by the fact that David had dubious origins. The tradition regarding David's Moabite connections subtly surfaces when he deposits his parents for safekeeping with the king of Moab as he flees Saul (1 Sam. 22:3–4). Let's face it—having a Moabite ancestor in ancient Israel would be like a Jew today admitting her grandmother was a voodoo priestess. Ruth's link to David was probably common knowledge, so David's scribes couldn't deny it. Instead, they may have chosen to spin it as a tale of how, thanks to Ruth's great virtuosity, God chose the house of David for the monarchy.

Today most scholars suggest that the book of Ruth was written in postexilic times. After the Jews returned from exile in Babylon, harsh measures against gentile wives and their children were instituted in order to eliminate foreign influence from the society of returnees. The story of Ruth the Moabitess may have served as a response to the sweeping condemnation of foreign wives. Not only was Ruth the model for the ideal convert, but her goodness was so rich and innate that she gave birth to the grandfather of the messianic dynasty.

7

The Levite and His Concubine at Gibeah

Judges 19

Societal breakdown in Israel leads to gang rape, murder, and dismemberment

See page 319 for visitor information.

WHERE ARE WE?

Tel el Ful (Hill of Beans) is the Arabic name for Gibeah, the administrative center of the biblical tribe of Benjamin in the days of the judges and its capital city in the days of King Saul onward (it is also known as Geva Binyamin and Givat Shaul). Exploratory excavations of the site have revealed remains of settlement from the early twelfth century BCE destroyed in the following century, and a subsequent eleventh-century BCE settlement built afterward. Although no archaeological remains are visible today, this ancient city is at the center of our story. Gibeah existed throughout the First Temple period and until the Roman conquest in the first century BCE.

After Israel's War of Independence in 1948, this hilltop served the Jordanian Legion as part of its defense system surrounding Jerusalem. The Jordanian army dug trenches and bunkers here because the site is located on an important road between Jerusalem and Samaria.

Fig. 7. King Hussein's unfinished villa at Tel el Ful (Gibeah)

SETTING THE SCENE

The shell of the modern building on the hilltop is the unfinished summer palace of the late King Hussein of Jordan. With its spectacular views of Jerusalem, the Old City, the lowlands, and on a clear day, the coastal plain, this site was chosen for the official holiday retreat of the Jordanian royal family. Construction commenced in 1966 but was halted abruptly when the Six-Day War broke out in June 1967. This hilltop was captured by Israel, together with east Jerusalem and the West Bank, in the war. Subsequently, the building's skeleton became a historical site in its own right.

THE CONTEXT

The book of Judges is about to come to a close. In the previous fourteen chapters (Judg. 3:7–16:31), we have learned of a series of charismatic but often flawed Israelite chieftains ("judges") who rose from anonymity to vanquish the enemies of the tribes of Israel and bring peace to their surroundings. A cyclic system emerges in the framework of the narratives and repeats itself throughout the book:

- The Israelites stray from the path of the Lord and violate the covenant by worshipping pagan gods.
- The Israelites are punished by a foreign oppressor who makes their lives miserable.
- The Israelites cry out to God to redeem them.
- A divinely appointed chieftain emerges from the Israelite tribes and leads the involved tribes in overcoming the enemy.
- Usually the chieftain rules for an extended period of quiet, but when he dies the Israelites revert to their idolatrous ways (sometimes the sinning even gets under way while he is still ruling).

The stories in Judges don't follow a clear chronological pattern. They seem to present a more geographical portrait of the Israelite tribulations, which often occurred simultaneously. We learn of the cruelty of the Moabites, the Canaanites, the Midianites, the Ammonites, and the Philistines, who harassed the tribes from every direction. These external enemies chipped away at the tribes' security, and the traditional Israelite leadership was unable to provide stability. Also, as the Israelites transitioned from nomadic herdsmen to sedentary settlers, they became loyal to the territories they had conquered. Each tribe was preoccupied with its own issues, and tension and strife between tribes pervaded the entire period.

The book of Judges describes a deep breakdown in the structures of traditional Israelite society. The tribal elders were elbowed aside by a new breed of ruler who galvanized people around him thanks to his divinely bestowed charisma, and not to a tribal pedigree. These chieftains stepped comfortably into the military roles that the traditional leadership had not succeeded in fulfilling in the face of Israel's many enemies. However, they were unable to establish long-lasting institutions that guaranteed the tribes' security and independence.

Judges traces the dizzying downward spiral of the Israelites as their traditional foundations unraveled and their society lost its direction. The five final chapters of the book (17–21) reveal the nadir of lawlessness and depravity to which the Israelites descended, at a time when "there was no king in Israel; everyone did as he pleased" (21:25).

- -

Judges 19

¹In those days, when there was no king in Israel, a Levite residing at the other end of the hill country of Ephraim took to himself a concubine from Bethlehem in Judah. ²Once his concubine deserted him, leaving him for her father's house in Bethlehem in Judah; and she stayed there a full four months. ³Then her husband set out, with an attendant and a pair of donkeys, and went after her to woo her and to win her back. She admitted him into her father's house; and when the girl's father saw him, he received him warmly. ⁴His father-in-law, the girl's father, pressed him, and he stayed with him three days; they ate and drank and lodged there. ⁵Early in the morning of the fourth day, he started to leave; but the girl's father said to his son-in-law, "Eat something to give you strength, then you can leave." ⁶So the two of them sat down and they feasted together. Then the girl's father said to the man, "Won't you stay overnight and enjoy yourself?" ⁷The man started to leave, but his father-in-law kept urging him until he turned back and spent the night there. ⁸Early in the morning of the fifth day, he was about to

leave, when the girl's father said, "Come, have a bite." The two of them ate, dawdling until past noon. ⁹Then the man, his concubine, and his attendant started to leave. His father-in-law, the girl's father, said to him, "Look, the day is waning toward evening; do stop for the night. See, the day is declining; spend the night here and enjoy yourself. You can start early tomorrow on your journey and head for home."

¹⁰But the man refused to stay for the night. He set out and traveled as far as the vicinity of Jebus—that is, Jerusalem; he had with him a pair of laden donkeys, and his concubine was with him. ¹¹Since they were close to Jebus, and the day was very far spent, the attendant said to his master, "Let us turn aside to this town of the Jebusites and spend the night in it." ¹²But his master said to him, "We will not turn aside to a town of aliens who are not of Israel, but will continue to Gibeah. ¹³Come," he said to his attendant, "let us approach one of those places and spend the night either in Gibeah or in Ramah." ¹⁴So they traveled on, and the sun set when they were near Gibeah of Benjamin.

¹⁵They turned off there and went in to spend the night in Gibeah. He went and sat down in the town square, but nobody took them indoors to spend the night. ¹⁶In the evening, an old man came along from his property outside the town. (This man hailed from the hill country of Ephraim and resided at Gibeah, where the townspeople were Benjaminites.) ¹⁷He happened to see the wayfarer in the town square. "Where," the old man inquired, "are you going to, and where do you come from?" ¹⁸He replied, "We are traveling from Bethlehem in Judah to the other end of the hill country of Ephraim. That is where I live. I made a journey to Bethlehem of Judah, and now I am on my way to the House of the LORD, and nobody has taken me indoors. ¹⁹We have both bruised straw and feed for our donkeys, and bread and wine for me and your handmaid, and for

the attendant with your servants. We lack nothing." ²⁰"Rest easy," said the old man. "Let me take care of all your needs. Do not on any account spend the night in the square." ²¹And he took him into his house. He mixed fodder for the donkeys; then they bathed their feet and ate and drank.

²²While they were enjoying themselves, the men of the town, a depraved lot, had gathered about the house and were pounding on the door. They called to the aged owner of the house, "Bring out the man who has come into your house, so that we can be intimate with him." ²³The owner of the house went out and said to them, "Please, my friends, do not commit such a wrong. Since this man has entered my house, do not perpetrate this outrage. ²⁴Look, here is my virgin daughter, and his concubine. Let me bring them out to you. Have your pleasure of them, do what you like with them; but don't do that outrageous thing to this man." ²⁵But the men would not listen to him, so the man seized his concubine and pushed her out to them. They raped her and abused her all night long until morning; and they let her go when dawn broke.

²⁶Toward morning the woman came back; and as it was growing light, she collapsed at the entrance of the man's house where her husband was. ²⁷When her husband arose in the morning, he opened the doors of the house and went out to continue his journey; and there was the woman, his concubine, lying at the entrance of the house, with her hands on the threshold. ²⁸"Get up," he said to her, "let us go." But there was no reply. So the man placed her on the donkey and set out for home. ²⁹When he came home, he picked up a knife, and took hold of his concubine and cut her up limb by limb into twelve parts. He sent them throughout the territory of Israel. ³⁰And everyone who saw it cried out, "Never has such a thing happened or been seen from the day the Israelites came out of the land of Egypt to this day! Put your mind to this; take counsel and decide."

The events of this chapter and the chapters that follow it seem more characteristic of a Coen brothers movie than the sacred text of the Bible. However, the shock value of the concubine's fate and the ensuing events of civil war against the tribe of Benjamin, the slaughter of the residents of Jabesh Gilead, and the sanctioned kidnapping of the daughters of Shiloh (read about all this in Judg. 20–21) is cleverly manipulated by the biblical writers in order to let us know that something is very rotten in Israel. (See also Judg. 17–18 for more choice examples of the problematic manner in which the Israelites built shrines and relations between tribes.)

The first clue that all hell has broken loose lies in the structure of the narrative. Thus far in Judges, most of the stories have followed the same five-stage cycle of idolatry-oppression-SOS-deliverance-quiet. In the final chapters of the book the pattern crumbles because rather than being threatened by invaders, now the enemy has come from within. The disintegration in the narrated material serves as a metaphor for the breakdown of Israelite society. Moreover, the narrator relates the events in cold, factual terms, almost without passing any judgment on the actions of the characters.

A second indication of the dire situation is the complete absence of names in the story of Gibeah; every single character remains anonymous (the only exception in Judg. 20:28 reinforces the rule). While this lack of identification universalizes the characters (there but for the grace of God, go I), more importantly, it dehumanizes them. If the narrator couldn't be bothered to identify the characters by name, we can infer that personal identity had lost its significance.

The cryptic information gleaned from the story about the Levite's relationship to his concubine also hints darkly at the dissolution of traditional family structure. We're told in the story that the concubine, a second-class wife, had run away from her husband. Although we never find out what caused her flight, we know she terminated their relationship and sauntered out into the public domain by herself to travel to her father's house. While the modern reader may cheer her feistiness, her actions grossly violated the accepted social codes of the time, which forbade women to venture out unchaperoned by a male. She was guilty of blatant sexual misconduct, and her behavior reflected poorly on her husband, who seemed incapable of controlling her.

A man who could not control his women was an object of ridicule and was unworthy of respect. The evil men of Gibeah who, behaving like the people of Sodom (see Gen. 19:4–5), demanded to have their way with the Levite were probably not a clutch of creepy perverts, but rather garden-variety heterosexuals who smelled a weak, ineffectual man they could humiliate by forcing him into the role of sexual object. Since the Levite was protected by his host, they settled instead for his concubine, an object that represented his lack of honor. Perhaps they turned down the offer of the host's daughter because in their eyes her father was a real man.

In fact, it's possible that when the Levite sent his concubine out to be ravished by the rabble, he was balancing accounts between them by punishing her for his lost honor. Perhaps in his gruesome dismemberment of her body, he wreaked his final act of revenge on her.

For readers familiar with the Pentateuch, a grim sense of foreboding hovers over this story. The events in Gibeah bear a striking similarity to an episode from Genesis 19:1–26 that describes the visit of two angels to Lot's house in Sodom. Lot, following in the tradition of his uncle Abraham, welcomes the guests warmly, but his house is surrounded by the town's men, who demand that the sojourners be sent out to them for their carnal pleasure. Lot and his family escape as God punishes the town by destroying it and all its inhabitants with a storm of fire and brimstone, whose sulfurous smell figuratively wafts over the story of the Levite and his concubine.

All these elements suggest a terrible turmoil in Israelite family life. The boundaries between the public and the private domain were blurred. Traditional codes of hospitality were trampled. Men could not be relied upon to protect the women under their responsibility. Women no longer respected male authority.

The dissolution of family values was probably the direct result of an overall collapse in the system of patriarchal authority and the Israelite commitment to the ethical laws of the covenant. The dimensions of the disintegration seep out between the lines of the story. We see it in the startling image of the abused concubine on the doorstep of the host's house in the early morning, helpless and abandoned; in the Levite's complete disregard of respect for the dead; in the brutal murder of the residents of Jabesh Gilead; in the sacrifice of the daughters of Shiloh to the remnant of the depraved Benjaminites; in the Benjaminites' choice of blind tribal loyalty over justice, which resulted in a cruel civil war and the near obliteration of one tribe.

THE K WORD

The picture of Israelite society painted by all the elements of the story is of a life-threatening emergency. The tribes were destroying themselves from within and were on the brink of no return. The special delivery of the concubine's mutilated appendages was the wake-up call. In previous chapters there is no record of a pan-tribal confederation for nonmilitary issues in Israel at this time. The record for galvanizing the tribes is held by Deborah, who brought together just six in a high point of national esprit de corps (Judg. 5:14–18). However, in the wake of the events of the last two chapters, all the tribes (except Benjamin) recognized the imminent catastrophe. They came together for the first time in the entire period chronicled in Judges and agreed to take decisive action despite the absence of any central leadership figure (Judg. 20:1–11). The Benjaminites were punished, nearly wiped out, and then saved at the final moment, the only response deemed fitting by the tribal confederation.

Yet after life returned to normal, the Israelites still found themselves deep in the throes of a leadership crisis. The multiple enemies and the breakdown of traditional society called for a dramatic new order. The Israelites decided they needed a king.

It wasn't an obvious solution. In fact, the demand for a king was slap in the face to God. The deal stipulated that the Israelites would abide by the covenant, and God would protect them. All their problems could be remedied easily, had they held up their part of the bargain. Instead, they wriggled out of the contract.

But their request was ultimately granted. In the eyes of the biblical redactors the monarchy was born in sin, but it was a necessary evil—even God was resigned (1 Sam. 8) The stories of the Levite and his concubine and the civil war between the tribes and Benjamin at the end of the period of the judges were uncontestable proof that Israel's days were numbered unless drastic action was taken.

8

David and Goliath in the Valley of Elah

1 Samuel 17

An anonymous shepherd boy defeats
the Philistine giant against all odds

See page 318 for visitor information.

WHERE ARE WE?

The brook of Elah seems to have been a strategic artery between Israelite and Philistine territory. The five Philistine cities—Gaza, Gath, Ashkelon, Ashdod, and Ekron—lay on the southern coastal plain, to the west. The Israelite population was firmly ensconced in the highlands to the east (if visibility is good you may be able to make out the city of Bethlehem on the ridge in the distance). The powerful Philistine army was determined to break through the Israelite chain of mountain settlements in order to take control of the Kings' Highway, a major thoroughfare of the ancient Middle Eastern road system. The brook of Elah marked the passageway through the lowlands toward the Judaean foothills, which the Philistines hoped to capture on their thrust eastward. The western part of the brook was already in their hands, as was the city of Azekah, the flat hilltop boasting a lone tree visible directly in front of you, on the western side of Route 38. The Philistines had advanced as far as Socoh, an ancient city on the hill behind you to the right, along the continuation of Route 375. (Socoh, a bare hilltop today, is known popularly as Givat HaTurmusim, or Lupine Hill. In the early spring the entire hill is covered with wild purple lupines, attracting hoards of weekend traffic.) Saul and his army were camped further east along the creek bed in order to block the Philistine advance eastward into Israelite territory via the brook of Elah.

When you've gotten your bearings on Socoh and Azekah, carefully descend down into the bed of the brook of Elah. Walk through the creek bed, away from the road, until you reach the deposits of stones left by the winter rains draining through the brook on their way to the Mediterranean. The length of your walk will vary, depending on the previous winter's rainfall and the number of visitors seeking stones like David's who have arrived before you. Find a place to sit and read the story.

THE CONTEXT

Samuel, the last of the judges, was educated as a priest and was also a prophet. He managed to convince the Israelites to abandon the practices of idol worship that they had adopted from their Canaanite neighbors. Immediately afterward the Israelite army successfully repelled an invasion by the Philistines, their most threatening enemy (1 Sam. 7:1–14). Samuel, charismatic and controlling, kept both the Israelites and their enemies on a short leash, but the Philistines loomed menacing on the horizon.

Until Samuel, nearing old age, set up his two corrupt sons to succeed him. Thinking ahead, the people of Israel realized that the moment Samuel disappeared from the scene and those two bozos took charge, the delicate balance he had maintained would fall to pieces in the face of the Philistine menace. Foreseeing a regression to the chaos and lawlessness that had characterized most of the era of

Fig. 8.1. The brook of Elah in the dry season

the judges, the Israelites petitioned Samuel to appoint a king—an undisputed leader who would raise a standing army and command it against the mighty Philistine host (1 Sam. 8:1–5).

With both reluctance and understanding, God chose Saul to inaugurate the monarchy. Although a modest peasant from Israel's smallest tribe, Benjamin, once filled with the spirit of the Lord Saul became a charismatic leader, his aura bolstered by his commanding height. God's choice of Saul seemed to convey the message that even the most unassuming man can be king over Israel—as long as it's in partnership with God.

As Israel's first divinely appointed monarch, Saul seemed to have potential. His father is described as "a man of substance" (1 Sam. 9:1), and Samuel announced that "there is none like (Saul) among all the people" (1 Sam. 10:24). "God gave him another heart" (1 Sam. 10:9),

Fig. 8.2. Stones in the brook of Elah

transforming him from a simple peasant into an instrument of God's will.

However, Saul was deeply insecure about his ability to fulfill the role that had been thrust on him. As the story progresses, we watch Saul as, again and again, he makes the wrong decision under pressure, disappointing Samuel, his soldiers, his family members, and of course, God.

Saul's worst mistake, from which there was no turning back, was to ignore the Lord's instructions. Samuel relayed God's specific orders to Saul to destroy Amalek, the ancient and deadly enemy of Israel, but he didn't deliver the goods (1 Sam.15:1–9). When God saw that Saul had not listened He was filled with remorse for having chosen him as king (1 Sam. 15:10–11). He withdrew His support from Saul and the first monarch of Israel became persona non grata. Samuel, the reluctant midwife of Israel's monarchy, took Saul's inadequacy very, very hard—so hard that he couldn't bear to see him again after the bitter and final disappointment of the Amalek fiasco (1 Sam. 15:34–35).

God, however, seemed to take this setback in stride. "Get over it," he admonished the bereft Samuel, perhaps gently reminding him that no one is perfect. "How long will you grieve over Saul, since I have rejected him as king over Israel? Fill your horn with oil and set out. I am sending you to Jesse the Bethlehemite, for I have decided on one of his sons to be king" (1 Sam.16:1).

Unbeknown to Saul as he arrayed his forces against the Philistines in the Valley of Elah, David, a low-level member of the royal court (1 Sam. 16:14–23), had already been secretly anointed as king over Israel (1 Sam. 16:1–13).

- -

1 Samuel 17

[1]The Philistines assembled their forces for battle; they massed at Socoh of Judah, and encamped at Ephes-dammim, between Socoh and Azekah. [2]Saul and the men of Israel massed and encamped in the valley of Elah. They drew up their line of battle against the Philistines, [3]with the Philistines stationed on one hill and Israel stationed on the opposite hill; the ravine was between them. [4]A champion of the Philistine forces stepped forward; his name was Goliath of Gath, and he was six cubits and a span tall. [5]He had a bronze helmet on his head, and wore a breastplate of scale armor, a bronze breastplate weighing five thousand shekels. [6]He had bronze greaves on his legs, and a bronze javelin [slung] from his shoulders. [7]The shaft of his spear was like a weaver's bar, and the iron head of his spear weighed six hundred shekels; and the shield-bearer marched in front of him.

[8]He stopped and called out to the ranks of Israel and he said to them, "Why should you come out to engage in

battle? I am the Philistine [champion], and you are Saul's servants. Choose one of your men and let him come down against me. ⁹If he bests me in combat and kills me, we will become your slaves; but if I best him and kill him, you shall be our slaves and serve us." And the Philistine ended, "I herewith defy the ranks of Israel. Get me a man and let's fight it out!" ¹¹When Saul and all Israel heard these words of the Philistine, they were dismayed and terror-stricken.

¹²David was the son of a certain Ephrathite of Bethlehem in Judah whose name was Jesse. He had eight sons, and in the days of Saul the man was already old, advanced in years. ¹³The three oldest sons of Jesse had left and gone with Saul to the war. The names of his three sons who had gone to the war were Eliab the first-born, the next Abinadab, and the third Shammah; ¹⁴and David was the youngest. The three oldest had followed Saul, ¹⁵and David would go back and forth from attending on Saul to shepherd his father's flock at Bethlehem.

¹⁶The Philistine stepped forward morning and evening and took his stand for forty days.

¹⁷Jesse said to his son David, "Take an ephah of this parched corn and these ten loaves of bread for your brothers, and carry them quickly to your brothers in camp. ¹⁸Take these ten cheeses to the captain of their thousand. Find out how your brothers are and bring some token from them." ¹⁹Saul and the brothers and all the men of Israel were in the valley of Elah, in the war against the Philistines.

²⁰Early next morning, David left someone in charge of the flock, took [the provisions], and set out, as his father Jesse had instructed him. He reached the barricade as the army was going out to the battle lines shouting the war cry. ²¹Israel and the Philistines drew up their battle lines opposite each other. ²²David left his baggage with the man in charge of the baggage and ran toward the

battle line and went to greet his brothers. ²³While he was talking to them, the champion, whose name was Goliath, the Philistine of Gath, stepped forward from the Philistine ranks and spoke the same words as before; and David heard him.

²⁴When the men of Israel saw the man, they fled in terror. ²⁵And the men of Israel were saying [among themselves], "Do you see that man coming out? He comes out to defy Israel! The man who kills him will be rewarded by the king with great riches; he will also give him his daughter in marriage and grant exemption to his father's house in Israel." ²⁶David asked the men standing near him, "What will be done for the man who kills that Philistine and removes the disgrace from Israel? Who is that uncircumcised Philistine that he dares defy the ranks of the living God?" ²⁷The troops told him in the same words what would be done for the man who killed him.

²⁸When Eliab, his oldest brother, heard him speaking to the men, Eliab became angry with David and said, "Why did you come down here, and with whom did you leave those few sheep in the wilderness? I know your impudence and your impertinence: you came down to watch the fighting!" ²⁹But David replied, "What have I done now? I was only asking!" ³⁰And he turned away from him toward someone else; he asked the same question, and the troops gave him the same answer as before.

³¹The things David said were overheard and were reported to Saul, who had him brought over. ³²David said to Saul, "Let no man's courage fail him. Your servant will go and fight that Philistine!" ³³But Saul said to David, "You cannot go to that Philistine and fight him; you are only a boy, and he has been a warrior from his youth!" ³⁴David replied to Saul, "Your servant has been tending his father's sheep, and if a lion or a bear came and carried off an animal

from the flock, ³⁵I would go after it and fight it and rescue it from its mouth. And if it attacked me, I would seize it by the beard and strike it down and kill it. ³⁶Your servant has killed both lion and bear; and that uncircumcised Philistine shall end up like one of them, for he has defied the ranks of the living God. ³⁷The LORD," David went on, "who saved me from lion and bear will also save me from that Philistine." "Then go," Saul said to David, "and may the LORD be with you!"

³⁸Saul clothed David in his own garment; he placed a bronze helmet on his head and fastened a breastplate on him ³⁹David girded his sword over his garment. Then he tried to walk; but he was not used to it. And David said to Saul, "I cannot walk in these, for I am not used to them." So David took them off. ⁴⁰He took his stick, picked a few smooth stones from the wadi, put them in the pocket of his shepherd's bag and, sling in hand, he went toward the Philistine.

⁴¹The Philistine, meanwhile, was coming closer to David, preceded by his shield-bearer. ⁴²When the Philistine caught sight of David, he scorned him, for he was but a boy, ruddy and handsome. ⁴³And the Philistine called out to David, "Am I a dog that you come against me with sticks?" The Philistine cursed David by his gods; ⁴⁴and the Philistine said to David, "Come here, and I will give your flesh to the birds of the sky and the beasts of the field."

⁴⁵David replied to the Philistine, "You come against me with sword and spear and javelin; but I come against you in the name of the LORD of Hosts, the God of the ranks of Israel, whom you have defied. ⁴⁶This very day the LORD will deliver you into my hands. I will kill you and cut off your head; and I will give the carcasses of the Philistine camp to the birds of the sky and the beasts of the earth. All the

earth shall know that there is a God in Israel. [47]And this whole assembly shall know that the LORD can give victory without sword or spear. For the battle is the LORD's, and He will deliver you into our hands."

[48]When the Philistine began to advance toward him again, David quickly ran up to the battle line to face the Philistine. [49]David put his hand into the bag; he took out a stone and slung it. It struck the Philistine in the forehead; the stone sank into his forehead, and he fell face down on the ground. [50]Thus David bested the Philistine with sling and stone; he struck him down and killed him. David had no sword; [51]so David ran up and stood over the Philistine, grasped his sword and pulled it from its sheath; and with it he dispatched him and cut off his head.

When the Philistines saw that their warrior was dead, they ran. [52]The men of Israel and Judah rose up with a war cry and they pursued the Philistines all the way to Gai and up to the gates of Ekron; the Philistines fell mortally wounded along the road to Shaarim up to Gath and Ekron. [53]Then the Israelites returned from chasing the Philistines and looted their camp.

[54]David took the head of the Philistine and brought it to Jerusalem; and he put his weapons in his own tent.

[55]When Saul saw David going out to assault the Philistine, he asked his army commander Abner, "Whose son is that boy, Abner?" And Abner replied, "By your life, Your Majesty, I do not know." [56]"Then find out whose son that young fellow is," the king ordered. [57]So when David returned after killing the Philistine, Abner took him and brought him to Saul, with the head of the Philistine still in his hand. [58]Saul said to him, "Whose son are you, my boy?" And David answered, "The son of your servant Jesse the Bethlehemite."

A CASE OF ROYAL AMNESIA

The contest between David and Goliath is arguably one of the most famous stories from the Bible and certainly one of the most beloved over the ages. The idea of the thundering giant vanquished by the resourceful, pure-of-heart shepherd boy aglow in the power of the Lord has inspired underdogs everywhere. But David's glorious victory is overshadowed by a bizarre turn of events. In the previous chapter we learned that after his secret anointment David was brought to the palace to serve Saul, first as a musician and then as an arms bearer. We are told, "Saul took a strong liking to (David) (1 Sam. 16:21). Yet King Saul, who sent David into battle following a long conversation (1 Sam. 17:31–40), professed not to recognize the lad as he sauntered off to fight Goliath. "Whose son is that boy, Abner?" (v. 55) Saul queried his defense minister. Was the sun in his eyes? What could possibly explain Saul's sudden case of amnesia regarding someone with whom he was well acquainted?

A TALE OF TWO SOURCES

It's actually not unusual to find accounts in the Bible that seem to contradict each other. In fact, the entire text is sprinkled with differing versions of the same event. For starters Genesis kicks off with two different creation stories (see Gen. 1 and 2). For another good example, skip ahead to 2 Samuel 21:19, where we're told that our very same Goliath is slain in battle by a dude from Bethlehem named Elhanan son of Jaare-oregim.

Scholars often clarify these inconsistencies in light of the different sources tapped to compile the biblical anthology as we know it. For example, one explanation is that the two Genesis creation stories, when read together, are complementary versions that flesh out the relationship between God and his human creations. Another explanation is that the two traditions were already sacred and the editor had to include both of them. It is also possible that the ancient editors were simply not bothered by inconsistencies. In the case of the identity of Goliath's slayer, some biblical scholars have suggested that Elhanan was David's original given name, before he became king and was renamed David ("beloved"). Others suggest that David's brother (they correct the text and read "Jaare" as "Jesse") killed Goliath, but in Samuel the story was attributed to David.

What about the discrepancy exposed when Saul draws a blank on David? One possible explanation is that the editors wanted to present two different stories about David's debut. In chapter 16 he is introduced as God's chosen, a gifted soul—the skilled musician and excellent warrior who appears on the scene to serve the king. In chapter 17 he is portrayed in a very different light, as an inexperienced but ambitious young man sent by his father on a delivery run to bring food to his brothers at the battlefield. Many scholars think it was imperative for the editors to present the accepted traditions and thus to create a multifaceted David; they were also convinced that the ancient editors were less concerned with the disparities between the stories.

THE "TRUTH" ABOUT SAUL

But perhaps, in this case, there is a plausible explanation for Saul's inability to identify David as he goes out to battle Goliath. Hints abound in the previous chapters when the narrator tells us that Saul exhibits some extremely erratic behavior. Eyebrows were raised when he went into an uncharacteristic ecstatic trance following his anointing as king over Israel by Samuel (1 Sam. 10:10–11). Yet when Samuel summoned all the people for Saul's official coronation a short while later, Saul never showed up. He was eventually located, hiding among the baggage (1 Sam. 10:17–24). Subsequently, following a frustrating confrontation with the Philistines, Saul became so distraught that he nearly killed his son Jonathan for unwittingly disobeying an order (1 Sam. 14:43–45). If by now the reader harbored any doubts about Saul's emotional stability, the biblical author dispenses with them unequivocally: "Now the spirit of the LORD had departed from Saul, and an evil spirit from the LORD began to terrify him" (1 Sam. 16:14).

Medical professionals have attempted to diagnose Saul's condition based on the descriptions of his behavior in the text. They have suggested he suffered from depression, bipolar disorder, or hypoglycemia brought on by a malfunction of the pituitary gland (which would also explain his unusual height). While he may very well have suffered from any of those illnesses, Saul was in the throes of an ongoing existential crisis, especially in the wake of his harsh confrontation with Samuel (1 Sam. 13, 15), who told him he had squandered his opportunity to be a successful king.

ENTER DAVID

Jesse was blessed with eight boys, seven of whom were paraded before Samuel for inspection. Samuel was immediately drawn to Eliab, the eldest of the brood and a handsome specimen of male attributes. "But the Lord said to Samuel, 'Pay no attention to his appearance or his stature, for I have rejected him. For not as man sees [does the LORD see]; man sees only what is visible, but the LORD sees into the heart'" (1 Sam. 16:7). We learn that David, the youngest of the brothers, was handsome without being tall, hinting at an inner radiance that projected outward—a man after God's own heart (1 Sam 13:14).

Perhaps here God was suggesting that he had failed with Saul and that Saul never had the right stuff. A king who is tall, drop-dead gorgeous, and a gifted warrior may impress the subjects (and the enemies), but ultimately it's what's inside that counts. God equipped Saul with his spirit, but evidently Saul never had what it took to be a successful king—that is, an innate, organic confidence in God's power to use him as a tool.

So when we finally meet Saul a while later, encamped on the battlefield in the Valley of Elah opposite the Philistines, he was in a bad way. Moody and dejected, he showed no leadership before his troops. For forty days Goliath had challenged the Israelite army, and although Saul was the tallest man in Israel and probably a Benjaminite expert with the slingshot himself, he made no move to engage the giant because he was just as intimidated as his soldiers.

Saul, obviously desperate, summoned David, who made the extraordinary claim that he could defeat the Philistine. Saul perfunctorily explained how unevenly matched David was against Goliath, sounding not like a stern father figure reprimanding a loose cannon but rather like a teacher hoping his star pupil would disprove his argument.

David spoke with the confidence of a person enveloped in the presence of God. His aura was so powerful that Saul, king of Israel, recognized immediately that this was the man who had been chosen by God to replace him. Yet he found it humanly impossible to internalize this resignation. Locked in a struggle between resentment and acknowledgment of David's rising star, Saul could not come to terms with the inevitable unfolding of events. His sudden amnesia can perhaps be explained as the expression of an emotional breakdown while David left behind Saul's armor and weapons and turned to approach Goliath with his character alone. When Saul asked Abner, "Whose son is that boy?" his right-hand man and military expert, unwilling to expose the king's vulnerability, played along. "By your life, Your Majesty, I do not know" (v. 55). Saul remained behind—rejected, defeated, humiliated, and no longer in his right mind.

The king's emotional instability would worsen in the days ahead. As his sanity unraveled, he would aim to pin David to the wall with his spear as David played the harp (1 Sam. 18:10–11). He would fly into a rage over Jonathan's friendship with David and attempt to murder his own son (1 Sam. 20:30–35). He would grow so single-mindedly obsessed with hunting down and eliminating David (1 Sam. 23–27) that he would neglect the imminent Philistine military threat and disregard the affairs of his kingdom.

POSTSCRIPT: THE UNDERDOG QUESTION

Over centuries the story of David and Goliath has warmed hearts, inspired countless meditations, and lifted innumerable dejected souls. Who among us has not, at some point, faced a menacing Goliath? Who doesn't love to cheer for David, the quintessential underdog, and delight in his victory against the odds? The much-loved Israeli pop song by the band Kaveret, "Goliath," which took first place in the 1975 hit parade, sums up the story in one unforgettable line: בפוני בול לו קלע (He [David] nailed him right in the bangs).

There's just one problem: According to some, David wasn't an underdog. For those who seek natural explanations for miraculous events in the Bible, a careful reading suggests a different conclusion. Moshe Dayan, perhaps Israel's most famous general, wrote that David was young, not particularly tall, and an inexperienced warrior. However, according to Dayan David was neither naive nor weak. He collected intelligence on his enemy, established exactly whom he was up against, and chose his weapons accordingly. It was impossible to ignore David's calculated advantages as he stood before Goliath: he was agile and mobile, while Goliath was weighed down with heavy armor. Goliath was expecting hand-to-hand combat, while David fired lethal ammunition from a distance. As explained in Moshe Dayan's *The Spirit of the Fighters*, David identified Goliath's weak point, his unprotected temples, and chose the right moment to turn his disadvantages into victory.

Indeed, the David and Goliath story is discussed in detail by Malcolm Gladwell in his 2013 book *David and Goliath*, which analyzes the classic misunderstandings of advantages and disadvantages. He claims that for ages, this story has been fundamentally misread and that David wasn't actually the underdog.

So, are you convinced? Most of us love this story in its traditional reading, with its message of eternal hope for the weak. Go tell one hundred thousand Israelis at two Kaveret reunion concerts in summer, 2013 singing, "He nailed him right in the bangs" that David wasn't an underdog.

9

David's Flight to En Gedi

1 Samuel 24

Saul and David unexpectedly come
face-to-face in a desert hideout

See page 312 for visitor information.

WHERE ARE WE?

En Gedi lies in the heart of the Judaean Wilderness, along the western shore of the Dead Sea. At 1,300 feet below sea level, this body of water is the lowest point on earth. This desert, part of the territory assigned to the Israelite tribe of Judah, was formed relatively late in geological time thanks to an enormous underground explosion that burst open the earth's surface and created a gigantic fissure known as the Syrian African Rift Valley. The pocket of warm air that hovers over the Dead Sea seals the rain clouds as they pass over it and move eastward, creating a vast area with almost no precipitation. However, much of the rainwater that falls on the high ridge to the west makes its way down to this basin, emptying into the Dead Sea and nourishing underground springs on the way as it seeps into the ground. En Gedi ("The Spring of the Goat") is fed by an aquifer where water has collected, drop by drop, after trickling down through the rock. A shift in the fault line created an opening for the water to flow down over the rocks and into the Dead Sea (although today the water is diverted to Kibbutz En Gedi for local use). The Nahal David walk follows the water uphill to the David Waterfall, where it emerges from the rock. The reserve also includes three additional springs.

The abundant source of water at En Gedi has attracted myriad forms of life to this oasis. Human remains from the Chalcolithic period five thousand years ago were found here, as well as a magnificent synagogue from the third century CE and signs of ancient agriculture indicating that En Gedi was an important center for the cultivation of dates and balsam. Flora and fauna abound in an impressive radius from the springs. You will see ferns, bamboo, acacia trees, Sodom's apple, giant reeds, capers, and numerous other plants that thrive in the desert. En Gedi is also home to many ibex, the wild mountain goat that gives the spring its name, and hyrax, a cute desert groundhog that is actually a very distant relative of the elephant. Nocturnal animals such as foxes, wolves, hyenas, and even leopards make their home at En Gedi too, but they will be asleep during your visit.

SETTING THE SCENE

Limestone is the basis for the terrain in the Judaean Desert, comprised of billions of tiny skeletons of marine animals that once lived in a giant sea covering this region. Limestone has varying degrees of hardness, but it can be dissolved by water over very long periods of time. This process, called Carstic action, results in the formation of natural caves in the rock. The cliffs overlooking the western shore of the Dead Sea are dotted with hundreds of these caves, many of which have been used over the ages as storerooms, caches, temporary shelters, and hiding places. The Judaean Desert has been well known as a haven for refugees in flight, and those not daunted by the harsh conditions here often found the craggy, inaccessible

Fig. 9.1. A waterfall at En Gedi. Photo courtesy of Susan Rheins.

caves to be quite hospitable. (The most famous Judaean desert caves at Qumran yielded hundreds of ancient scrolls stored or hidden over two thousand years ago, and documents and artifacts have been found in many others. They all survived thanks to the extreme aridity of the Dead Sea area.) Look beyond the trees on the right side of the path going into the reserve, and you will see a number of natural caves in the steep face of the rock. From this vantage point they appear completely inaccessible, but clear evidence of human presence has been found in those caves. They might very well be the caves that David and his men chose to hide in at En Gedi.

THE CONTEXT

We first meet David as he is secretly anointed king of Israel by Samuel in Bethlehem, and shortly afterward he is called

Fig. 9.2. A cave at En Gedi

to play a relatively minor role in King Saul's court (1 Sam. 16:14–23). A young shepherd with extraordinary musical talent, his job was to soothe the king's bad moods by playing the lyre. However, after David defeated the Philistine giant Goliath (see chapter 8), he was catapulted from anonymity to center stage. Saul took him under his wing and assigned him increasing missions and responsibility, which David carried out with great success and devotion. David also established a unique friendship with Jonathan, Saul's eldest son and heir apparent. David's meteoric rise to prominence appeared safely ensconced within the military hierarchy subordinate to King Saul—until the women of Israel started singing a certain song.

News of the victory over Goliath and the Philistines spread rapidly, and as Saul and the troops returned home from fighting, they were welcomed with a celebratory parade. Women cheered and ululated to the joyful music of tambourines and lutes, and as they cavorted they sang a little ditty:

"Saul has slain his thousands; David, his tens of thousands!" (1 Sam. 18:7)

The song shot immediately to the number one slot on the late second millennium BCE hit parade. Most scholars agree that the lyrics were probably composed according to a standard formula for celebratory odes, but Saul wasn't buying it. When he heard that David was credited with a larger number than he, he was incensed. The refrain awakened in him a deep vein of paranoia. Almost instantaneously his pride and admiration of David morphed into jealousy and suspicion. The fear that David would usurp the throne from him and his descendants rapidly grew into an obsession that blinded him to the responsibilities of running the kingdom.

Saul made numerous attempts to liquidate David, but none succeeded. He threw his spear at him as he played the harp, but David dodged it (1 Sam. 18:10–11). He sent him away on dangerous military missions, but David returned home triumphant each time (1 Sam. 18:12–15). When Saul's daughter Michal fell in love with David, Saul demanded a bride price of one hundred Philistine foreskins, calculating that David would die collecting them. Instead, David presented him with a basket of two hundred uncircumcised penises (1 Sam. 18:20–27). The more successful and the more beloved David became, the more threatened Saul grew in his shadow. Even his own children pledged their allegiance to David. David was warned by Jonathan that his father was planning to kill him (1 Sam. 19:1–2), and with the help of Michal he escaped and went into hiding (1 Sam. 19:11–17). Saul was so bent on eliminating David that he tried to kill Jonathan when he stood up for David (1 Sam. 20:30–34).

David feared for his family's safety and arranged for his parents to take refuge in Moab (1 Sam. 22:3–4). Then, operating according to the wisdom that the enemy of my enemy is my friend, in desperation David fled to the Philistine city of Gath in the hope finding asylum there. He had planned to plead his case with King Achish as an artless refugee from King Saul, but before he could speak, the palace servants recognized him. "Isn't he the one they sing about in their dances: 'Saul has slain his thousands, and David his tens of thousands?'" (By now David was probably really hating that song.) Dangerously identified, in a moment of brilliant improvisation David played the lunatic, drooling into his beard and scratching at the wood work, until he was summarily ejected from the palace by order of the king (1 Sam. 21:11–16).

Meantime, when Saul discovered that Ahimelech the priest of Nob had provided David with food and weapons in his flight, Saul slaughtered all the town's residents in a rage (1 Sam. 22:9–19). Desperate for sanctuary, David retreated into the desert, gathering around him a band of four hundred relatives, sympathizers, and outlaws. Saul refused to call off the chase and pursued him with thousands of men whenever he received news of David's whereabouts. Following a close call in the wilderness of Maon, when Saul was called away to fight the Philistines just as he closed in on David and his men, David found refuge at En Gedi, an oasis on the shores of the Dead Sea.

----

1 Samuel 24

[1]David went from there and stayed in the wildernesses of En-gedi.

²When Saul returned from pursuing the Philistines, he was told that David was in the wilderness of En-gedi. ³So Saul took three thousand picked men from all Israel and went in search of David and his men in the direction of the rocks of the wild goats; ⁴and he came to the sheepfolds along the way. There was a cave there, and Saul went in to relieve himself. Now David and his men were sitting in the back of the cave.

⁵David's men said to him, "This is the day of which the LORD said to you, 'I will deliver your enemy into your hands; you can do with him as you please.'" David went and stealthily cut off the corner of Saul's cloak. ⁶But afterward David reproached himself for cutting off the corner of Saul's cloak. ⁷He said to his men, "The LORD forbid that I should do such a thing to my lord—the LORD's anointed—that I should raise my hand against him; for he is the LORD's anointed." ⁸David rebuked his men and did not permit them to attack Saul.

Saul left the cave and started on his way. ⁹Then David also went out of the cave and called after Saul, "My lord king!" Saul looked around and David bowed low in homage, with his face to the ground. ¹⁰And David said to Saul, "Why do you listen to the people who say, 'David is out to do you harm?' ¹¹You can see for yourself now that the LORD delivered you into my hands in the cave today. And though I was urged to kill you, I showed you pity; for I said, 'I will not raise a hand against my lord, since he is the LORD's anointed.' ¹²Please, sir, take a close look at the corner of your cloak in my hand; for when I cut off the corner of your cloak, I did not kill you. You must see plainly that I have done nothing evil or rebellious, and I have never wronged you. Yet you are bent on taking my life. ¹³May the LORD judge between you and me! And may He take vengeance upon you for me, but my hand will never touch you. ¹⁴As the ancient proverb has it: 'Wicked deeds come from wicked men!' My hand will never touch you. ¹⁵Against whom has the king of Israel come out? Whom are you pursuing? A dead dog? A single flea? ¹⁶May the LORD be arbiter and may He judge between you and me! May He take note and uphold my cause, and vindicate me against you."

¹⁷When David finished saying these things to Saul, Saul said, "Is that your voice, my son David?" And Saul broke down and wept. ¹⁸He said to David, "You are right, not I; for you have treated me generously, but I have treated you badly. ¹⁹Yes, you have just revealed how generously you treated me, for the LORD delivered me into your hands and you did not kill me. ²⁰If a man meets his enemy, does he let him go his way unharmed? Surely, the LORD will reward you generously for what you have done for me this day ²¹I know now that you will become king, and that the kingship over Israel will remain in your hands. ²²So swear to me by the LORD that you will not destroy my descendants or wipe out my name from my father's house." ²³David swore to Saul, Saul went home, and David and his men went up to the strongholds.

A TROUBLED MAN

Saul was in a bad way, and everyone knew it. He was depressed, irrational, and unpredictable. While the infamous song represented a turning point in his relationship with David, Saul's star had been in a free fall since his scathing failure to destroy Amalek back in 1 Samuel 15. Rebuked by Samuel, rejected by God, shadowed by the successful David in his palace, and yet still king of Israel, he couldn't help but wake up each day in a bad mood.

He recognized David as the divinely ordained successor to the throne because it was impossible to ignore the incredible force field that enveloped him, but his maniacal pursuit of David was a form of denial of his fate. He was determined to hunt him down, no matter what the cost, even while the war with the Philistines raged in the background.

THE DESERT AS REFUGE

Young David understood Saul's tragic dilemma but was not willing to sacrifice his life, and the throne, on the altar of Saul's angst. He proved to be admirably adept at surviving for long periods in the isolation of the desert. Inhospitable as it may seem, the desert has often served as a haven for fugitives and nonconformists on the run from mainstream society. Throughout time prophets, subversives, sectarians, and hermits have sought refuge in the desert expanse that comprised a significant chunk of the territory of ancient (and modern) Israel.

The loneliness of the desert can be demoralizing, but it may also be conducive to inspiration and spirituality. Moses and Elijah sought the presence of the Lord in the desert. The covenant between the people of Israel and God was forged in the desert. An apocryphal psalm relates that as a shepherd in the solitude of the desert, David taught himself to fashion and play musical instruments in order to sing the praises of God to the silent landscape (Ps. 151, the Psalms Scroll of Qumran Cave 11).

As a professional shepherd, David would have felt quite at home in the desert, typically defined as an area lacking the rainfall needed for agriculture but with enough scrub brush to graze sheep and goats. He no doubt knew how to find water, how to navigate his way through the disorienting terrain, and how to fend off wild animals. It's not surprising that the role of shepherd was idealized by the prophets, an admiration reflected in the first line of Psalm 23, "The Lord is my shepherd." In fact, David's long, lonely sojourns in the desert with his family's flocks served as a kind of Outward Bound experience that prepared him for the leadership training he would ultimately undergo as the head of a ragtag band of outlaws. Keeping the flocks away from farmers' fields, getting to know each animal's personality, and identifying hidden, hard-to-reach caves in which to take shelter were all skills that undoubtedly served him well while he was on the lam from Saul with four hundred desperados.

THIS IS A TEST

So when Saul strolled into the cave at En Gedi, he was as good as dead. His security detail had completely failed to protect the king by allowing him to wander into an area that had not yet been sterilized; he was alone and outnumbered. Could David have killed Saul in the cave and then claimed self-defense? An oft-quoted rabbinic legal ruling on a passage from Exodus 22 about theft says, "If someone comes to kill you, rise up and kill him (first)." (*b. Sanhedrin* 72.1) Since Saul made his intention to kill David very clear, theoretically David would have been off the hook, although David himself chose a different course of action. It was Saul's great fortune that his enemy David harbored a deep respect for the Lord's anointed, even though that same man posed a very real threat to him. David did not perceive Saul's arrival in the cave as a gift from God, as his men did, or his murder as an act of self-preservation. Instead, he understood that only he would bear responsibility for the unfolding events. He may have even viewed the situation as a test. As a fugitive living from hand to mouth, David was still humble, still circumspect. He probably calculated that killing Saul would not be an act looked kindly upon by the subjects of the kingdom he was about to inherit.

Instead, he chose the next-best option and tore off a piece of the king's garment. In ancient times the hem of a garment was not simply a piece of clothing but rather a personal insignia. It represented the character and the power of the person who wore it, and to rip off a piece of it was an unmistakable challenge to its owner's authority. The act of violating Saul's robe was a way for David to assert his claim to the throne without harming a single hair on Saul's head. Everyone, including Saul, understood its symbolic meaning.

In this story David emerges as a valiant hero precisely because he submits to the authority of a supreme master. However, when later on David becomes king and finds himself in a position of absolute power, he too will succumb to the hubris of one who knows no limits, to disastrous consequences (see 2 Sam. 11–20). Nonetheless, the Davidic monarchy was here to stay—for better or for worse—for over four hundred years.

10

King Saul at Mount Gilboa

1 Samuel 28:3–25, 31

*The king of Israel tragically succumbs to
defeat by the Philistines and death*

See page 325 for visitor information.

WHERE ARE WE?

Mount Gilboa, an 18-kilometer-long ridge
(or 11 miles), rises to a height of 650 meters
(2,100 feet) above sea level. Its southeastern edge borders on the West Bank highlands and the Bet Shean Valley and on its
northwestern side the Jezreel Valley. The
Mount Gilboa Scenic Route traverses the entire length of
the ridge. It is the place where King Saul died in battle, and
many significant locations here, such as the communities
of Malkishua and Merav, Jonathan Hill and Mount Avi-
nadav, are named for members of Saul's family. It is also
home to the Gilboa iris, *Iris haynei*, which can be found
blooming in the wild during March and April.

SETTING THE SCENE

From the vantage point of this overlook we see just what
King Saul would have seen from Mount Gilboa as he prepared to go to battle with the Philistine army. As we look
across the valley to the left we see the Hill of Moreh, and
nestled near the southwestern foot of its slope is the Arab
village of Sulam, known in biblical times as Shunem. This
was where the Philistine army was bivouacked. En-Dor,

Fig. 10. Tel Bet She'an, where the Philistines hanged Saul's body

where Saul visited the witch, was on the other side of the Hill of Moreh, not far from its northeastern edge, but not visible from here. Off in the distance is the rounded top of Mount Tabor, and down in the valley below us are the modern agricultural communities of Kfar Yehezkel, Geva, and En Harod.

THE CONTEXT

King Saul was on the brink of catastrophe. His reign, which began with so much promise, had spiraled downward in the wake of many poor decisions. While earlier on he was able to defeat the Philistines, Israel's most threatening enemy, at both Michmash and the Valley of Elah it was now clear that he had lost divine support. The Philistines had successfully penetrated Israelite territory in the Jezreel Valley, and their multitudes were encamped in an intimidating display, poised to push eastward and to isolate the Galilee in the north from the central highlands.

Who would help Saul? Terrified and alone, with no worthy counsel and no one to confide in, Saul was desperate for contact with the only person he believed could rescue him—the prophet Samuel, his estranged spiritual mentor. Unfortunately, Samuel was unavailable because he was dead. The king ordered the court prophets to seek a message from him, but they came up empty-handed. He consulted the priests, who used Urim and Thummim and other techniques to divine the future, but they were silent. He went to sleep each night clinging to the hope that Samuel would appear to the prophets in a dream they could interpret for him, but Samuel never showed (1 Sam. 28:6).

Frantic, Saul decided to avail himself of the services of a medium—a conjurer who would summon the spirit of Samuel up from the dead. In the ancient world, and even in the modern one, it was widely acknowledged that certain people were capable of contacting ghosts. However, these channels were deemed off-limits in Israel, and Saul himself had adopted a zero-tolerance approach to this phenomenon by declaring it a capital offense and driving out anyone dealing in necromancy in Israel (1 Sam. 28:3).

Yet because God did not answer him, in his desperation Saul was prepared to violate his own decree. He enlisted the help of two servants, who located a ghost wife in the village of En-Dor (1 Sam. 28:7–8).

It was imperative that the king's identity remain hidden to the witch of En-Dor, so Saul prepared to visit her by disguising himself as a commoner. However, there were additional risks involved in this imprudent escapade: the danger that he would be recognized by his own subjects on the way to this hypocritical, illegal rendezvous or the chance that his identity would be discovered by the Philistines, whose camp lay dangerously close to the road to En-Dor. Saul's two most loyal and trustworthy servants were the only ones privy to this masquerade; his partners to the crime, they led him safely to the woman's door. Interestingly, they remain nameless, but they would ultimately play a pivotal role in the upcoming harrowing scene.

Consider for a moment Saul's state of mind at this juncture. He was abandoned and isolated; a powerful army was practically on top of him; he was about to engage in an act that was despicable in his own eyes; and he was petrified that he would be seen and identified. He must have been a wreck. His digestive system was no doubt paralyzed and completely dysfunctional. His stomach was tied up in a thousand knots, and he couldn't even look at food. He must have set out for the journey to En-Dor without having eaten for the entire day, perhaps even longer.

- -

1 Samuel 28

³Now Samuel had died and all Israel made lament for him; and he was buried in his own town of Ramah. And Saul had forbidden [recourse to] ghosts and familiar spirits in the land.

⁴The Philistines mustered and they marched to Shunem and encamped; and Saul gathered all Israel, and they encamped at Gilboa. ⁵When Saul saw the Philistine force, his heart trembled with fear. ⁶And Saul inquired of the LORD, but the LORD did not answer him, either by dreams or by Urim or by prophets. ⁷Then Saul said to his courtiers, "Find me a woman who consults ghosts, so that I can go to her and inquire through her." And his courtiers told him that there was a woman in En-dor who consulted ghosts.

⁸Saul disguised himself; he put on different clothes and set out with two men. They came to the woman by night,

and he said, "Please divine for me by a ghost. Bring up for me the one I shall name to you." 9But the woman answered him, "You know what Saul has done, how he has banned [the use of] ghosts and familiar spirits in the land. So why are you laying a trap for me, to get me killed?" 10Saul swore to her by the LORD: "As the LORD lives, you won't get into trouble over this." 11At that, the woman asked, "Whom shall I bring up for you?" He answered, "Bring up Samuel for me." 12Then the woman recognized Samuel, and she shrieked loudly, and said to Saul, "Why have you deceived me? You are Saul!" 13The king answered her, "Don't be afraid. What do you see?" And the woman said to Saul, "I see a divine being coming up from the earth." 14"What does he look like?" he asked her. "It is an old man coming up," she said, "and he is wrapped in a robe." Then Saul knew that it was Samuel; and he bowed low in homage with his face to the ground.

15Samuel said to Saul, "Why have you disturbed me and brought me up?" And Saul answered, "I am in great trouble. The Philistines are attacking me and God has turned away from me; He no longer answers me, either by prophets or in dreams. So I have called you to tell me what I am to do." 16Samuel said, "Why do you ask me, seeing that the LORD has turned away from you and has become your adversary? 17The LORD has done for Himself as He foretold through me: The LORD has torn the kingship out of your hands and has given it to your fellow, to David, 18because you did not obey the LORD and did not execute His wrath upon the Amalekites. That is why the LORD has done this to you today. 19Further, the LORD will deliver the Israelites who are with you into the hands of the Philistines. Tomorrow your sons and you will be with me; and the LORD will also deliver the Israelite forces into the hands of the Philistines."

20At once Saul flung himself prone on the ground, terrified by Samuel's words. Besides, there was no strength in him, for he had not eaten anything all day and all night. [21]The woman went up to Saul and, seeing how greatly disturbed he was, she said to him, "Your handmaid listened to you; I took my life in my hands and heeded the request you made of me. [22]So now you listen to me: Let me set before you a bit of food. Eat, and then you will have the strength to go on your way." [23]He refused, saying, "I will not eat." But when his courtiers as well as the woman urged him, he listened to them; he got up from the ground and sat on the bed. [24]The woman had a stall-fed calf in the house; she hastily slaughtered it, and took flour and kneaded it, and baked some unleavened cakes. [25]She set this before Saul and his courtiers, and they ate. Then they rose and left the same night.

31

[1]The Philistines attacked Israel, and the men of Israel fled before the Philistines and [many] fell on Mount Gilboa. [2]The Philistines pursued Saul and his sons, and the Philistines struck down Jonathan, Abinadab, and Malchishua, sons of Saul. [3]The battle raged around Saul, and some of the archers hit him, and he was severely wounded by the archers. [4]Saul said to his arms-bearer, "Draw your sword and run me through, so that the uncircumcised may not run me through and make sport of me." But his arms-bearer, in his great awe, refused; whereupon Saul grasped the sword and fell upon it. [5]When his arms-bearer saw that Saul was dead, he too fell on his sword and died with him. [6]Thus Saul and his three sons and his arms-bearer, as well as all his men, died together on that day. [7]And when the men of Israel on the other side of the valley and on the other side of the Jordan saw that the men of Israel had fled and that Saul and his sons were dead,

they abandoned the towns and fled; the Philistines then came and occupied them.

⁸The next day the Philistines came to strip the slain, and they found Saul and his three sons lying on Mount Gilboa. ⁹They cut off his head and stripped him of his armor, and they sent them throughout the land of the Philistines, to spread the news in the temples of their idols and among the people. ¹⁰They placed his armor in the temple of Ashtaroth, and they impaled his body on the wall of Beth-shan. ¹¹When the inhabitants of Jabesh-gilead heard about it—what the Philistines had done to Saul—¹²all their stalwart men set out and marched all night; they removed the bodies of Saul and his sons from the wall of Beth-shan and came to Jabesh and burned them there. ¹³Then they took the bones and buried them under the tamarisk tree in Jabesh, and they fasted for seven days.

THE SÉANCE

When confronted with Saul's request to hold a séance, the medium, not surprisingly, played the indignant, law-abiding citizen, accusing the stranger of setting her up. Somehow, however, she innately sensed her potential client's desperation. No money changed hands here; she agreed to call up the spirit for him, as long as she was assured that no harm would come to her. The stranger placed his order: "Bring up Samuel for me" (1 Sam. 28:11). The witch got to work and handily produced results.

When the image of Samuel appeared to her, the medium let out a bloodcurdling scream—not because she had just seen a ghost, but because she immediately realized that her client was none other than King Saul. Her other patrons typically requested contact with the spirits of little-known country folk—a deceased child tragically plucked from life by disease or an ancient relative privy to dark family secrets. The intimidating visage of the prophet Samuel would not rise from his restless slumbers for any old Tom, Dick, or Harry. If he was here, it was for Saul, and if this was Saul then she was in big trouble.

But the king reassured her that she had nothing to fear, and the séance proceeded. Although the conversation took place directly between Samuel and Saul, the medium was the medium—she heard every word and understood, together with Saul, the imminence of the terrible tragedy that would take place the following day: the armies of Israel would be slaughtered by the Philistines, and Saul and his three sons would all die.

THE BREAKDOWN

Once again, consider Saul's state of mind now. His last glimmer of hope for an encouraging message from Samuel had been cruelly shattered. There was no longer any way to get around the terrible events that awaited him. His powerful physique collapsed beneath the weight of this knowledge, and Saul fell to the ground, sprawled in all his height and girth on the floor (1 Sam. 28:20). He was in a state of shock. All his strength had been drained out of him. The world was ending.

The medium quickly pulled herself together and took charge of the situation, hoping to revive Saul with a bite to eat. Acutely aware of his compromising position, she subserviently appealed to the king's sense of fairness. Just as she had done what he requested, now he must reciprocate by eating something so he would have strength for his journey back to camp.

But Saul was defiantly uncooperative. "I will not eat."

The medium and the two servants understood that the king of Israel was in the midst of a breakdown. He was both physically and emotionally depleted, incapable of thinking rationally. They had a dire emergency on their hands—what should they do? They couldn't call for help—their loyalty to Saul would not allow anyone else to see him in this humiliating state. There were no medical remedies that would magically cure Saul's suffering. None of them would dare to administer a sharp slap to the king's cheek under any circumstances. There was only one option.

They must hold an intervention.

The text keeps their exhortations private, but we can imagine what they may have said:

"Everyone is counting on you to lead us against the enemy, just as you did in Jabesh-Gilead and the Valley of Elah."

"How can you send your sons into battle alone? What kind of an example will you be setting as a father?"

"Is this how you wish to be remembered in Israel—as one who surrendered to the uncircumcised without fighting?"

"Would the armies of Israel have assembled with you at Gilboa if they did not trust you?"

"No one can replace you. We are lost without you."

FOOD IS LOVE

Lying there on the floor, Saul experienced his defining moment. He internalized the inevitability of his destiny and accepted it. He could not abandon his sons and the Israelite army on the battlefield. Even though he knew they would lose and die tomorrow, he pulled himself together and picked himself up off the floor. He sat down on the couch and said, "You're right. I should eat something."

The woman hurried off to get dinner. She prepared a scrumptious feast. While she was cooking, Saul no doubt conferred with his men about the upcoming battle, still recovering from the trauma of seeing into his future, still weak, yet level-headed.

The medium put the meal on the table, and Saul and his two servants began to eat. The food was delicious, not only because Saul was ravenous but because food is love—he could taste the woman's care and concern for him in every morsel.

In his darkest moment Saul was literally scraped off the floor by these three simple folk. They showed him that the people of Israel had not yet given up on him. Although the end would be catastrophic, as king he was obligated to complete the task. Quitting was not an option. Saul's comprehension of his responsibility to them provided him with the final boost of strength he needed to face his destiny.

THE BITTER END

Much has been written about Saul's suicide, one of six mentioned in the Bible. Although suicide is condemned in traditional Jewish law, the sages have justified Saul's actions before the inevitability of Philistine abuse (*Shulchan Aruch* YD 345:3). Given that Saul was faced with forced conversion by the enemy, endangering the lives of others as a result of torture, and making a mockery of the Israelite kingship by being paraded through the Philistine cities, the rabbis have condoned his choice to die by his own hand. The Jewish historian Josephus Flavius, writing over one thousand years later, lavished effusive praise on Saul's exemplary heroism and strength of character (*Jewish Antiquities* 6.340–350).

Some scholars, however, challenge the assumption that Saul in fact committed suicide, arguing that the mortal wound inflicted by the bowmen was the actual cause of his death, even if Saul chose ultimately to fall on his sword. Conversely, the acclaimed Bible critic Robert Alter favors a translation of the text that emphasizes Saul's fear rather than his wound, implying in *The David Story* that his injury wasn't necessarily life-threatening.

The divergent interpretations of Saul's death also reflect an additional complexity: the account in 1 Samuel 31 is actually one of three different versions of the story in the Bible, and each rendering seems to harbor its own subtle agenda. The version in our passage, related by the omniscient biblical narrator, presents Saul's death as the tragic demise of a noble hero. The second version immediately follows the first, in 2 Samuel 1:1–16, when David is notified of Israel's defeat in battle and the death of Saul and his sons by a young Amalekite who was present at the scene. His account does not differ greatly from the first version, but it firmly establishes David's absence from the battlefield at the time of Saul's death. It also serves as a platform for David's reaction to the news, allowing the reader to witness his grief and anger over his rival's demise. A cover story in *People* magazine cleverly placed by a twenty-first-century spin doctor could not have surpassed this public relations accomplishment.

The third version of the story appears in the pro-Davidic book of Chronicles (1 Chron. 10:1–14). Discreet differences in the telling sniff disapprovingly at Saul, and ultimately the Chronicler leaves no room for doubt by the end of the passage. He condemns Saul as a sinner who received his just desserts: death and the loss of the kingdom to the house of David.

The multiple accounts of Saul's death and their identifiable differences exemplify the terrific challenge inherent in the writing and editing of the Bible: many stories have more than one version, so which one do we tell? The answer is include them all, and allow the reader the freedom to choose.

Saul seemed to have an uncanny premonition about the future preoccupation with his demise. What's notable about the final scene on Mount Gilboa in all three versions is that at the end, Saul's worst fear was not his inevitable death but rather the manner in which he would die. In this concern lies his true nobility. The Israelite army had been disgracefully routed, Saul's three sons were dead, and now he was seriously wounded by the Philistine archers. He knew that if the Philistines abused and tortured him while still alive, the Israelite monarchy would forever bear the black mark of his dishonorable death. In the midst of this terrible tragedy, Saul was thinking ahead to the future generations of Israel. His ultimate wish was to die in a way that would make Israel proud to retell the story of his death.

11

Bathsheba in the City of David

2 Samuel 11:1–12:24

*King David violates sacred moral
codes to satisfy his carnal desire*

See page 306 for visitor information.

WHERE ARE WE?

The small ridge known today as the City of David was the first hilltop settled in the primeval city of Jerusalem. Although not the highest hill in the area, it boasted two major advantages appealing to the ancients who arrived here at least five thousand years ago: the ridge is surrounded on three sides by valleys that provide an excellent natural defense system, and the Gihon spring, an abundant water source, sits at its foot. Two millennia later, in approximately 1000 BCE, King David chose this city, known then as Jebus and afterward as the City of David, to be the newly crowned capital of the united kingdom of the twelve tribes of Israel. Situated smack on the border of the tribal lands of Judah and Benjamin and formerly an enclave of Jebusites probably of Hittite origin, this ridge was politically neutral ground. In the days of David the historical circle was closed, and the city was known by its original name, Jerusalem.

The City of David expanded north and west over the centuries, and this narrow ridge became distant from the city's center. It was eventually left outside the walls when the Crusaders rebuilt the city 2,100 years after David's

Fig. 11. Silwan village, the mirror image of the City of David

time, at the turn of the twelfth century CE. The present city walls, constructed by the Ottoman Turks in the mid-16th century CE, cemented the isolation of the City of David by excluding it once again.

SETTING THE SCENE

The steep Kidron Valley beneath us dramatically separates the City of David from the Mount of Olives ridge across the way to the east. The Arab village of Silwan, which sits directly opposite the City of David, is its mirror image and a superb visual aid. Silwan's dense construction of houses built right into the cliff side is probably almost identical to the urban setting of David's city. David's palace would have been situated on the highest part of the ridge. As he strolled on the rooftop, David would have enjoyed a bird's-eye view of all his subjects' roofs and their activities in this outdoor space that often functioned as an additional room of the house. He may have observed them doing laundry, sun-drying fruits and legumes, weaving, grinding grains, and sometimes, bathing.

THE CONTEXT

After many difficult years as an outlaw, David had successfully claimed the throne of the people of Israel. An outstanding warrior and superb politician, he had overcome his adversaries and had consolidated the different estranged tribes of Judah and northern Israel under his leadership. His coronation was celebrated in the presence of the elders of all the tribes, and he was now the undisputed king of Israel (2 Sam. 5:3).

Firmly ensconced in the seat of power, David turned his attention to other important objectives. After establishing Jerusalem as the political capital of his kingdom (2 Sam. 5:7), he built himself a fortified residence (2 Sam. 5:11), brought the ark of the covenant up to the city permanently (2 Sam. 6:2–5, 12–17), and gave Jerusalem the status of a king's sanctuary and royal palace.

David also put most of his enemies out of business. In addition to defeating the Philistines, the Moabites, the Edomites, Amalek, the Aramaean-Ammonite coalition, and a few other choice foes (2 Sam. 8:1–14), David ensured that no one from the house of Saul, Israel's first king, would come back to haunt him. In a bloody civil war that preceded his coronation, most of Saul's living relatives were brutally executed (2 Sam. 3:27; 4:5–8). He declined intimacy with his wife Michal, Saul's daughter, so she would not produce children (2 Sam. 6:23). Only Mephibosheth, Jonathan's crippled son, was spared, as his handicap disqualified him for the monarchy. Since he posed no threat, he was invited to eat at the king's table (2 Sam. 9).

All the while David was busy producing heirs, siring eleven sons (2 Sam. 5:14–15) and probably at least as many daughters by his numerous wives and concubines.

David could allow himself to feel confident in his accomplishments. They were virtually guaranteed by God, who promised him that his descendants would forever rule over Israel (2 Sam. 7). At this point David had comfortably completed the transition from warrior to statesman. After years of hiding out in caves and sleeping in battlefields, he could sit back and admire his accomplishments from the plush comfort of the throne room. Victorious over his adversaries, middle-aged, perhaps sporting a pair of love handles, he could now turn his energies inward to his own domain from the comfort of his regal abode.

The biblical narrator hangs the Chekhovian gun on the wall at the beginning of the story when he announces, "At the turn of the year, the season when kings go out [to battle], David sent Joab . . ." (2 Sam. 11:1). War was a seasonal occupation, waged only after the rainy months and their hazards were safely over. One of an ancient Middle Eastern king's most important responsibilities was the command of his army, but David seemed to have retired himself from this nuisance. When it was time to head back out to the battlefield, the king remained in the comfort of the palace and sent his deputy in his place. Now he had some spare time on his hands. And that's when the trouble began.

- -

2 Samuel 11

¹At the turn of the year, the season when kings go out [to battle], David sent Joab with his officers and all Israel with him, and they devastated Ammon and besieged Rabbah; David remained in Jerusalem. ²Late one afternoon, David rose from his couch and strolled on the roof of the royal

palace; and from the roof he saw a woman bathing. The woman was very beautiful, ³and the king sent someone to make inquiries about the woman. He reported, "She is Bathsheba daughter of Eliam [and] wife of Uriah the Hittite." ⁴David sent messengers to fetch her; she came to him and he lay with her—she had just purified herself after her period—and she went back home. ⁵The woman conceived, and she sent word to David, "I am pregnant." ⁶Thereupon David sent a message to Joab, "Send Uriah the Hittite to me"; and Joab sent Uriah to David.

⁷When Uriah came to him, David asked him how Joab and the troops were faring and how the war was going. ⁸Then David said to Uriah, "Go down to your house and bathe your feet." When Uriah left the royal palace, a present from the king followed him. ⁹But Uriah slept at the entrance of the royal palace, along with the other officers of his lord, and did not go down to his house. ¹⁰When David was told that Uriah had not gone down to his house, he said to Uriah, "You just came from a journey; why didn't you go down to your house?" ¹¹Uriah answered David, "The Ark and Israel and Judah are located at Succoth, and my master Joab and Your Majesty's men are camped in the open; how can I go home and eat and drink and sleep with my wife? As you live, by your very life, I will not do this!" ¹²David said to Uriah, "Stay here today also, and tomorrow I will send you off." So Uriah remained in Jerusalem that day. The next day, ¹³David summoned him, and he ate and drank with him until he got him drunk; but in the evening, [Uriah] went out to sleep in the same place, with his lord's officers; he did not go down to his home.

¹⁴In the morning, David wrote a letter to Joab, which he sent with Uriah. ¹⁵He wrote in the letter as follows: "Place Uriah in the front line where the fighting is fiercest; then fall back so that he may be killed." ¹⁶So when Joab was

besieging the city, he stationed Uriah at the point where he knew that there were able warriors. [17]The men of the city sallied out and attacked Joab, and some of David's officers among the troops fell; Uriah the Hittite was among those who died.

[18]Joab sent a full report of the battle to David. [19]He instructed the messenger as follows: "When you finish reporting to the king all about the battle, [20]the king may get angry and say to you, 'Why did you come so close to the city to attack it? Didn't you know that they would shoot from the wall? [21]Who struck down Abimelech son of Jerubbesheth? Was it not a woman who dropped an upper millstone on him from the wall at Thebez, from which he died? Why did you come so close to the wall?' Then say: 'Your servant Uriah the Hittite was among those killed.'"

[22]The messenger set out; he came and told David all that Joab had sent him to say. [23]The messenger said to David, "First the men prevailed against us and sallied out against us into the open; then we drove them back up to the entrance to the gate. [24]But the archers shot at your men from the wall and some of Your Majesty's men fell; your servant Uriah the Hittite also fell." [25]Whereupon David said to the messenger, "Give Joab this message: 'Do not be distressed about the matter. The sword always takes its toll. Press your attack on the city and destroy it!' Encourage him!"

[26]When Uriah's wife heard that her husband Uriah was dead, she lamented over her husband. [27]After the period of mourning was over, David sent and had her brought into his palace; she became his wife and she bore him a son.

12

But the LORD was displeased with what David had done, [1]and the LORD sent Nathan to David. He came to him and said,

"There were two men in the same city, one rich and one poor. ²The rich man had very large flocks and herds, ³but the poor man had only one little ewe lamb that he had bought. He tended it and it grew up together with him and his children: it used to share his morsel of bread, drink from his cup, and nestle in his bosom; it was like a daughter to him. ⁴One day, a traveler came to the rich man, but he was loath to take anything from his own flocks or herds to prepare a meal for the guest who had come to him; so he took the poor man's lamb and prepared it for the man who had come to him."

⁵David flew into a rage against the man, and said to Nathan, "As the LORD lives, the man who did this deserves to die! ⁶He shall pay for the lamb four times over, because he did such a thing and showed no pity." ⁷And Nathan said to David, "That man is you! Thus said the LORD, the God of Israel: 'It was I who anointed you king over Israel and it was I who rescued you from the hand of Saul. ⁸I gave you your master's house and possession of your master's wives; and I gave you the House of Israel and Judah; and if that were not enough, I would give you twice as much more. ⁹Why then have you flouted the command of the LORD and done what displeases Him? You have put Uriah the Hittite to the sword; you took his wife and made her your wife and had him killed by the sword of the Ammonites. ¹⁰Therefore the sword shall never depart from your House—because you spurned Me by taking the wife of Uriah the Hittite and making her your wife.' ¹¹Thus said the LORD: 'I will make a calamity rise against you from within your own house; I will take your wives and give them to another man before your very eyes and he shall sleep with your wives under this very sun. ¹²You acted in secret, but I will make this happen in the sight of all Israel and in broad daylight.'"

¹³David said to Nathan, "I stand guilty before the LORD!" And Nathan replied to David, "The LORD has remitted your

sin; you shall not die. ¹⁴However, since you have spurned the enemies of the LORD by this deed, even the child about to be born to you shall die."

¹⁵Nathan went home, and the LORD afflicted the child that Uriah's wife had borne to David, and it became critically ill. ¹⁶David entreated God for the boy; David fasted, and he went in and spent the night lying on the ground. ¹⁷The senior servants of his household tried to induce him to get up from the ground; but he refused, nor would he partake of food with them. ¹⁸On the seventh day the child died. David's servants were afraid to tell David that the child was dead; for they said, "We spoke to him when the child was alive and he wouldn't listen to us; how can we tell him that the child is dead? He might do something terrible." ¹⁹When David saw his servants talking in whispers, David understood that the child was dead; David asked his servants, "Is the child dead?" "Yes," they replied.

²⁰Thereupon David rose from the ground; he bathed and anointed himself, and he changed his clothes. He went into the House of the LORD and prostrated himself. Then he went home and asked for food, which they set before him, and he ate. ²¹His courtiers asked him, "Why have you acted in this manner? While the child was alive, you fasted and wept; but now that the child is dead, you rise and take food!" ²²He replied, "While the child was still alive, I fasted and wept because I thought: 'Who knows? The LORD may have pity on me, and the child may live.' ²³But now that he is dead, why should I fast? Can I bring him back again? I shall go to him, but he will never come back to me."

²⁴David consoled his wife Bathsheba; he went to her and lay with her. She bore a son and she named him Solomon. The LORD favored him, ²⁵and He sent a message through the prophet Nathan: and he was named Jedidiah at the insistence of the LORD.

Two pats on the lap

Two claps

Two alternating horizontal hand slices

Two alternating vertical fist knocks

Two alternating touch-your-elbow-and-wiggle-
your-fingers

These are the hand movements many of us learned in religious school to accompany our raucous singing of "David, melech Yisrael, hai, hai v'kayam" (David, King of Israel, he's alive and well). Would we have been gesturing so wildly had we known, in our preadolescent naïveté, that the hero we were celebrating was actually a philandering, conniving murderer? Why didn't anyone tell us that David, king of Israel, broke at least three of the Ten Commandments?

David's integrity is further thrown into question when he is compared to the chivalrous Uriah. In town on an errand for the king, Uriah refused to partake of the pleasures of his lovely wife out of solidarity with his comrades-in-arms, who remained in the field (2 Sam. 11:11). It seemed there could be no soldier purer in heart and more devoted to the king and his cause than Uriah. David's devious attempts to force him into the arms of Bathsheba to cover for his reprehensible behavior do not reflect well on His Majesty. Any last remnants of sympathy for David dissipate when David sends Uriah back to the front bearing his own execution order.

THE MESSIAH CONNECTION

So it is puzzling that David has the undisputed role, according to the biblical tradition, as the progenitor of the Messiah—the savior of humanity and the redeemer at the end of days (see, e.g., Isa. 11:1–10). With the arrival of this savior who can trace his roots back to David, the world will finally be cured of its imperfections. Evil and disease will be eradicated, universal peace and social justice will prevail, the Jewish people will be ingathered in the land of Israel, and the world's harmony will be restored. The Messiah represents the aspirations of generations for a perfect world. The hope for the Messiah's arrival has been an integral element of Jewish belief for centuries; many Jewish prayer services include an expression of this longing, which has strengthened Jews over centuries of persecution.

So who air-brushed the felonious David into the father of the messianic line? Throughout the ages David has emerged again and again as one of the most beloved protagonists of the Bible, probably because so many readers identify with his heroic imperfection. The majority have preferred to remember David in the spirit of the old Johnny Mercer song "Accentuate the Positive, Eliminate the Negative" when they read and reread those stories. In their eyes, and ultimately in the Jewish national consciousness they nurtured, the golden epoch of David's reign was the model for the messianic age. Through David, God brought the nation of Israel to the best of times: prosperity, tribal unity, and justice, and his military victories promised an era of peace. Most readers would not allow the Bathsheba affair, in their eyes simply a minor transgression on David's part, to overshadow the hope that a new David would one day restore perfection to the world.

THE MAN WHO HAD EVERYTHING

Yet after reading the disturbing story of David, Bathsheba, and Uriah, we may still find it hard to accept David in such a pivotal role in the future of the Jewish people. Indeed, many prefer to remember David as he was before this shocking turn of events—the sweet singer of Israel, the underdog warrior aglow in the spirit of the Lord. Before the Bathsheba imbroglio, David was the golden boy. He had everything—empire, power, wealth, women, and, most important, a deeply intimate relationship with the Creator. But the story must be read to its conclusion, where we learn that David was ultimately corrupted by his unbridled power. He came to believe that as king he could blatantly defy any law to satisfy his own desires.

It might be helpful to view David as a symbol of the human capacity for egoism, the tendency to consider only oneself and one's own interests. Somewhere along the way the divinely appointed king of Israel lost the understanding that he was a tool for the greater good of everyone, a process experienced by countless individuals who have reached positions of power. David's hubris and his subsequent fall from grace may suggest that trust in political leadership is a disappointment waiting to happen—if King David couldn't resist the urge, then no one is incorruptible. Sooner or later, even the most noble of spirits will succumb to the temptation that absolute power affords. The great question then becomes, now that you've screwed up royally, how do you fix it?

REPAIR WHAT IS BROKEN

In the Jewish tradition the answer is *teshuva*, or repentance—acknowledging you have erred and resolving never to make the same mistake again. However, David was so drunk with power that he was incapable of judging his own behavior. He had to be manipulated by Nathan into looking in the mirror (2 Sam. 12:1–25), but once he glimpsed himself in all his ugliness, he understood the gravity of his actions. He searched inward and arrived at the inevitable conclusion that he had sinned, big time, and verbally confessed.

Some sages posit that the process David experienced represents the human aspiration to perfection. All mortals are flawed, and no one can be perfect—even David, who ostensibly had everything going for him. Therefore, the human ability to soul search, to recognize errors, and to attempt to remedy them is our only chance for redemption.

The hope for the Messiah's arrival is based on the understanding that the world and all who inhabit it are imperfect. Therefore, the person who will fulfill the role of the savior of the world must be a paragon of the human aspiration to perfection. For many people David represents that ideal.

POSTSCRIPT: THE LEGACY OF BATHSHEBA

While Bathsheba plays a pivotal role in this story, little about her can be inferred from the text in which she speaks only one sentence: "I'm pregnant." Was she a modest woman whose privacy was violated by the lustful, voyeuristic king, or a conniving temptress who deliberately exposed herself to David in the hope of gaining entrance to the corridors of power? Was she an obedient subject who respected the king's authority or a lonely wife neglected by her absent husband (or both)? Did David simply have his way with her, or was she a party to their emotional entanglement? Her character as a pushy Jewish mother is fleshed out somewhat by the biblical authors later in the narrative when she convinces the elderly King David to choose her son Solomon to succeed him (1 Kings 1–2:40), but at this stage in her life her personality remains an enigma to the reader. Bathsheba brings to mind David's actions, and not a three-dimensional character of her own.

Perhaps this is why her name was appropriated to

describe a phenomenon known as the Bathsheba Syndrome. A term coined by two American business professors, Dean C. Ludwig and Clinton O. Longenecker, in 1993, the Bathsheba Syndrome is defined as the moral corruption of those who are powerful. It has nothing to do with Bathsheba and everything to do with King David, the paradigm for intelligent, ethical people of integrity who, once they reach the pinnacle of success, throw it all away by doing something grossly unethical that they believe they can conceal. It turns out that David, like many successful people today, was probably ill prepared to deal with the fruit of his accomplishments. After reaching the apex of power, he became complacent and lost his strategic focus (he should have been out there on the battlefield with his officers, instead of lounging around the palace, spying on other men's wives). He abused the privileged access to people and information that came with his success (the view from the palace was for the good of the kingdom's security, not a tool to indulge his personal fantasy). He used his organization's resources for his own needs (he sent the servants to get Bathsheba and used Uriah to deliver his own execution warrant). He was confident that he could make the problem go away (his ultimate solution compounded his initial crime of adultery with murder).

So, what's to be done to avoid the pitfalls of success? Business psychologists' first recommendation is to inculcate the awareness that it can happen to anybody. They also recommend a healthy lifestyle of family, friends, and interests outside work that will balance the negative aspects of success and keep leaders down-to-earth and in touch with reality. Complacency is dangerous—evaluate strategic direction constantly, and surround yourself with a good team of ethical managers who will both support and challenge you.

Absalom's Flight to Geshur

2 Samuel 13

Rape and murder in the royal family

See page 331 for visitor information.

WHERE ARE WE?

The ancient cities of Geshur and Bethsaida were located here, on the southern slopes of the Golan Heights at the northeastern shore of Lake Kinneret. The excavations at the site have unearthed two significant settlement periods: tenth century BCE and first century CE. The remains of the first-century CE fishing village have been identified as Bethsaida, a town mentioned significantly in the Gospel narrative. It was the home of three of Jesus's disciples—Philip, Andrew, and Peter (John 1:44)—and Jesus visited here many times. Bethsaida (which may mean "house of the hunt") was the place where Jesus healed the blind man (Mark 8:22–26), where he first met the disciple Bartholomew (aka Nathanael) (John 1:43–51), and where he performed the second miracle of the feeding of the multitude (Luke 9:10–17). The people of Bethsaida were ultimately cursed by Jesus, together with those of the neighboring towns of Korazim and Kfar Nahum, for not repenting after witnessing the miracles he performed there (Luke 10:13–15).

The first-century town was built by Herod Philip, a son of Herod the Great, with a pluralistic bent. Judging by the Greek names of the Bethsaida Jewish disciples, the town

Fig. 12. The city gate of ancient Geshur (Bethsaida). Photo courtesy of Moti Dolev.

probably had a mixed population of both Jews and gentiles. On your tour of the tel you will encounter a number of finds from this period, including a paved road and the homes of two local tradesmen, a fisherman and a winegrower.

SETTING THE SCENE

The gate plaza you are standing in and the massive fortifications (over 10 meters/32 feet wide!) surrounding the city have been dated by archaeologists to the tenth century BCE. At this time a small state known as Geshur was established by one of the Aramean tribes on the slopes of the Golan Heights and the eastern shore of Lake Kinneret. This city served as its capital.

This gate, its main entrance, boasted a huge cultic platform temple measuring 36 square meters (118 square feet). One of the site's most magnificent finds was unearthed here, a stele (an upright stone slab) carved with a bull wearing a dagger, the principle representation of the Aramean moon god Haddad (view the stele in the archaeological wing of the Israel Museum). The outer gateway, flanked by two enormous towers, led to four inner rooms inside the gate, the largest of its kind from the biblical period discovered in Israel. The king's palace stood to the north of the gate, complete with a throne room.

Settlement in Geshur came to an abrupt halt in 734 BCE, when the city was destroyed by the Assyrian king Tiglath Pileser III. Evidence of the destruction can be seen inside the gate in the charred bricks and carbonized wood, hints of the enormous conflagration that wiped the city off the map for hundreds of years.

THE CONTEXT

At the time this story takes place King David, well established in his capital city of Jerusalem, had seven wives (1 Chron. 3:1–5) and probably over twenty children (not counting the offspring of his ten concubines, who had lower status). We may imagine that each wife lived in a private residence within the palace complex, together with her children.

Amnon was David's eldest son by his second wife, Achinoam of Jezreel. Since David's first wife, Michal, had no children, Amnon was the crown prince—the officially acknowledged successor to David.

Tamar and Absalom were the children of Maacah, the daughter of Talmai, king of Geshur and David's fourth wife. David and King Talmai shared mutual military interests, probably in connection with the coalition of Aramean states ultimately defeated by David. The two kings signed a treaty and sealed it, as was common in ancient times, with a marriage. Talmai's daughter, Princess Maacah, packed her things and went off to live in Jerusalem as the wife of King David, thereby ensuring Talmai an inside influence in his ally's palace and grandchildren to claim their slice of the pie.

However, despite her regal lineage Maacah probably remained an outsider in her husband's extended family. A non-Israelite of royal birth, she no doubt provoked the resentment of the hometown wives. It's not hard to imagine them turning their noses up at the foreign princess, perhaps even ostracizing her and her children. As the royal progeny grew old enough to understand the palace hierarchy, the rivalry and intrigue only intensified.

David is almost completely absent as an authority figure in this story, probably because he was still in the throes of a deep emotional crisis following the Bathsheba calamity and the death of their infant son (2 Sam. 11–12:25). Left to their own devices, David's children took matters into their own hands.

- -

2 Samuel 13

¹This happened sometime afterward: Absalom son of David had a beautiful sister named Tamar, and Amnon son of David became infatuated with her. ²Amnon was so distraught because of his [half] sister Tamar that he became sick; for she was a virgin, and it seemed impossible to Amnon to do anything to her. ³Amnon had a friend named Jonadab, the son of David's brother Shimah; Jonadab was a very clever man. ⁴He asked him, "Why are you so dejected, O prince, morning after morning? Tell me!" Amnon replied, "I am in love with Tamar, the sister of my brother Absalom!" ⁵Jonadab said to him, "Lie down in your bed and pretend you are sick. When your father comes to see you, say to him, 'Let my sister Tamar come and give me something to

eat. Let her prepare the food in front of me, so that I may look on, and let her serve it to me.'"

⁶Amnon lay down and pretended to be sick. The king came to see him, and Amnon said to the king, "Let my sister Tamar come and prepare a couple of cakes in front of me, and let her bring them to me." ⁷David sent a message to Tamar in the palace, "Please go to the house of your brother Amnon and prepare some food for him." ⁸Tamar went to the house of her brother Amnon, who was in bed. She took dough and kneaded it into cakes in front of him, and cooked the cakes. ⁹She took the pan and set out [the cakes], but Amnon refused to eat and ordered everyone to withdraw. After everyone had withdrawn, ¹⁰Amnon said to Tamar, "Bring the food inside and feed me." Tamar took the cakes she had made and brought them to her brother inside. ¹¹But when she served them to him, he caught hold of her and said to her, "Come lie with me, sister." ¹²But she said to him, "Don't, brother. Don't force me. Such things are not done in Israel! Don't do such a vile thing! ¹³Where will I carry my shame? And you, you will be like any of the scoundrels in Israel! Please, speak to the king; he will not refuse me to you." ¹⁴But he would not listen to her; he overpowered her and lay with her by force.

¹⁵Then Amnon felt a very great loathing for her; indeed, his loathing for her was greater than the passion he had felt for her. And Amnon said to her, "Get out!" ¹⁶She pleaded with him, "Please don't commit this wrong; to send me away would be even worse than the first wrong you committed against me." But he would not listen to her. ¹⁷He summoned his young attendant and said, "Get that woman out of my presence, and bar the door behind her."—¹⁸She was wearing an ornamented tunic, for maiden princesses were customarily dressed in such garments.—His attendant took her outside and barred the door after her. ¹⁹Tamar

put dust on her head and rent the ornamented tunic she was wearing; she put her hands on her head, and walked away, screaming loudly as she went. 20Her brother Absalom said to her, "Was it your brother Amnon who did this to you? For the present, sister, keep quiet about it; he is your brother. Don't brood over the matter." And Tamar remained in her brother Absalom's house, forlorn. 21When King David heard about all this, he was greatly upset. 22Absalom didn't utter a word to Amnon, good or bad; but Absalom hated Amnon because he had violated his sister Tamar.

23Two years later, when Absalom was having his flocks sheared at Baal-hazor near Ephraim, Absalom invited all the king's sons. 24And Absalom came to the king and said, "Your servant is having his flocks sheared. Would Your Majesty and your retinue accompany your servant?" 25But the king answered Absalom, "No, my son. We must not all come, or we'll be a burden to you." He urged him, but he would not go, and he said good-bye to him. 26Thereupon Absalom said, "In that case, let my brother Amnon come with us," to which the king replied, "He shall not go with you." 27But Absalom urged him, and he sent with him Amnon and all the other princes. 28Now Absalom gave his attendants these orders: "Watch, and when Amnon is merry with wine and I tell you to strike down Amnon, kill him! Don't be afraid, for it is I who give you the order. Act with determination, like brave men!" 29Absalom's attendants did to Amnon as Absalom had ordered; whereupon all the other princes mounted their mules and fled. 30They were still on the road when a rumor reached David that Absalom had killed all the princes, and that not one of them had survived. 31At this, David rent his garment and lay down on the ground, and all his courtiers stood by with their clothes rent. 32But Jonadab, the son of David's brother Shimah, said, "My lord must not think that all the young princes have been killed. Only Amnon is dead; for this has been decided by Absalom ever since his sister Tamar was violated. ³³So my lord the king must not think for a moment that all the princes are dead; Amnon alone is dead."

³⁴Meanwhile Absalom had fled.

The watchman on duty looked up and saw a large crowd coming from the road to his rear, from the side of the hill. ³⁵Jonadab said to the king, "See, the princes have come! It is just as your servant said." ³⁶As he finished speaking, the princes came in and broke into weeping; and David and all his courtiers wept bitterly, too.

³⁷Absalom had fled, and he came to Talmai son of Ammihud, king of Geshur. And [King David] mourned over his son a long time. ³⁸Absalom, who had fled to Geshur, remained there three years. ³⁹And King David was pining away for Absalom, for [the king] had gotten over Amnon's death.

WOMEN AS PROPERTY

The rabbinic discussion of this story largely focuses on the nature of the family relationship between Amnon and Tamar (*b. Sanhedrin* 21a). The underlying motivation behind this question was to determine whether Amnon's crime was incest (perish the thought) or rape. Although Levitical law expressly prohibits the union of siblings with one common parent (Lev. 18:9), the sages generally agreed that this law did not apply to Tamar, the daughter of an erstwhile non-Israelite woman. Therefore, the crime was not incest. It was only a rape.

What a relief.

There is no word for "rape" as we understand it today in biblical Hebrew, although the Bible relates incidents of rape (e.g., the concubine in Gibeah). The concept of sexual intercourse with a woman against her will as a crime did not exist then. In biblical times the crime was the theft of property from the man who held the rights to a woman's sexuality—her father, brother, or husband, but never the woman herself. Tamar, in this context, is an object whose life trajectory is determined by the men in her family, and as such she is cruelly betrayed by four of the males responsible for her safety.

GOODFELLAS

Tamar's first betrayal comes in the supporting role of Jonadab, David's nephew. He is described as shrewd or clever (2 Sam. 13:3) and was no doubt a careful observer of the cast of characters roaming the palace compound. He provided Amnon with the pretext to get Tamar into the inner chambers of his bedroom. Although scholars have exonerated him of any role in the rape through a careful semantic examination of his advice to Amnon, Jonadab must have been aware that he was playing with fire by suggesting such a devious plan. If he was indeed as smart as the biblical author made sure to point out, he would have certainly known his cousin Amnon for the creep that he was and steered him safely away from his other cousin, Tamar. Perhaps he viewed Amnon's predicament as a way to tweak the beautiful, uppity, half-foreign princess, never imagining things would go so awry. Whether his plan was a silly prank or an ill-advised scheme, Jonadab clearly did not have Tamar's interest in mind.

Tamar's half brother Amnon can only be described as a sleazebag. The first of David's sons, born with the silver spoon of the crown prince in his mouth, Amnon was most certainly spoiled and coddled, rapidly morphing into the biggest brat in the palace. We can imagine that his every demand was fulfilled, and his wishes were never denied. Nothing was out of his reach—except his beautiful and exotic half sister, Tamar. "Amnon was so distraught because of his [half] sister Tamar that he became sick; for she was a virgin, and it seemed impossible for Amnon to do anything to her " (2 Sam. 13:2). The "lovesick" Amnon was confronted, probably for the first time in his life, with an object beyond his reach, a situation that was incomprehensible to him. He had the run of the palace; he could "do" anything he wanted to anyone in the compound. We will never know how many servant girls were knocked up by the spoiled prince or how many rapes preceded Tamar's. What's clear is that the moment Amnon achieved the object of his desire, it no longer held any value for him.

Interestingly, biblical law provided a loophole for wanton men who preyed on unbetrothed virgins. Deuteronomy states that a man can rectify the rape of a virgin by paying her father fifty shekels of silver and then marrying her, with no option for divorce (Deut. 22:28–29). Ironically, this law was designed to protect the victim by guaranteeing her economic support and the status of a married woman (no one asked her how she felt about marrying her rapist—irrelevant).

Amnon, however, was not at all concerned with the consequences of his actions. Void of any emotion or sense of responsibility and driven solely by egotistical urges, David's eldest son was the poster child for moral depravity. The circumstances surrounding his betrayal of Tamar raise very disturbing questions about the royal family.

Which brings us to David, the king and father of this sinister brood, who seems to have been largely absent during the upbringing of his many offspring. The Bible stories about David make mention on several occasions of his fatherly love for his children, but he could not have been more than barely involved in their day-to-day lives. David seemed to have forfeited the privilege of intimate acquaintance with his sons and daughters. He had fulfilled his duty by producing heirs, and besides, he had a complicated kingdom to run. Thus, David may have had a few moments in the morning to pop in, see the ailing Amnon, and ask if there was anything his son needed. However, it seems he was so marginally involved in the goings-on of his own family that he was clueless about the true motivation behind Amnon's request. Obliviously, David sent his daughter Tamar directly into the hands of her brother the fiend. Sure, he was furious when he heard about it— but the damage was done. To add insult to injury, ultimately David chose to take no action to rectify the crimes against Tamar.

Tamar's final betrayal was seemingly furnished by her full-blood brother Absalom, presumably her closest ally in the wasps' nest of the palace milieu. It appears from Absalom's reaction to Tamar that he was not at all concerned with his sister's welfare—it was all about him. Out loud he downplayed the importance of the event and entreated her to remain quiet in order to protect the family's reputation. There were no kind words for the battered and humiliated Tamar, no promise to seek justice and restore her dignity. Instead, she was told to shut up and forget about it.

But could Absalom have remained so callous at the sight of his violated sister? No doubt, he was incensed by the abuse of Tamar. Yet, there is an undertone of sympathy and loyalty in his words to her: "For the present, sister, keep quiet about it, he is your brother. Don't brood over the matter" (2 Sam. 13:20). Absalom seems to be hinting to Tamar that the action he is planning to take requires a subtle approach to the incident, and in fact he lay low for two years, silently plotting his revenge. In the face of Absalom's passivity, Amnon probably thought the rape had been swept under the rug. He was confident enough to let his guard down and accept Absalom's invitation to join him for a sheep-shearing party. When he had imbibed enough alcohol to blur his senses, Absalom's men fell upon him and murdered him (2 Sam. 13:23–34).

Absalom had to flee, but where does a son take refuge from an angry father? Often, with his loving and sympathetic grandparents. Absalom escaped to Geshur, where he hid out for three years (2 Sam. 13:37–38). During this time he married and had a family—three sons and a daughter he named Tamar after his beloved, damaged sister (2 Sam. 14:27).

THE DARK SIDE OF THE ROYAL FAMILY

King David's household can be described as dysfunctional at best and in the darkest light as deeply abusive. In fact, the story of Amnon, Tamar, and Absalom reveals intimate details about the royal relations that frighteningly correspond to the classic profile of an abusive family. These families are not always poor white trash; often large, they appear normal, even exemplary on the outside, while usually remaining socially isolated from the community at large. Natural emotions are denied and distorted, and there is no healthy intimacy between the family members. They are governed by strict rules dictating that all needs be met within the family and a deep fear of family breakdown. Victims of abuse are blamed and humiliated. All the family members adhere to a code of silence.

It's hard not to wonder why the biblical authors and editors chose to air the house of David's dirty laundry so publicly. To what end are the most sordid secrets of the royal family divulged? Not to teach us a lesson—Tamar's story is one of the strongest biblical examples of justice not being served, and it certainly doesn't conclude with a happy ending.

In fact, while the story begins with Tamar at the center, as it unfolds she recedes into the background and the spotlight moves to Absalom, the real protagonist. The biblical writer announces as much by mentioning Absalom in the first verse (2 Sam. 13:1). Although he doesn't appear on the scene until much later, he ultimately safeguards his sister and takes revenge. One reason for this focus may be an attempt by the narrator to help us sympathize with the troubled youth Absalom, who will go on to lead an armed rebellion against his father, David (see chapter 15).

However, we have to know the story of Tamar in order to understand why Amnon, the crown prince, was murdered by his brother Absalom, and why Absalom fled to the protection of his grandparents in Geshur, eventually returned to Jerusalem, rebelled against David, and was killed. These stories are part of the wider scope of the David story known as the succession narrative, which tells the story of David's rise to power, his years as king, the untimely demise of his older sons, and the rise of Solomon to the throne in the wake of his father's death (2 Sam. 9–20 and 1 Kings 1–2). Amnon and Absalom are important links in this chain of events; what happens between them and to them is the fulfillment of Nathan's prophecy to David that "the sword shall never depart from your house" (2 Sam. 12:10), the punishment for David's sins against Uriah and Bathsheba. Moreover, in the succession narrative we learn that kings, no matter how blessed or powerful, do not determine the world order and that all is controlled by the hand of God. It is the laws laid down by the Creator that determine the rule of the house of David, the pattern of monarchic rule, and the concept of the divinely appointed role of the king, the nation, and the city of Jerusalem. All these ideas come to us through the succession narrative, a pivotal element of the biblical literary canon.

Tragically, then, Tamar is betrayed once again: first by the male members of her family who were unwilling to protect her, and then by the compilers of the Bible, who used her rape and humiliation to tell, first and foremost, someone else's story.

13

Absalom's Rebellion in the Kidron Valley

2 Samuel 15–19:9

*King David's disgruntled son Absalom
raises an army against his father*

See page 305 for visitor information.

WHERE ARE WE?

We are standing in the Kidron Valley, which separates the Mount of Olives to the east from the City of David and the Temple Mount to the west. This valley, which was thirty to sixty feet deeper in biblical times, was an important element in the natural defense system of the City of David, which can be seen on the spur south of the Temple Mount. During the rainy season water flows through the Kidron and eventually makes its way to the Dead Sea, beyond the Mount of Olives to the east. When David fled Jerusalem in fear of his son Absalom and his army, he came down barefoot through this valley and up the slope of the Mount of Olives on his way to the desert.

SETTING THE SCENE

Although a popular Jewish legend associates the monument known as Absalom's Pillar with David's rebellious son, Absalom, this tomb was actually built about one thousand years after Absalom and King David lived in Jerusalem.

The Kidron Valley and the slopes of the Mount of Olives have been used as burial grounds since the time of King Solomon. (Some of the first temple period tombs can still be seen carved out of the rock beneath the lower level of houses in Silwan, the Arab village on the eastern side of the valley, across from the City of David.) Outside the city walls yet close enough to visit, this area went on to become the necropolis of ancient Jerusalem. During the late Second Temple period (165 BCE–70 CE) several elaborate tombs were built in this section of the Kidron Valley, including the one attributed to Absalom. We don't know who was actually buried here, but he was probably a wealthy man. In the tomb's architecture he incorporated both Hellenistic and Egyptian elements popular at the time, but in keeping with Jewish tradition there are no graven images in the stonework. The grave, the square lower part, is carved out of the hillside's natural rock, while the upside-down funnel on the top is the monument. This style reflected the popular Hellenistic notion that body and soul should be memorialized separately.

Despite the tomb's late date, its stubborn association with Absalom assured that no other tombs would be dug in the vicinity, for who would choose to be linked to a rebellious son in the world to come?

In the fifteenth century a fascinating male-bonding tradition developed here. Jewish and Muslim fathers would bring their sons to Absalom's Pillar and pelt the monument with stones while the fathers admonished their progeny not to follow in the treacherous footsteps of the rebellious son.

THE CONTEXT

This story is the tragic denouement of a series of extremely disturbing incidents in King David's household. The eldest son, Amnon, brutally raped and humiliated his half sister

Fig. 13. Absalom's Pillar in the Kidron Valley, Jerusalem

Tamar, the daughter of a different mother, the Geshurite princess Maacah. Although David was furious over what happened, he evidently took no action, either to punish Amnon or to compensate Tamar. Absalom, her brother, took Tamar into his house and seethed for two years following the rape, no doubt deeply hurt by his father David's inability or refusal to dispense justice. Finally, Absalom took revenge and murdered Amnon. He then fled to the safety of his grandparents in the northeastern kingdom of Geshur (2 Sam. 13).

Absalom may very well have been received as a hero in Geshur. We can imagine he was warmly welcomed by King Talmai, who no doubt applauded his grandson's bravery in defending the honor of his Geshurite family. Absalom remained in the cozy embrace of his grandparents for three years (2 Sam. 13:38), during which time he married and had children (2 Sam. 14:27). Yet Absalom would have been unwise to burn the bridges to Jerusalem behind him. With Amnon dead and Chileab, the son next in line, absent from the narrative, Absalom was set to inherit the throne.

More importantly, Absalom was probably expecting a showdown with his father. He had murdered his brother, and it was inconceivable to him that David wouldn't come after him. Demanding his day in court, Absalom desperately wanted a chance to state his case. He probably spent hours in front of the mirror, rehearsing what he would say to his father when he finally stood before him, face-to-face.

But David never came. For three years the runaway, rebellious son marked time, waiting for a sign that his father cared about him, missed him, was angry with him, but there was only silence. This silence served to deepen Absalom's anger and resentment toward his father.

Meantime, back in Jerusalem, "King David mourned over his son a long time. . . . And [King David] was pining away for Absalom, for [the king] had gotten over Amnon's death" (2 Sam. 13:37, 39). David had come to terms with Amnon's death and sought reconciliation with Absalom, whom he appears to have forgiven. However, David was torn and could not bring himself to initiate contact. Joab, David's army commander and close confidant, recognized the king's anguish. To help resolve the dilemma he sent a woman to request the king's mediation in resolving a fictional dispute involving her two sons, one of whom had killed the other. By cleverly compelling David to rule that the murdering son must not be harmed by those who wished to avenge his brother's blood, Joab successfully convinced David that his son's predicament was no different (2 Sam. 14:1–21).

Consequently David gave his permission for Absalom to return home, but at the same time he gave him an icy welcome. David refused to see him, and Joab, his principle ally, largely ignored him as well. Absalom languished in the capital for two years (2 Sam. 14:28), until finally, in frustration and desperation, he set fire to Joab's crops to attract his attention, demanding he arrange a face-off (2 Sam. 14:30). After murdering his half brother Amnon, all in all Absalom waited for seven years until he was summoned by his father to a tête-à-tête, yet no meaningful conversation is recorded at their reunion. There was no screaming and yelling, no exchange of accusations, no trial, and no catharsis. Just a cold, formal, kiss-on-the-cheek (2 Sam. 14:33). Absalom probably realized that the father who had been absent for him all these years would never fulfill his hopes and expectations. Bitterly disappointed, he probably lost respect for David. Absalom was a rebellion waiting to happen.

- -

2 Samuel 15

¹Sometime afterward, Absalom provided himself with a chariot, horses, and fifty outrunners. ²Absalom used to rise early and stand by the road to the city gates; and whenever a man had a case that was to come before the king for judgment, Absalom would call out to him, "What town are you from?" And when he answered, "Your servant is from such and such a tribe in Israel," ³Absalom would say to him,

"It is clear that your claim is right and just, but there is no one assigned to you by the king to hear it." ⁴And Absalom went on, "If only I were appointed judge in the land and everyone with a legal dispute came before me, I would see that he got his rights." ⁵And if a man approached to bow to him, [Absalom] would extend his hand and take hold of him and kiss him. ⁶Absalom did this to every Israelite who came to the king for judgment. Thus Absalom won away the hearts of the men of Israel.

⁷After a period of forty years had gone by, Absalom said to the king, "Let me go to Hebron and fulfill a vow that I made to the LORD. ⁸For your servant made a vow when I lived in Geshur of Aram: If the LORD ever brings me back to Jerusalem, I will worship the LORD." ⁹The king said to him, "Go in peace"; and so he set out for Hebron.

¹⁰But Absalom sent agents to all the tribes of Israel to say, "When you hear the blast of the horn, announce that Absalom has become king in Hebron." ¹¹Two hundred men of Jerusalem accompanied Absalom; they were invited and went in good faith, suspecting nothing. ¹²Absalom also sent [to fetch] Ahithophel the Gilonite, David's counselor, from his town, Giloh, when the sacrifices were to be offered. The conspiracy gained strength, and the people supported Absalom in increasing numbers.

¹³Someone came and told David, "The loyalty of the men of Israel has veered toward Absalom." ¹⁴Whereupon David said to all the courtiers who were with him in Jerusalem, "Let us flee at once, or none of us will escape from Absalom. We must get away quickly, or he will soon overtake us and bring down disaster upon us and put the city to the sword." ¹⁵The king's courtiers said to the king, "Whatever our lord the king decides, your servants are ready." ¹⁶So the king left, followed by his entire household, except for ten concubines whom the king left to mind the palace.

¹⁷The king left, followed by all the people, and they stopped at the last house. ¹⁸All his followers marched past him, including all the Cherethites and all the Pelethites; and all the Gittites, six hundred men who had accompanied him from Gath, also marched by the king. ¹⁹And the king said to Ittai the Gittite, "Why should you too go with us? Go back and stay with the [new] king, for you are a foreigner and you are also an exile from your country. ²⁰You came only yesterday; should I make you wander about with us today, when I myself must go wherever I can? Go back, and take your kinsmen with you, [in] true faithfulness." ²¹Ittai replied to the king, "As the LORD lives and as my lord the king lives, wherever my lord the king may be, there your servant will be, whether for death or for life!" ²²And David said to Ittai, "Then march by." And Ittai the Gittite and all his men and all the children who were with him marched by.

²³The whole countryside wept aloud as the troops marched by. The king crossed the Kidron Valley, and all the troops crossed by the road to the wilderness. ²⁴Then Zadok appeared, with all the Levites carrying the Ark of the Covenant of God; and they set down the Ark of God until all the people had finished marching out of the city. Abiathar also came up. ²⁵But the king said to Zadok, "Take the Ark of God back to the city. If I find favor with the LORD, He will bring me back and let me see it and its abode. ²⁶And if He should say, 'I do not want you,' I am ready; let Him do with me as He pleases." ²⁷And the king said to the priest Zadok, "Do you understand? You return to the safety of the city with your two sons, your own son Ahimaaz and Abiathar's son Jonathan. ²⁸Look, I shall linger in the steppes of the wilderness until word comes from you to inform me." ²⁹Zadok and Abiathar brought the Ark of God back to Jerusalem, and they stayed there.

³⁰David meanwhile went up the slope of the [Mount of] Olives, weeping as he went; his head was covered and he walked barefoot. And all the people who were with him covered their heads and wept as they went up. ³¹David [was] told that Ahithophel was among the conspirators with Absalom, and he prayed, "Please, O LORD, frustrate Ahithophel's counsel!"

³²When David reached the top, where people would prostrate themselves to God, Hushai the Archite was there to meet him, with his robe torn and with earth on his head. ³³David said to him, "If you march on with me, you will be a burden to me. ³⁴But if you go back to the city and say to Absalom, 'I will be your servant, O king; I was your father's servant formerly, and now I will be yours,' then you can nullify Ahithophel's counsel for me. ³⁵You will have the priests Zadok and Abiathar there, and you can report everything that you hear in the king's palace to the priests Zadok and Abiathar. ³⁶Also, their two sons are there with them, Zadok's son Ahimaaz and Abiathar's son Jonathan; and through them you can report to me everything you hear." ³⁷And so Hushai, the friend of David, reached the city as Absalom was entering Jerusalem.

16

¹David had passed a little beyond the summit when Ziba the servant of Mephibosheth came toward him with a pair of saddled asses carrying two hundred loaves of bread, one hundred cakes of raisin, one hundred cakes of figs, and a jar of wine. ²The king asked Ziba, "What are you doing with these?" Ziba answered, "The asses are for Your Majesty's family to ride on, the bread and figs are for the attendants to eat, and the wine is to be drunk by any who are exhausted in the wilderness." ³"And where is your master's son?" the king

asked. "He is staying in Jerusalem," Ziba replied to the king, "for he thinks that the House of Israel will now give him back the throne of his grandfather." ⁴The king said to Ziba, "Then all that belongs to Mephibosheth is now yours!" And Ziba replied, "I bow low. Your Majesty is most gracious to me."

⁵As King David was approaching Bahurim, a member of Saul's clan—a man named Shimei son of Gera—came out from there, hurling insults as he came. ⁶He threw stones at David and all King David's courtiers, while all the troops and all the warriors were at his right and his left. ⁷And these are the insults that Shimei hurled: "Get out, get out, you criminal, you villain! ⁸The LORD is paying you back for all your crimes against the family of Saul, whose throne you seized. The LORD is handing over the throne to your son Absalom; you are in trouble because you are a criminal!"

⁹Abishai son of Zeruiah said to the king, "Why let that dead dog abuse my lord the king? Let me go over and cut off his head!" ¹⁰But the king said, "What has this to do with you, you sons of Zeruiah? He is abusing [me] only because the LORD told him to abuse David; and who is to say, 'Why did You do that?'" ¹¹David said further to Abishai and all the courtiers, "If my son, my own issue, seeks to kill me, how much more the Benjaminite! Let him go on hurling abuse, for the LORD has told him to. ¹²Perhaps the LORD will look upon my punishment and recompense me for the abuse [Shimei] has uttered today." ¹³David and his men continued on their way, while Shimei walked alongside on the slope of the hill, insulting him as he walked, and throwing stones at him and flinging dirt. ¹⁴The king and all who accompanied him arrived exhausted, and he rested there.

¹⁵Meanwhile Absalom and all the people, the men of Israel, arrived in Jerusalem, together with Ahithophel.

¹⁶When Hushai the Archite, David's friend, came before Absalom, Hushai said to Absalom, "Long live the king! Long live the king!" ¹⁷But Absalom said to Hushai, "Is this your loyalty to your friend? Why didn't you go with your friend?" ¹⁸"Not at all!" Hushai replied. "I am for the one whom the LORD and this people and all the men of Israel have chosen, and I will stay with him. ¹⁹Furthermore, whom should I serve, if not David's son? As I was in your father's service, so I will be in yours."

²⁰Absalom then said to Ahithophel, "What do you advise us to do?" ²¹And Ahithophel said to Absalom, "Have intercourse with your father's concubines, whom he left to mind the palace; and when all Israel hears that you have dared the wrath of your father, all who support you will be encouraged." ²²So they pitched a tent for Absalom on the roof, and Absalom lay with his father's concubines with the full knowledge of all Israel.— ²³In those days, the advice which Ahithophel gave was accepted like an oracle sought from God; that is how all the advice of Ahithophel was esteemed both by David and by Absalom.

17

¹And Ahithophel said to Absalom, "Let me pick twelve thousand men and set out tonight in pursuit of David. ²I will come upon him when he is weary and disheartened, and I will throw him into a panic; and when all the troops with him flee, I will kill the king alone. ³And I will bring back all the people to you; when all have come back [except] the man you are after, all the people will be at peace." ⁴The advice pleased Absalom and all the elders of Israel. ⁵But Absalom said, "Summon Hushai the Archite as well, so we can hear what he too has to say." ⁶Hushai came to Absalom, and Absalom said to him, "This is what

Ahithophel has advised. Shall we follow his advice? If not, what do you say?"

⁷Hushai said to Absalom, "This time the advice that Ahithophel has given is not good. ⁸You know," Hushai continued, "that your father and his men are courageous fighters, and they are as desperate as a bear in the wild robbed of her whelps. Your father is an experienced soldier, and he will not spend the night with the troops; ⁹even now he must be hiding in one of the pits or in some other place. And if any of them fall at the first attack, whoever hears of it will say, 'A disaster has struck the troops that follow Absalom'; ¹⁰and even if he is a brave man with the heart of a lion, he will be shaken—for all Israel knows that your father and the soldiers with him are courageous fighters. ¹¹So I advise that all Israel from Dan to Beer-sheba—as numerous as the sands of the sea—be called up to join you, and that you yourself march into battle. ¹²When we come upon him in whatever place he may be, we'll descend on him [as thick] as dew falling on the ground; and no one will survive, neither he nor any of the men with him. ¹³And if he withdraws into a city, all Israel will bring ropes to that city and drag its stones as far as the riverbed, until not even a pebble of it is left."

¹⁴Absalom and all Israel agreed that the advice of Hushai the Archite was better than that of Ahithophel.—The LORD had decreed that Ahithophel's sound advice be nullified, in order that the LORD might bring ruin upon Absalom.

¹⁵Then Hushai told the priests Zadok and Abiathar, "This is what Ahithophel advised Absalom and the elders of Israel; this is what I advised. ¹⁶Now send at once and tell David, 'Do not spend the night at the fords of the wilderness, but cross over at once; otherwise the king and all the troops with him will be annihilated.'" ¹⁷Jonathan

and Ahimaaz were staying at Enrogel, and a slave girl would go and bring them word and they in turn would go and inform King David. For they themselves dared not be seen entering the city. [18]But a boy saw them and informed Absalom. They left at once and came to the house of a man in Bahurim who had a well in his courtyard. They got down into it, [19]and the wife took a cloth, spread it over the mouth of the well, and scattered groats on top of it, so that nothing would be noticed. [20]When Absalom's servants came to the woman at the house and asked where Ahimaaz and Jonathan were, the woman told them that they had crossed a bit beyond the water. They searched, but found nothing; and they returned to Jerusalem.

[21]After they were gone, [Ahimaaz and Jonathan] came up from the well and went and informed King David. They said to David, "Go and cross the water quickly, for Ahithophel has advised thus and thus concerning you." [22]David and all the troops with him promptly crossed the Jordan, and by daybreak not one was left who had not crossed the Jordan.

[23]When Ahithophel saw that his advice had not been followed, he saddled his ass and went home to his native town. He set his affairs in order, and then he hanged himself. He was buried in his ancestral tomb.

[24]David had reached Mahanaim when Absalom and all the men of Israel with him crossed the Jordan. [25]Absalom had appointed Amasa army commander in place of Joab; Amasa was the son of a man named Ithra the Israelite, who had married Abigal, daughter of Nahash and sister of Joab's mother Zeruiah. [26]The Israelites and Absalom encamped in the district of Gilead. [27]When David reached Mahanaim, Shobi son of Nahash from Rabbath-ammon, Machir son of Ammiel from Lo-debar, and Barzillai the Gileadite from Rogelim [28]presented couches, basins, and earthenware; also wheat, barley, flour, parched grain, beans,

lentils, parched grain, 29honey, curds, a flock, and cheese from the herd for David and the troops with him to eat. For they knew that the troops must have grown hungry, faint, and thirsty in the wilderness.

18

1David mustered the troops who were with him and set over them captains of thousands and captains of hundreds. 2David sent out the troops, one-third under the command of Joab, one-third under the command of Joab's brother Abishai son of Zeruiah, and one-third under the command of Ittai the Gittite. And David said to the troops, "I myself will march out with you." 3But the troops replied, "No! For if some of us flee, the rest will not be concerned about us; even if half of us should die, the others will not be concerned about us. But you are worth ten thousand of us. Therefore, it is better for you to support us from the town." 4And the king said to them, "I will do whatever you think best."

So the king stood beside the gate as all the troops marched out by their hundreds and thousands. 5The king gave orders to Joab, Abishai, and Ittai: "Deal gently with my boy Absalom, for my sake." All the troops heard the king give the order about Absalom to all the officers.

6The troops marched out into the open to confront the Israelites, and the battle was fought in the forest of Ephraim. 7The Israelite troops were routed by David's followers, and a great slaughter took place there that day—twenty thousand men. 8The battle spread out over that whole region, and the forest devoured more troops that day than the sword.

9Absalom encountered some of David's followers. Absalom was riding on a mule, and as the mule passed under the tangled branches of a great terebinth, his hair got caught in the terebinth; he was held between heaven and earth as the mule under him kept going. ¹⁰One of the men saw it and told Joab, "I have just seen Absalom hanging from a terebinth." ¹¹Joab said to the man who told him, "You saw it! Why didn't you kill him then and there? I would have owed you ten shekels of silver and a belt." ¹²But the man answered Joab, "Even if I had a thousand shekels of silver in my hands, I would not raise a hand against the king's son. For the king charged you and Abishai and Ittai in our hearing, 'Watch over my boy Absalom, for my sake.' ¹³If I betrayed myself—and nothing is hidden from the king— you would have stood aloof." ¹⁴Joab replied, "Then I will not wait for you." He took three darts in his hand and drove them into Absalom's chest. [Absalom] was still alive in the thick growth of the terebinth, ¹⁵when ten of Joab's young arms-bearers closed in and struck at Absalom until he died. ¹⁶Then Joab sounded the horn, and the troops gave up their pursuit of the Israelites; for Joab held the troops in check. ¹⁷They took Absalom and flung him into a large pit in the forest, and they piled up a very great heap of stones over it. Then all the Israelites fled to their homes.— ¹⁸Now Absalom, in his lifetime, had taken the pillar which is in the Valley of the King and set it up for himself; for he said, "I have no son to keep my name alive." He had named the pillar after himself, and it has been called Absalom's Monument to this day.

¹⁹Ahimaaz son of Zadok said, "Let me run and report to the king that the LORD has vindicated him against his enemies." ²⁰But Joab said to him, "You shall not be the one to bring tidings today. You may bring tidings some other day, but you'll not bring any today; for the king's son is dead!" ²¹And Joab said to a Cushite, "Go tell the king what you have seen." The Cushite bowed to Joab and ran off.

²²But Ahimaaz son of Zadok again said to Joab, "No matter what, let me run, too, behind the Cushite." Joab asked, "Why should you run, my boy, when you have no news worth telling?" ²³"I am going to run anyway." "Then run," he said. So Ahimaaz ran by way of the Plain, and he passed the Cushite.

²⁴David was sitting between the two gates. The watchman on the roof of the gate walked over to the city wall. He looked up and saw a man running alone. ²⁵The watchman called down and told the king; and the king said, "If he is alone, he has news to report." As he was coming nearer, ²⁶the watchman saw another man running; and he called out to the gatekeeper, "There is another man running alone." And the king said, "That one, too, brings news." ²⁷The watchman said, "I can see that the first one runs like Ahimaaz son of Zadok"; to which the king replied, "He is a good man, and he comes with good news." ²⁸Ahimaaz called out and said to the king, "All is well!" He bowed low with his face to the ground and said, "Praised be the LORD your God, who has delivered up the men who raised their hand against my lord the king." ²⁹The king asked, "Is my boy Absalom safe?" And Ahimaaz answered, "I saw a large crowd when Your Majesty's servant Joab was sending your servant off, but I don't know what it was about." ³⁰The king said, "Step aside and stand over there"; he stepped aside and waited.

³¹Just then the Cushite came up; and the Cushite said, "Let my lord the king be informed that the LORD has vindicated you today against all who rebelled against you!" ³²The king asked the Cushite, "Is my boy Absalom safe?" And the Cushite replied, "May the enemies of my lord the king and all who rose against you to do you harm fare like that young man!"

19

¹The king was shaken. He went up to the upper chamber of the gateway and wept, moaning these words as he went, "My son Absalom! O my son, my son Absalom! If only I had died instead of you! O Absalom, my son, my son!"

²Joab was told that the king was weeping and mourning over Absalom. ³And the victory that day was turned into mourning for all the troops, for that day the troops heard that the king was grieving over his son. ⁴The troops stole into town that day like troops ashamed after running away in battle. ⁵The king covered his face and the king kept crying aloud, "O my son Absalom! O Absalom, my son, my son!"

⁶Joab came to the king in his quarters and said, "Today you have humiliated all your followers, who this day saved your life, and the lives of your sons and daughters, and the lives of your wives and concubines, ⁷by showing love for those who hate you and hate for those who love you. For you have made clear today that the officers and men mean nothing to you. I am sure that if Absalom were alive today and the rest of us dead, you would have preferred it. ⁸Now arise, come out and placate your followers! For I swear by the LORD that if you do not come out, not a single man will remain with you overnight; and that would be a greater disaster for you than any disaster that has befallen you from your youth until now." ⁹So the king arose and sat down in the gateway; and when all the troops were told that the king was sitting in the gateway, all the troops presented themselves to the king.

ME AND MY DAD

The biblical text invites us into the most intimate chambers of the lauded King David. In striking contrast to official accounts of other ancient rulers, the Bible doesn't attempt to portray King David as a perfect, irreproachable savior sent as a gift from God to his people. Instead, the foibles and shortcomings of this very mortal ruler are nakedly exposed. In the story of Absalom's revolt we observe David under the microscope as parent and king, and the slide isn't pretty.

According to the biblical account David had nineteen sons (1 Chron. 3:1–9). Only one daughter is mentioned by name, but the law of averages leads us to believe that he sired a similar number of girls. The text pointedly mentions that this list does not include the children of his concubines, of which he was in possession of at least ten, as we learn in the Absalom story. If we allot them a minimum of two children each, we can calculate that David was the father of around sixty children.

We can fairly assume that David was not a hands-on kind of dad. He had a kingdom to run, an army to command, and many subjects seeking his rulings and advice. David's children were no doubt important to him, but it is unlikely that he told them bedtime stories and played games with them—there were servants for that. It's doubtful whether David knew his children well or was familiar with the day-to-day goings on in their lives. He was so oblivious to the true nature of his children's personalities that he unwittingly sent his daughter Tamar into the hands of her brother Amnon, her rapist, and Amnon into the hands of his brother Absalom, his murderer.

FATHER, WHERE ART THOU?

And [King David] was pining away for Absalom, for [the king] had gotten over Amnon's death." (2 Sam. 13:37, 39)

So, why didn't he go to him? Why was David the father unable to reach out to his son?

Could he be one of those emotionally stunted men incapable of revealing his feelings for fear of being perceived as weak? Not David. His public relations efforts notwithstanding, the biblical text is replete with examples of David's outward and uninhibited expression of emotions. He danced wildly when the ark was brought up to Jerusalem (2 Sam. 6:5, 14–15). He comforted Bathsheba over the death of their infant son (2 Sam. 12:24). He wept openly when he parted from Jonathan (1 Sam. 20:41), when he and his men discovered the devastation at Ziklag (1 Sam. 30:1–4), when he received news of the death of Saul and his sons (2 Sam. 1:11–12), and over Abner son of Ner's grave (2 Sam. 3:32). David was a lover, a warrior, an outlaw, an extortionist, an adulterer, and a murderer—but he wasn't a cold fish.

Perhaps he managed to delude himself that Absalom was safe in Geshur. If his son returned to Jerusalem, David might have to try and convict him of murder in the first degree, a crime punishable by death. However, the wise woman of Tekoa cleverly dispatched by Joab successfully undermined that excuse by posing a similar dilemma, albeit fictional, concerning fratricide. David, unaware that it was a ruse, ruled that the murdering brother was not to be harmed, a precedent that thereby exonerated his own son. In the wake of this clever manipulation, David reluctantly agreed to allow Absalom to return home to Jerusalem but stipulated immediately that he would not see him. What prevented David from reconciling with Absalom?

It would be fair to assume that at this point in the narrative David was in a ravaged emotional state. His infant son with Bathsheba was dead, his daughter Tamar had been brutally raped by her brother Amnon, and Amnon had been murdered by his brother Absalom. Awash in sorrow, guilt, self-loathing, and remorse, David was a broken vessel. He was probably emotionally incapable of reconciling with Absalom because he would have to admit he had failed yet again as a father. Unable to face this raw truth, David chose instead to avoid it by completely distancing himself from his son, subsequently widening the painful gap between them. He never initiated contact, denying Absalom an opportunity to address the terrible events that had transpired. Absalom was deeply hurt by his father's cold shoulder. His heart was out on his sleeve as he stood by the city gate and greeted people on their way to see the king. "If only I were appointed judge in the land and everyone with a legal dispute came before me, I would see that he got his rights" (2 Sam. 15:4).

The sneering Absalom doesn't always invite sympathy. He vandalizes property to get attention, he undermines his father's authority in public, and he probably preens and prances around so everyone in the kingdom can admire his perfect complexion and unparalleled good looks. So what if he's a hunk—who can feel sorry for a guy who weighs his own hair (2 Sam. 14:26)?

However, Absalom had a legitimate case against his father, and evidently he wasn't the only one disappointed in David's leadership. There seems to have been a groundswell of reinforcement for Absalom. How else can we explain why "the people supported Absalom in increasing numbers" (2 Sam. 15:12)? This distress appears to be widespread, as later we will learn of another attempted coup on David by a Benjaminite named Sheba son of Bichri. Although the narrative refers to him as a scoundrel, it goes on to note that "all the men of Israel left David and followed Sheba son of Bichri" (2 Sam. 20:1-2). If so many of David's subjects defected to a questionable leader, they must have had a significant ax to grind. Absalom, backed by many disgruntled men and David's best advisor (2 Sam. 15:12), was able to raise an army and march on Jerusalem. A blood-bath appeared imminent.

It is hard to read the account of David's flight from Jerusalem without wincing at the king's vulnerability. With a brood of helpless women and children behind him, David escaped from the city, abandoning his weeping subjects along the road as he made his way over the Kidron brook and up the Mount of Olives. His crown and regal bearing were hastily forgotten in the palace, and he was barefoot, his face partially hidden by a scarf. Himself in tears, he was cursed and pelted with stones and dirt by the ranting Shimei, a member of Saul's family, who no longer feared David's authority (2 Sam. 16:5–14). Meanwhile back in Jerusalem, in a symbolic move understood by all, his son was publicly laying claim to the kingdom by bedding David's ten concubines in a tent on the roof of the palace while everyone watched.

Amid these painful circumstances many a parent would be mumbling @#$&*$#*!!, cursing the rebellious child and the day he was born. Yet David never expressed any animosity toward Absalom and did not hold him accountable for his humiliation. He was almost fatalistic, acknowledging his own powerlessness in the face of God's will and urging his allies to save themselves. Even when David managed to turn the situation around, reorganizing his men to go on the offensive against Absalom's soldiers, he specifically commanded them to "deal gently with my boy Absalom, for my sake" (2 Sam. 18:5).

There are those who say, "We get the children we deserve." Implicit in David's treatment of Absalom was the recognition that he himself was to blame for his son's errant behavior. Absalom was a child crying out for attention, but by the time his father listened to him it was too late. David fell apart when he heard Absalom had been killed. Devastated, he completely forgot the enormous sacrifice his men had made for him and turned the victory party into a funereal sob fest. The kingdom and David's power over it had been saved, but they were no longer of any value to him when compared to what he had lost—an honest and meaningful relationship with his son.

POSTSCRIPT: THE PUNISHMENT OF REBELLIOUS SONS

If your kids are giving you a hard time too, check out Deuteronomy 21:18–21 for the biblical solution to problem children:

> If a man has a wayward and defiant son, who does not heed his father or mother and does not obey them even after they discipline him, his father and mother shall take hold of him and bring him out to the elders of his town at the public place of his community. They shall say to the elders of his town, "This son of ours is disloyal and defiant; he does not heed us. He is a glutton and a drunkard." Thereupon the men of his town shall stone him to death. Thus you will sweep out evil from your midst: all Israel will hear and be afraid.

If the rebellious son was indeed condemned to death, his sentence had to be published everywhere, and the stoning had to take place in Jerusalem during a pilgrimage festival for maximum exposure (*Tosefta Sanhedrin* 11:7). The execution was not to punish him for his evil deeds but to prevent him from ruining his parents and living a life of robbery and murder (*Sanhedrin* 72a; *TJ, Sanhedrin* 8:7).

Pretty harsh, huh? Relax—no need to call in the welfare authorities. There is no recorded execution of this law, ever. In fact, the rabbinic sages interpreted it so restrictively that it was virtually impossible to implement. They determined that the "son" had to be thirteen years old but with no pubic hair (which would categorize him as a man) (*Sanhedrin* 8:1), a period usually lasting no longer than three months by the majority opinion (*Sanhedrin* 69a; *Yad, Mamrim* 7:6). They also drew up minimum quantities for the food and drink consumed in gluttony, amounts that no thirteen-year-old son could afford unless he stole the money (*Sanhedrin* 8:3, 71a; *Yad, Mamrim* 7:2). Either parent could withdraw the complaint at any time (*Sif. Deuteronomy* 218; *Sanhedrin* 88b; *TJ, Sanhedrin* 8:6; *Yad, Mamrim* 7:8). If the son escaped before sentencing and his hair had grown, he had to be released (*Sanhedrin* 71b; *Yad, Mamrim* 7:9).

If the law was unlikely to be carried out, what was its purpose? First of all, it limited the authority of the head of the household, who was forced to bring an unruly child before the elders instead of devising his own punishment. More importantly, it was there in writing as a warning that desperate parents could use to educate their poorly behaved children.

In times ancient and modern, parenting has never been easy.

14

Jeroboam in Dan

1 Kings 11:42–12:33

Lines between politics and religion blur
as the Israelite kingdom splits

See page 332 for visitor information.

WHERE ARE WE?

The Tel Dan Nature Reserve lies in the northeastern corner of Israel, in the area known as the land of the headwaters of the Jordan River. Flanked by Lebanon to the north and the Golan Heights to the east, three rivers come together in this region to form the Jordan: the Snir (Banias), the Hermon (Hatzbani), and the Dan, the largest and most important. The Dan River's waters are fed by snow and rain that fall on nearby Mount Hermon, trickle down the mountain, and reemerge as springs at Tel Dan. The main spring here is the largest of its kind in the Middle East.

The abundant source of water and the surrounding fertile lands were what attracted the biblical tribe of Dan to settle here. Dan's original land portion stretched from the Judaean foothills out to the coastal plain, the region today known as the Tel Aviv metropolitan area. It was marked by the Mediterranean Sea in the west, the Yarkon River in the north, Nahal Sorek in the south, and the border with Judah, Benjamin, and Ephraim in the east. However, the Danites were unable to settle in this region for a long time because of the Philistines. They tried unsuccessfully to evict them (see the Samson stories in Judg. 13–16) and ultimately chose to move on in search of an alternate location to settle. They singled out this spot, formerly known as Laish, attacked and evicted its isolated and unsuspecting citizens, and built the city of Dan, ancient Israel's northernmost outpost (Judg. 18). From this time onward the borders of Israel are often referred to as stretching "from Dan to Beersheba" (e.g., Judg. 20.1; 1 Sam. 3:20, and many more).

SETTING THE SCENE

At the tel's summit lie the remains of the cultic center of the ancient city of Dan. The aluminum structure on the lower level is a reconstruction of the altar; its size was based on a stone horn from the original altar found here during the excavations. The adjacent staircase led up to the "high place," the main platform that served as the local sanctuary at Dan. High places were commonly used by all the Israelite tribes before the book of Deuteronomy centralized worship at the temple in Jerusalem (Deut. 12:1–7), and King Josiah shut down those that were still in use in the late seventh century BCE (2 Kings 23:1–25). The high place you see here was probably built by King Ahab in the mid-ninth century BCE, and the staircase was the handiwork of Jeroboam II in the mid-eighth century BCE. Remains of earlier structures were found underneath, which we may presume were built by Jeroboam I. It seems this site was used continuously for cultic purposes until the Assyrian invasion of 732 BCE, when it was destroyed together with the city of Dan. The ancient Greeks returned four hundred years later to reestablish a temple here; they built the wall that surrounds the ritual site to this day.

Fig. 14.1. The ancient cultic site at Tel Dan

THE CONTEXT

The Jeroboam affair actually begins with Solomon, the third king of Israel who followed Saul and David. Universally Solomon is most renowned for his wisdom. In the beginning of his reign God appeared to him in a dream and offered to give him anything he wished for. Rather than riches or a long life, Solomon requested "an understanding mind to judge Your people, to distinguish between good and bad" (1 Kings 3:9). God granted his wish (and then threw in all the things he didn't ask for as a bonus). Solomon's great wealth of knowledge was unprecedented in his time, and his fame still reverberates. Is there a religious-school graduate who is unfamiliar with the line, "Cut the baby in half!"?

However, Sunday school teachers usually choose not to tell the rest of the story. It is true that Solomon had formi-

Fig. 14.2. A pool in the Tel Dan Nature Reserve. Photo courtesy of Susan Rheins.

dable accomplishments such as the construction of the first temple and his private palace in Jerusalem (1 Kings 6–7), the refortification of three major cities (1 Kings 9:15), the building of chariot cities (1 Kings 9:19), and his encounter with the duly impressed (and incredibly sexy) Queen of Sheba. An intellectual in her own right, the queen was so dazzled by Solomon's wisdom, wealth, and taste she was left breathless (1 Kings 10:1–10) (and, as the Ethiopian legend goes, pregnant). However, his achievements were eventually overshadowed by his material and moral excesses. Ultimately he devolved into a depraved despot who was completely disconnected from his subjects.

How did this happen? The answer seems to be found in the text's details. For starters Solomon was born into a lifestyle of great privilege. King David left him a vast, wealth-generating empire. Solomon was able to rest comfortably on the laurels of his father, an outstanding warrior and excellent military strategist who, according to the biblical account, had subdued the entire region between the Euphrates and the western coast of Israel (1 Kings 5:1, 4–5). Conquered nations and vassal kings kept the tribute flowing, so that Solomon drank from goblets fashioned of gold (1 Kings 10:21), filled his stables with imported horses (1 Kings 10:28), and sat on a throne inlaid with ivory and gold (1 Kings 10:18–20). Also, anyone who arrived in Jerusalem seeking his wisdom brought gifts, so the royal coffers were literally overflowing with treasures. Solomon didn't seem terribly bothered by the law code of Deuteronomy that specifically prohibited the king from acquiring great wealth and large numbers of horses (Deut. 17:14–17). Rather, he seemed more preoccupied by his material affluence and by the ways he might most conspicuously consume it.

Despite his flashy international reputation, Solomon wouldn't have won any popularity contests at home. The rift between the northern and the southern tribes that would ultimately lead to the breakup of the union was largely precipitated by King Solomon. He imposed onerous taxes (1 Kings 4:7), drafted men into forced labor gangs (1 Kings 5:27–30), appointed governors who overruled tribal leaders, ignored tribal boundaries and redrew district lines (1 Kings 4:7–19), gave away northern territory (1 Kings 9:10–11), and unabashedly favored his own tribe of Judah at the expense of the other tribes (1 Kings 4:7–29).

The biblical author preferred to downplay the hardship created by Solomon's taxation. He indicates that Solomon's immense riches were a by-product of his God-given wisdom, implying they were somehow legitimate (1 Kings 10:23–25). He doesn't bat an eyelash when he succinctly lists the daily provisions required by the king: "30 kors of semolina, and 60 kors of {ordinary} flour, 10 fattened oxen, 20 pasture-fed oxen, and 100 sheep and goats, besides deer and gazelles, roebucks and fatted geese" (1 Kings 5:2–3).

However, in the eyes of the biblical author the buck stopped abruptly when it came to women. Deuteronomy states, "[The king] shall not have many wives, lest his heart go astray"(17:17). Yet through his treaties, crafty King Solomon accumulated seven hundred wives of aristocratic lineage and three hundred concubines, all of whom were foreign and therefore off-limits to him as an Israelite, according to the law. Nonetheless, "such Solomon clung to and loved"(1 Kings 11:1–2). Was it the drive of an insatiable libido? Was it a search for warmth and intimacy? Was it a collector's obsession? Whatever it was that Solomon sought from these women, it is told that in his later years he allowed himself to be enticed by them into worshiping their foreign gods (1 Kings 11:4–8). Wise King Solomon, the man who had everything, turned his back on the Creator.

The punishment was not long in coming. God informed Solomon in no uncertain terms that his descendants would not inherit the kingdom. Instead, a man who was not from the house of David would rule over Israel. Only the tribe of Judah (which by now had probably absorbed his brother Simon's tribe) would remain in the hands of Solomon's progeny, as a gesture to David's loyalty (1 Kings 11:9–13). It may have been the debauchery of the harem, and it may have been the merciless taxation; whatever the reason, when Solomon died the united kingdom died with him.

- -

1 Kings 11

[42]The length of Solomon's reign in Jerusalem, over all Israel, was forty years. [43]Solomon slept with his fathers and was

buried in the city of his father David; and his son Rehoboam succeeded him as king.

12

¹Rehoboam went to Shechem, for all Israel had come to Shechem to acclaim him as king. ²Jeroboam son of Nebat learned of it while he was still in Egypt; for Jeroboam had fled from King Solomon, and had settled in Egypt. ³They sent for him; and Jeroboam and all the assembly of Israel came and spoke to Rehoboam as follows: ⁴"Your father made our yoke heavy. Now lighten the harsh labor and the heavy yoke which your father laid on us, and we will serve you." ⁵He answered them, "Go away for three days and then come back to me." So the people went away.

⁶King Rehoboam took counsel with the elders who had served his father Solomon during his lifetime. He said, "What answer do you advise [me] to give to this people?" ⁷They answered him, "If you will be a servant to those people today and serve them, and if you respond to them with kind words, they will be your servants always." ⁸But he ignored the advice that the elders gave him, and took counsel with the young men who had grown up with him and were serving him. ⁹"What," he asked, "do you advise that we reply to the people who said to me, 'Lighten the yoke that your father placed upon us'?" ¹⁰And the young men who had grown up with him answered, "Speak thus to the people who said to you, 'Your father made our yoke heavy, now you make it lighter for us.' Say to them, 'My little finger is thicker than my father's loins. ¹¹My father imposed a heavy yoke on you, and I will add to your yoke; my father flogged you with whips, but I will flog you with scorpions.'"

¹²Jeroboam and all the people came to Rehoboam on the third day, since the king had told them: "Come back

on the third day." ¹³The king answered the people harshly, ignoring the advice that the elders had given him. ¹⁴He spoke to them in accordance with the advice of the young men, and said, "My father made your yoke heavy, but I will add to your yoke; my father flogged you with whips, but I will flog you with scorpions." ¹⁵(The king did not listen to the people; for the LORD had brought it about in order to fulfill the promise that the LORD had made through Ahijah the Shilonite to Jeroboam son of Nebat.) ¹⁶When all Israel saw that the king had not listened to them, the people answered the king:

"We have no portion in David,
No share in Jesse's son!
To your tents, O Israel!
Now look to your own House, O David."

So the Israelites returned to their homes. ¹⁷But Rehoboam continued to reign over the Israelites who lived in the towns of Judah.

¹⁸King Rehoboam sent Adoram, who was in charge of the forced labor, but all Israel pelted him to death with stones. Thereupon King Rehoboam hurriedly mounted his chariot and fled to Jerusalem. ¹⁹Thus Israel revolted against the House of David, as is still the case.

²⁰When all Israel heard that Jeroboam had returned, they sent messengers and summoned him to the assembly and made him king over all Israel. Only the tribe of Judah remained loyal to the House of David.

²¹On his return to Jerusalem, Rehoboam mustered all the House of Judah and the tribe of Benjamin, 180,000 picked warriors, to fight against the House of Israel, in order to restore the kingship to Rehoboam son of Solomon. ²²But the word of God came to Shemaiah, the man of God: ²³"Say to King Rehoboam son of Solomon of Judah, and to all the House of Judah and Benjamin and the rest of the people:

²⁴Thus said the LORD: You shall not set out to make war on your kinsmen the Israelites. Let every man return to his home, for this thing has been brought about by Me." They heeded the word of the LORD and turned back, in accordance with the word of the LORD.

²⁵Jeroboam fortified Shechem in the hill country of Ephraim and resided there; he moved out from there and fortified Penuel. ²⁶Jeroboam said to himself, "Now the kingdom may well return to the House of David. ²⁷If these people still go up to offer sacrifices at the House of the LORD in Jerusalem, the heart of these people will turn back to their master, King Rehoboam of Judah; they will kill me and go back to King Rehoboam of Judah." ²⁸So the king took counsel and made two golden calves. He said to the people, "You have been going up to Jerusalem long enough. This is your god, O Israel, who brought you up from the land of Egypt!" ²⁹He set up one in Bethel and placed the other in Dan. ³⁰That proved to be a cause of guilt, for the people went to worship [the calf at Bethel and] the one at Dan. ³¹He also made cult places and appointed priests from the ranks of the people who were not of Levite descent. ³²He stationed at Bethel the priests of the shrines that he had appointed to sacrifice to the calves that he had made. And Jeroboam established a festival on the fifteenth day of the eighth month; in imitation of the festival in Judah, he established one at Bethel, and he ascended the altar [there]. ³³On the fifteenth day of the eighth month— the month in which he had contrived of his own mind to establish a festival for the Israelites—Jeroboam ascended the altar that he had made in Bethel.

THE PARTY'S OVER

When Solomon's son Rehoboam informed the northerners that he intended to ratchet up their misery a few more notches, not surprisingly they decided to get rid of him and appoint their own king, effectively seceding from the union.

Jeroboam found himself in an ideal position to claim the throne of the newly formed northern kingdom. After rebelling against Solomon while in his employ as an overseer of forced laborers (1 Kings 11:26–28), he received God's blessing through the Shilonite prophet Ahijah (1 Kings 11:29–39). Now he was back from Egypt, where he had fled to escape Solomon's death sentence (1 Kings 11:40). A natural leader, he represented the will of the people when he led them first to query Rehoboam in all fairness and then to reject his sovereignty over them. The ten tribes of the north unanimously confirmed his appointment (1 Kings 12:20). Young, ambitious, charismatic, and empowered by a great sense of justice, he had virtually no enemies in the north.

From Jeroboam's perspective, his secession policy achieved exactly what he had hoped for: a clean and final break for the northern tribes from Judah. Never again were the two kingdoms to unite, and their reunification became an aspiration reserved for the messianic era.

And yet according to the biblical account, Jeroboam lost no time in tainting religion with politics. He immediately came down with a serious case of paranoia, surmising his position would soon be threatened. In an attempt to solidify his power and to prevent the northerners from journeying to Jerusalem, he put two golden calves in Dan and Bethel. The northern Israelites soon flocked to the shrines at Dan and Bethel. The narrator tells us that to make matters worse, Jeroboam defied religious convention by appointing his own priests and determining his own holidays.

POINT, COUNTERPOINT

A closer look is instructive. Let's take the golden calves, whose mere mention sends a shudder down the spine of every monotheist. The second commandment reads, "You shall not make for yourself a sculptured image, or any likeness of what is in the heavens above, or on the earth below, or in the waters under the earth. You shall not bow down to them or serve them" (Exod. 20:4–5).

This is a far-reaching prohibition against human and animal representation of any kind. However, the old Israelite guard was much less neurotic about the possibility of mistaking a statue for a divine image. In fact, the Holy of Holies, the inner sanctum of Solomon's temple where the ark of the covenant was kept, was decorated with two enormous cherubs (1 Kings 6:25–30). These were statues of winged animals with human heads that formed the platform of God's throne. In ancient Middle Eastern cultures deities were always portrayed sitting on a throne supported by animals or standing on animals' backs. In Jeroboam's time the calf probably represented the *presence* of God, just as the ark up in Jerusalem did. When Jeroboam said, "This is your god, O Israel, who brought you out of the land of Egypt" (Exod. 32:4) he was reciting word-for-word what the Israelites exclaimed before the golden calf, a formula well known to everyone in the congregation, the basic creed of the Israelites. The calf was an indication of God's nearness, as it was to those at Sinai. By building shrines in Dan and Bethel Jeroboam didn't introduce new cultic practices; rather he reclaimed important ancient worship centers and gave them the status of royal shrines or temples.

How about those sleazy priests with no Levitical genealogy that Jeroboam appointed? Priests were no doubt very carefully selected by the king because a charismatic priest could make or break his position. In much the same way that a newly elected American president will replace members of opposing parties in key positions with his own people, Jeroboam cleaned the northern stables of priests who may have remained loyal to the house of David and replaced them with men who supported the establishment of the northern kingdom. Jeroboam's changes notwithstanding, much earlier on, in the account of the establishment of the city of Dan in the book of Judges, the text notes that "Jonathan son of Gershom, the son of Manasseh, and his descendants served as priests to the Danite tribe until the land went into exile" (18:30). The footnote to this text remarks that "Manasseh" as it is written here with the letter "nun" bumped up half a line indicates an earlier version reading "Moses." Evidently, the biblical redactors critical of Jeroboam were uncomfortable with the idea that the progeny of Moses might be associated with the problematic Danites' temple. Indeed, could a priest who traced his family tree back to Moses really be considered illegitimate?

Similarly, Jeroboam's establishment of a new holiday can also be logically explained, especially since Exodus and Deuteronomy are not explicit about the exact date for the Feast of Tabernacles (Sukkot) (Exod. 23:1–14; Deut. 16:1–17). It is possible that Jeroboam simply reinstated a northern tribal festival previously annulled by Solomon. Holiday cycles determine life rhythms. Jeroboam's change in calendar may have been intended to underscore the separation between the two states.

All the changes that Jeroboam instigated can be rationally explained within the political and religious reality of the time. Yet everything he did is presented in an extremely negative light. Whoever recorded the story of the breakup of the twelve tribes and the establishment of the divided monarchy wanted us to understand these events as catastrophic for the people of Israel. The narrator, whoever he was, had an agenda.

So who was he? Who, in fact, wrote the early history of Israel, from Deuteronomy to the end of Kings, and what was he trying to tell us? For ages the tradition identified Moses as the author of the Torah, and Joshua, Samuel, Jeremiah, Ezra, and others as the authors of the books that came afterwards (*Bava Batra* 15a). The medieval Jewish scholar Ibn Ezra was the first to hint that Moses could not be the author of the Torah. The seventeenth-century Dutch Jewish philosopher Baruch Spinoza stated this unequivocally and attributed its authorship to Ezra the Scribe. Since the eighteenth century scholars have concurred that the Torah was compiled at a much later date. A mid-twentieth-century theory by the German scholar Martin Noth states that Genesis, Exodus, Leviticus, and Numbers were probably written by different authors and editors. The book of Deuteronomy, the final volume of the Torah, and the six books that follow it, Joshua, Judges, 1 Samuel, 2 Samuel, 1 Kings, and 2 Kings, all bear the stylistic hallmarks of a single school. This school has come to be known as the Deuteronomist school, or in shorthand, Dtr.

In order to understand Dtr.'s agenda, we must first review some seminal events in Israelite history. The ten northern tribes broke off and formed their own kingdom under Jeroboam in approximately 922 BCE. They remained at odds, and often at war, with the southern kingdom of Judah, but neither managed to completely overpower the other. Eventually the Assyrians, a far mightier regional adversary, appeared on the scene and invaded the northern kingdom in 722 BCE. Many of the northern Israelites there were forced into exile in faraway lands. Two hundred years after it had been founded, the northern kingdom of Israel was pulverized, and what was left of it was relegated to the status of an Assyrian province.

The southern kingdom of Judah boasted a more stable monarchy that enabled it to survive a similar Assyrian attempt at conquest a few years later, but it was severely weakened following numerous rebellions and deeply affected by the new reality. Judah was vulnerable, lacking influence and subjugated by the big powers. Ultimately the southerners too were unable to prevent a forceful foreign incursion. The kingdom of Judah was destroyed and dispersed by the Babylonians in 586 BCE, 136 years after the demise of the northern kingdom of Israel.

It seems that Dtr. completed its history after the destruction of Judah. They began to write under the influence of the book of Deuteronomy during a period of great religious rehabilitation, but in what turned out to be the waning days of the southern kingdom of Judah. They probably lived to witness the Babylonian destruction and the demise of Judah. The cataclysmic events of their time significantly influenced their understanding of the people of Israel, the kings who led them, and the God they worshipped. Therefore, the story they tell has a beginning and an end and attempts to explain historical events in a meaningful context. Quite simply, their presentation embodies a very clear message to the reader.

Dtr. wrote from a deeply religious point of view. A central theme woven through their story is the idea of covenant, the special contract the people of Israel have with God that requires them to be loyal and to combat idolatry. The covenant is expressed by the laws in the book of Deuteronomy, which was probably written over an extended period of time. Dtr. measured every king according to his obedience to this code and explained all the events that befell the people of Israel based on whether they were faithful to it. When they were true to their God, they were rewarded, and when they strayed from the path, they were punished.

Dtr. also placed strong emphasis on God's promise to David that one of his descendants would always be king, but only if they remained faithful to the Lord. Likewise, the Davidic line would continue to rule only if the people of Israel were true to the covenant. According to Dtr.'s understanding of history, the only way to ensure that Israel kept the faith was to have a king from the house of David ruling over all the tribes and one place of worship in Jerusalem.

For Dtr. the fall of the northern kingdom was not to be explained by the political constellations and the balance of power in the ancient Middle East. Instead, they related the Jeroboam story, and all that came after it, in theological terms. Solomon's mania for foreign women and their gods was the first crack that led to the disintegration. By breaking away from the union, appointing their own priests, and worshipping calves at multiple shrines, the northern tribes had strayed from the path of the covenant. Their demise was unavoidable.

If Jeroboam could provide a rebuttal to Dtr.'s version of the story, what would he say? Perhaps he would posit that he had rightfully reclaimed the trampled independence of the northern tribes. Perhaps he would insist that his religious institutions reflected the true Israelite faith. Perhaps he would accuse the Deuteronomist school of poisoning religion with politics. Perhaps he would implore us not to believe everything we read.

POSTSCRIPT: AN IMPORTANT DISCOVERY AT TEL DAN

During excavations at Tel Dan in 1993 archaeologists discovered a large fragment of a dedicatory stone embedded within a section of the ancient city wall. The inscription, written in Aramaic and dating to the late ninth century BCE, was written by an Aramean king of Damascus whose name does not appear on the fragment. The dedicatory stone, known as a stele, was probably erected at the entrance of the city of Dan following the Aramean king's victory over Israel, and then smashed to pieces when the Israelites regained control later on. It is the first extrabiblical source for the Israelite-Aramean wars of the tenth–eighth centuries BCE. In the inscription's text the kingdom of Judah is referred to as the "house of David."

The discovery created waves of excitement because it remains the first and only textual reference to David found outside the Bible. However, it also fueled a heated controversy in the academic community. Scholars who understand the biblical text as a subjective yet fairly historical document were delighted by what they deemed uncontested proof of David and his dynasty. However, archaeological evidence may be interpreted in more than one way. Scholars who question the historical authenticity of the Bible have claimed that the letters reading "house of David" actually mean something else.

However, today there is no reason to doubt the authenticity of the Tel Dan inscription. The controversy over its interpretation represents an ongoing argument in the academic community over the nature of the biblical text. Most scholars are convinced that the inscription is historical evidence for the existence of the house of David and for the wars between northern Israel and the Arameans.

Elijah at Mount Carmel

15

1 Kings 18:1–8, 16–40

A prophet on the lam challenges
idolaters to a tournament of faith

See page 322 for visitor information.

WHERE ARE WE?

The Carmelite monastery Mukhraka com-memorates the spot on Mount Carmel where tradition places the contest between Elijah and the prophets of Baal. (Mukhraka in Arabic means burnt offering—more on that in the story.) The Carmelites are a Catholic monastic order founded here in the twelfth cen-tury during the time of the Crusaders by monks who were inspired by the prophet Elijah. They chose to emulate his asceticism by living as hermits in caves (Mount Carmel is chock-full of them); later some took a vow of poverty (the word "discalced" on the sign at the entrance means bare-foot). Today there are communities of Carmelite monks and nuns around the world. The order's second signifi-cant location in Israel is the Stella Maris church on Mount Carmel in Haifa.

Mount Carmel, affectionately referred to by the ancient Egyptians as "the doe's nose," is a 15-kilometer-long (or 24-mile-long) mountain ridge with two sections. The upper Carmel rises to an altitude of 546 meters (1,791 feet). The city of Haifa sits on its northwestern end overlooking the Mediterranean Sea, and the Mukhraka, where we are now,

Fig. 15. A garden nook at the Carmelite Monastery on Mount Carmel

towers over the Jezreel Valley at its southeastern point. The lower Carmel continues southeast from here at about half the altitude.

The highly fissured rock of Mount Carmel was inhospitable to many crops, and the place was largely unsettled in biblical times (in fact, few chose to live here until the Druze arrived in the seventeenth century). However, in many ancient cultures mountains, in their loftiness, were sanctified; as a holy place, Mount Carmel served as a magnet for prophets such as Elisha, who established a base there (2 Kings 4:23–25). The "resident" god at Mount Carmel at the time of this story was probably Baal, which is why Elijah chose this location to prove the supremacy of the Israelite God.

SETTING THE SCENE

From the observation deck on the monastery's roof, looking out from the right side of the balcony as you come up, you will see the Mediterranean Sea off to the west; if the visibility is good, you will be able to make out the four tall smokestacks of the Yitzhak Rabin electrical power station on the coast near Caesaria.

To the east, on the left side of the balcony, lies the lush patchwork of the Jezreel Valley. Down at the bottom on the right is the town of Yokneam, and at its edge is Tel Yokneam, the excavated ruins of an ancient city. Off in the distance to the east you will see the landing strip of a large air force base, the rounded hill of Mount Tabor, the Hill of Moreh to its south, and on the far horizon the mountains of biblical Gilead (today the Hashemite Kingdom of Jordan). It was from a point further south along those eastern highlands that the Israelites crossed into the promised land with clear instructions: the land you are about to enter is flowing with milk and honey, but it is watered with rain from the heavens. If you are faithful to God, the land will provide everything you need. If you stray from the path, the skies will dry up, and there will be no rain. (For the complete rendition of the agricultural part of the covenant, see Deuteronomy 11:8–17.)

THE CONTEXT

In ancient times the land of Israel produced a great variety of agricultural crops such as wine, olive oil, grains, fruit, honey, and balsam. Although this produce often grew in generous abundance and was in high demand in the region, the naturally smooth Mediterranean coastline of Israel was notably lacking in deep-water harbors necessary for an export industry.

The Israelites' northern neighbors, the Phoenicians, had exactly the opposite predicament. Their mountainous terrain was poor in arable land but rich in natural ports along the coast. The Phoenicians were excellent shipbuilders and seamen, and they had access to all the international markets around the Mediterranean (see Ezek. 27). The two economies neatly complemented each other, and consequently the kings of ancient Israel always sought an alliance with their Phoenician neighbors in order to ensure prosperity and cement their power.

To this end in the first part of the ninth century BCE, the Israelite king Ahab, son of the great builder Omri, apparently signed a treaty with the Phoenician king Ethbaal of Sidon. As was the custom in ancient times, they sealed the agreement with a marriage (1 Kings 16:31). The Sidonian princess Jezebel was shipped off to the boondocks, no doubt rolling her eyes, to marry the provincial Israelite king Ahab and take up residence with him in his country palace in the Samarian hills.

In her new home Jezebel established and maintained a hefty entourage of 850 prophets of Baal and Asherah (1 Kings 18:19). Not surprisingly, her husband Ahab was perfectly agreeable. In the ancient Middle East Baal was understood to be a cosmic god, and not a national one. He was the god of wind, rain, and most importantly, fertility, and he was worshipped by all the peoples of the region, including Israel. Not only did Ahab tolerate Jezebel's Baal worship; he even built his own temple to him in Samaria (1 Kings 16:30–32). According to the book of Kings, in matters of faith Jezebel appears to have completely elbowed her husband out of the way and launched a relentless campaign to give Baal priority over the Israelite God. The Israelite subjects of the northern kingdom were quite amenable to Jezebel's missionary zeal, probably because Baal worship was nothing new to them. When faced with opposition from the Israelite prophets who spoke out against her, Jezebel systematically hunted them down and liquidated them (1 Kings 18:1).

The consequences were predictable. We are told that God punished the people of Israel for their unfaithfulness with a drought. Food and drinking water were scarce, and people all throughout the region were on the verge of starvation. However, after three years God took pity on his people and dispatched Elijah the prophet to meet King Ahab and to inform him that it would rain—conditional on the Israelite acknowledgment that it was sent by the Israelite God, and not Baal.

----

1 Kings 18

¹Much later, in the third year, the word of the LORD came to Elijah: "Go, appear before Ahab; then I will send rain upon the earth." ²Thereupon Elijah set out to appear before Ahab.

The famine was severe in Samaria. ³Ahab had summoned Obadiah, the steward of the palace. (Obadiah revered the LORD greatly. ⁴When Jezebel was killing off the prophets of the LORD, Obadiah had taken a hundred prophets and hidden them, fifty to a cave, and provided them with food and drink.) ⁵And Ahab had said to Obadiah, "Go through the land, to all the springs of water and to all the wadis. Perhaps we shall find some grass to keep horses and mules alive, so that we are not left without beasts."

⁶They divided the country between them to explore it, Ahab going alone in one direction and Obadiah going alone in another direction. ⁷Obadiah was on the road, when Elijah suddenly confronted him. [Obadiah] recognized him and flung himself on his face, saying, "Is that you, my lord Elijah?" ⁸"Yes, it is I," he answered. "Go tell your lord: Elijah is here!"

¹⁶Obadiah went to find Ahab, and informed him; and Ahab went to meet Elijah. ¹⁷When Ahab caught sight of Elijah, Ahab said to him, "Is that you, you troubler of Israel?"

¹⁸He retorted, "It is not I who have brought trouble on Israel, but you and your father's House, by forsaking the commandments of the LORD and going after the Baalim. ¹⁹Now summon all Israel to join me at Mount Carmel, together with the four hundred and fifty prophets of Baal and the four hundred prophets of Asherah, who eat at Jezebel's table."

²⁰Ahab sent orders to all the Israelites and gathered the prophets at Mount Carmel. ²¹Elijah approached all the people and said, "How long will you keep hopping between two opinions? If the LORD is God, follow Him; and if Baal, follow him!" But the people answered him not a word. ²²Then Elijah said to the people, "I am the only prophet of the LORD left, while the prophets of Baal are four hundred and fifty men. ²³Let two young bulls be given to us. Let them choose one bull, cut it up, and lay it on the wood, but let them not apply fire; I will prepare the other bull, and lay it on the wood, and will not apply fire. ²⁴You will then invoke your god by name, and I will invoke the LORD by name; and let us agree: the god who responds with fire, that one is God." And all the people answered, "Very good!"

²⁵Elijah said to the prophets of Baal, "Choose one bull and prepare it first, for you are the majority; invoke your god by name, but apply no fire." ²⁶They took the bull that was given them; they prepared it, and invoked Baal by name from morning until noon, shouting, "O Baal, answer us!" But there was no sound, and none who responded; so they performed a hopping dance about the altar that had been set up. ²⁷When noon came, Elijah mocked them, saying, "Shout louder! After all, he is a god. But he may be in conversation, he may be detained, or he may be on a journey, or perhaps he is asleep and will wake up." ²⁸So they shouted louder, and gashed themselves with knives and spears, according to their practice, until the blood

streamed over them. 29When noon passed, they kept raving until the hour of presenting the meal offering. Still there was no sound, and none who responded or heeded.

30Then Elijah said to all the people, "Come closer to me"; and all the people came closer to him. He repaired the damaged altar of the LORD. 31Then Elijah took twelve stones, corresponding to the number of the tribes of the sons of Jacob—to whom the word of the LORD had come: "Israel shall be your name"—32and with the stones he built an altar in the name of the LORD. Around the altar he made a trench large enough for two seahs of seed. 33He laid out the wood, and he cut up the bull and laid it on the wood. 34And he said, "Fill four jars with water and pour it over the burnt offering and the wood." Then he said, "Do it a second time"; and they did it a second time. "Do it a third time," he said; and they did it a third time. 35The water ran down around the altar, and even the trench was filled with water.

36When it was time to present the meal offering, the prophet Elijah came forward and said, "O LORD, God of Abraham, Isaac, and Israel! Let it be known today that You are God in Israel and that I am Your servant, and that I have done all these things at Your bidding. 37Answer me, O LORD, answer me, that this people may know that You, O LORD, are God; for You have turned their hearts backward."

38Then fire from the LORD descended and consumed the burnt offering, the wood, the stones, and the earth; and it licked up the water that was in the trench. 39When they saw this, all the people flung themselves on their faces and cried out: "The LORD alone is God, The LORD alone is God!"

40Then Elijah said to them, "Seize the prophets of Baal, let not a single one of them get away." They seized them, and Elijah took them down to the Wadi Kishon and slaughtered them there.

Who was that masked man? Elijah didn't wear a disguise, but he did have an aura of mystery about him not unlike a superhero. He probably lived between 920 and 850 BCE, but we know very little about his origins. The text tells us he was from a town called Tishbe in the land of Gilead across the Jordan, but no next-of-kin are mentioned. He wasn't your typical prophet-of-the-cult who hung around a shrine or a king's court, and he didn't have a house or home where he was known to reside regularly and where people seeking his help could find him. Rather, he was an itinerant man of God, roaming about Israel and suddenly appearing from nowhere. This vague personal history, the handy execution of several impressive miracles, and his theatrical departure from the earthly world in a fiery chariot (2 Kings 2:1–12) have given rise to lots of interesting conjecture about Elijah's real identity. Some say he was a direct descendent of Pinhas, the religiously zealous grandson of Aaron, which would mean Elijah was a priest as well as a prophet (*Pirkei de-Rabbi Eliezer* El.xlvii; *Targum Yerushalmi* on Numbers 25.12). According to the Kabbala, Elijah wasn't actually mortal but rather an angel in human form, which would explain why he had no parents or children (*Yalkut Reubeni, Bereshit* 9a). Legend equates him with Sandalphon, one of the cherubs of the ark, who gathers the prayers of the faithful and sends them to God.

In his own day Elijah no doubt cut a striking figure, clothed in a loose cloak sewn from hairy animal skins and girded with a leather belt (2 Kings 1:7–8). A radical believer in the concept that the Israelite God was the only god, he was on a crusade to eliminate idolatry from the Israelite religious practice. He was convinced that he was almost the only God-fearing Israelite left in Israel, and he was probably gruff, morose, and intimidating. Overzealous, when God assigned him the straightforward mission to go to Ahab and inform him that he would send rain to the parched Israelites, Elijah took it one step further. He thought the gift of rain should come with an impressive show of God's presence so the Israelites would understand it had come from him, and not the Canaanite god Baal. In short, Elijah invented the gimmick.

In the name of fair play he gave his opponents first shot at choosing the sacrificial animal and establishing contact with their god, but it turns out he was a masterful showman. Well-acquainted with the myths that attributed power over rain to Baal, Elijah set up the contest to mercilessly humiliate the Baal worshippers. It seems that no turn of phrase was too insulting. When relating his mocking sarcasm, most English translations prefer the more tasteful taunt, "He may be in conversation, he may be detained" (v. 27), but a closer linguistic analysis suggests that Elijah's biting irony was expressed in crass, graphic terms that left no room for interpretation. Scholars of ancient Hebrew quote Elijah saying, "Maybe he's defecating or urinating" (allow your mind to go wild in the vernacular). He gave them all the time they needed, waiting patiently until they had exhausted their efforts. Only then did Elijah call the people around him.

By receiving fire from heaven Elijah demonstrated that the dominion over life and death rested with the Israelite God alone, thus successfully convincing the people to turn their hearts back to him. This fantastic performance was topped off by a violent, bloody encore of the slaughter of Jezebel's false prophets. Now it could rain because everyone understood that the water was a gift, special delivery, from the God of Israel.

However, when Jezebel heard how Elijah had disposed of her precious prophets she vowed to kill him and he was forced to flee (1 Kings 19:1–2). A short time after the contest at Mount Carmel, we find Elijah in a cave in the desert at Horeb, the mountain of God, otherwise known as Mount Sinai. Depressed, dejected, and borderline suicidal, Elijah, when God asked what he was doing there, complained that the Israelites had rejected God and that he alone was the only true follower left (1 Kings 19:1–10). The painful truth was that despite the drama and pyrotechnics, the contest of prophets had failed to effect significant change among the errant Israelites.

It is interesting to note that Elijah is often compared to Moses. Both men had many similar experiences as leaders, as we can see from several of many examples: they confronted evil kings (Exod. 5:1–5; 1 Kings 18:17–18), fled to the wilderness for their lives (Exod. 2:11–15; 1 Kings 17:1–6; 19:1–3), were miraculously fed (Exod. 16:1–16; 1 Kings 17:1–6; 19:3–8), gathered their people (Deut. 29:9–12; 1 Kings 18:19), parted the waters (Exod. 14; 2 Kings 2:8), and much more. Both had revelations at Sinai (Exod. 19:1–6; 1 Kings 19:8–13), but the most notable difference between the two leaders was their approach to God in time of crisis. When Moses came down from Sinai and found the Israelites worshipping the golden calf, he was furious. Yet when he went back to God, he advocated for them, asking forgiveness for their sins (Exod. 32:30–34).

Elijah, however, completely despaired of the Israelites. He didn't attempt to defend his "clients" but rather hurled a litany of complaints about them to the Judge (1 Kings 19:9–10). He was a champion of God but not of his own people. He was fanatical, self-righteous, and drowning in self-pity, and clearly in need of some serious attitude readjustment.

In response God put on a show of his own, complete with all his best special effects. He asked Elijah to step outside, for he would soon pass by: "There was a great and mighty wind, splitting mountains and shattering rocks by the power of the LORD; but the LORD was not in the wind. After the wind—an earthquake; but the LORD was not in the earthquake. After the earthquake—fire; but the LORD was not in the fire" (1 Kings 19:11–12).

This revelation must have been terrifying. Yet throughout it all the presence of God was significantly absent. It came only after the fire, and it is described in Hebrew as "*kol d'mama dakik*" (1 Kings 19:12). The authors of the King James version of the Bible famously translated this phrase as "a still, small voice." Later translations have offered "the sound of a gentle whisper," "a soft murmuring sound," or "the sound of sheer silence." This puzzling yet beautifully moving communication was immediately identifiable to Elijah, who covered his face with his cloak and went out to stand at the cave's entrance, in the presence of the Lord at last (1 Kings 19:13).

ELIJAH REDUX

After this revelation, when God asked yet again, "What are you doing here, Elijah?" we can almost hear the exasperation in his voice. But the prophet, hardheaded, obstinate, and notably untransformed by what he had just witnessed, reread his list of complaints (1 Kings 19:13–14).

He didn't get it.

The driven, impatient Elijah hoped to achieve instant results at Mount Carmel by his bang-up, spectacular performance. He was unable to accept the notion that perhaps he had chosen the wrong tactic to imbue the Israelites with lasting spiritual transformation. Instead of Elijah attempting to turn the Israelites' hearts back to their God with a command performance, perhaps this enormous challenge would be achieved more effectively with soft, low-key, one-on-one encounters.

But Elijah could not deliver the goods. Instead, he was instructed to go back the way he had come, to appoint new kings in Aram and Israel and to anoint Elisha as the man who would succeed him (1 Kings 19:15–16). In other words—Elijah was fired.

The Jewish sages were tough on Elijah, condemning him for his overzealousness (*Mekhilta de-Rabbi Yishmael, Piska* 1:88–97). Some say he has been sentenced to be present at an eternity of circumcisions and Passover seders as a punishment for prophesying the end of the people of Israel. You were sure it was all over? Well, here's proof you were wrong—again and again.

Yet until today Elijah remains a popular Jewish folk hero. Bourne up to heaven in a whirlwind of fire, he never actually died and purportedly may still visit with mortals on earth. Throughout the ages he has been spotted in the guise of a poor beggar come to help the righteous in need, to sip from the Passover wine, to cradle baby boys at the circumcision ceremony, and to bestow a kiss on every groom who marries the right woman. He may be serving an eternal life sentence, but he may also be the model of a man who has come full circle. The once severe prophet who had lost all faith in Israel has perhaps been transformed into a watchful and tender nurturer of his people.

POSTSCRIPT: THIRSTY ISRAEL

Elijah's audience at Mount Carmel must have cringed as they witnessed the prophet ceremoniously dump ten gallons of precious water onto his altar in the fourth consecutive year of a terrible drought. Inhabitants of the land of Israel both ancient and modern have been hypersensitive about water conservation in the never-ending struggle to manage meager water resources.

Israel sits on the edge of a desert belt. While its climate is defined as subtropical, 60 percent is arid or semiarid, and rainfall often fluctuates wildly in the more temperate zones. In a good year the average rainfall between November and March reaches 900 millimeters (35.4 inches) in the center and north of the country, replenishing streams, springs, aquifers, and Lake Kinneret. However, since there is no guarantee of a good year, every drop must be utilized to its maximum potential. The farmers of ancient Israel developed numerous conservation techniques, such as cisterns, catchment basins hewn from the rock to store rainwater; terraces, leveled agricultural plots on hillsides that hold water; and channels for the efficient transportation of water over ground.

In modern Israel fulfilling the prophecy of Isaiah to make the deserts bloom has been a central element of the Zionist enterprise, but creative solutions continue to be sought for the ongoing water shortage. The slow-drip irrigation system developed in Beersheba in the 1960s is probably Israel's best-known technology for water conservation in agriculture. By laying a perforated hose pipe along each row of plants and dripping a predetermined amount of water from each hole, 50–70 percent of water used in conventional trench-flooding methods is saved, enabling farmers even in desert areas to raise crops successfully.

Other large-scale innovations undertaken by Israel's national water company include storage for floodwater catchment in reservoirs and aquifers; water recycling at the highest rate in the world (70 percent of Israel's wastewater is treated, reclaimed, and used for agriculture); reverse osmosis and electrodialysis in the desalinization of sea water and brackish well water; and rain enhancement by seeding clouds with silver iodide to increase precipitation. Water-efficient appliances, dual flush toilets, and faucet attachments can be found in most households today in Israel, but modern conveniences can only mildly alleviate the timeless challenge of living in a land flowing with goats' milk and date honey, but not much water.

16

Naboth's Vineyard at Jezreel

1 Kings 21:1–29

King Ahab is denied possession of a subject's vineyard

See page 326 for visitor information.

WHERE ARE WE?

Tel Jezreel sits about one hundred meters (three hundred feet) above the Jezreel Valley, affording it excellent command of the surrounding area and control of the ancient highway that passed from Megiddo to Bet Shean. The site has been excavated twice, in 1987 and then more extensively in 1990-95. The finds are exposed and visible, but the tel has not been transformed into an official tourist site.

SETTING THE SCENE

Standing on the tel, we can see the town of Afula to the left, in the west. The city of Nazareth rises on the ridge to its north. The ridge across the way is the Hill of Moreh. Kibbutz Merhavia and Moshav Merhavia lie at its foot, and the Arab village of Sulam sits behind them. The Jezreel spring is located at the foot of the tel, beneath a cluster of trees, and the Harod creek runs through the fields.

THE CONTEXT

At the time of the disturbing incident of Naboth's vineyard, the northern kingdom of Israel was ruled by the husband-and-wife team of Ahab and Jezebel. Omri, Ahab's father

Fig. 16. Tel Jezreel

and predecessor, chose to model himself after King David. When he became king, he built himself a new capital city on a hilltop in Samaria. His son Ahab, however, looked to David's son Solomon for inspiration. Not only did Ahab enable the worship of foreign gods in his kingdom as did Solomon, but he took it one step further and made this practice official by building a monumental temple to the god Baal in the capital city of Samaria.

In effect a tug of war was taking place between the Israelite and the Canaanite religions, each one vying for dominance. Most scholars agree that at this time Asherah worship, a central element of the Canaanite cult, had long been integrated into the Israelite religion. Most Israelites seemed comfortable with this adoption, but a small group of prophets viewed it as a serious threat to the religious traditions of Israel. The tension over this issue reached a critical mass under Ahab.

According to the biblical author, a shadow was cast over Ahab's regime right from the get-go thanks to his Phoenician bride Jezebel. The Phoenicians, Israel's seafaring northern Canaanite neighbors, had great experience with foreign cultures and were fashionably cosmopolitan for their time. They viewed the Israelites as country bumpkins but important allies nonetheless. By marrying his daughter to the provincial neighboring king, the Phoenician ruler Ethbaal gained access to the Kings Highway, a major trade route. Although Jezebel was packed off and sent to the sticks, she probably engendered a strong sense of mission in her new role as wife to the Israelite king. She was able both to champion her own country's interests and to enlighten the natives as to the true identity of the gods. Jezebel was the polar opposite of Ruth, the gentile woman who married into an Israelite family and subsequently relinquished her foreign gods, converted to the faith of her husband, and remained steadfastly devoted to her mother-in-law. Rather, Jezebel was a devout adherent of her Phoenician religion and insisted on promoting her faith with great zeal in her new home. Raised to worship the universal gods Baal and Asherah, Jezebel viewed the Israelite devotion to a singular parochial male God as primitive, restrictive, and exclusionary.

In previous chapters Jezebel had already proven that she was a headstrong, outspoken woman not to be messed with. She successfully hunted down and murdered most of the Israelite prophets in the kingdom in a zero-tolerance campaign (1 Kings18:4). During the three-year drought she fed and cared for an entourage of 950 of her own religious personnel while her subjects teetered on the brink of starvation (1 Kings 18:19). After the defiant Elijah humiliated and murdered her prophets, she ran him out of town in fear of his life (1 Kings 19:1–3).

Although Jezebel was an outsider and a woman, when she chose to act no one could stand in her way—not even

Ahab. But a closer look at the story of Naboth's vineyard reveals that the principle protagonist in this morality play isn't Jezebel—it's her husband, the king of Israel.

- -

1 Kings 21

[1][The following events] occurred sometime afterward: Naboth the Jezreelite owned a vineyard in Jezreel, adjoining the palace of King Ahab of Samaria. [2]Ahab said to Naboth, "Give me your vineyard, so that I may have it as a vegetable garden, since it is right next to my palace. I will give you a better vineyard in exchange; or, if you prefer, I will pay you the price in money." [3]But Naboth replied, "The LORD forbid that I should give up to you what I have inherited from my fathers!" [4]Ahab went home dispirited and sullen because of the answer that Naboth the Jezreelite had given him: "I will not give up to you what I have inherited from my fathers!" He lay down on his bed and turned away his face, and he would not eat. [5]His wife Jezebel came to him and asked him, "Why are you so dispirited that you won't eat?" [6]So he told her, "I spoke to Naboth the Jezreelite and proposed to him, 'Sell me your vineyard for money, or if you prefer, I'll give you another vineyard in exchange'; but he answered, 'I will not give my vineyard to you.'" [7]His wife Jezebel said to him, "Now is the time to show yourself king over Israel. Rise and eat something, and be cheerful; I will get the vineyard of Naboth the Jezreelite for you."

[8]So she wrote letters in Ahab's name and sealed them with his seal, and sent the letters to the elders and the nobles who lived in the same town with Naboth. [9]In the letters she wrote as follows: "Proclaim a fast and seat Naboth at the front of the assembly. [10]And seat two scoundrels opposite him, and let them testify against him:

'You have reviled God and king!' Then take him out and stone him to death."

11His townsmen—the elders and nobles who lived in his town—did as Jezebel had instructed them, just as was written in the letters she had sent them: 12They proclaimed a fast and seated Naboth at the front of the assembly. 13Then the two scoundrels came and sat down opposite him; and the scoundrels testified against Naboth publicly as follows: "Naboth has reviled God and king." Then they took him outside the town and stoned him to death. 14Word was sent to Jezebel: "Naboth has been stoned to death." 15As soon as Jezebel heard that Naboth had been stoned to death, she said to Ahab, "Go and take possession of the vineyard which Naboth the Jezreelite refused to sell you for money; for Naboth is no longer alive, he is dead." 16When Ahab heard that Naboth was dead, Ahab set out for the vineyard of Naboth the Jezreelite to take possession of it.

17Then the word of the LORD came to Elijah the Tishbite: 18"Go down and confront King Ahab of Israel who [resides] in Samaria. He is now in Naboth's vineyard; he has gone down there to take possession of it. 19Say to him, 'Thus said the LORD: Would you murder and take possession? Thus said the LORD: In the very place where the dogs lapped up Naboth's blood, the dogs will lap up your blood too.'"

20Ahab said to Elijah, "So you have found me, my enemy?" "Yes, I have found you," he replied. "Because you have committed yourself to doing what is evil in the sight of the LORD, 21I will bring disaster upon you. I will make a clean sweep of you, I will cut off from Israel every male belonging to Ahab, bond and free. 22And I will make your house like the House of Jeroboam son of Nebat and like the House of Baasha son of Ahijah, because of the provocation you have caused by leading Israel to sin. 23And the LORD has also spoken concerning Jezebel: 'The dogs shall devour Jezebel in the field of Jezreel. ²⁴All of Ahab's line who die in the town shall be devoured by dogs, and all who die in the open country shall be devoured by the birds of the sky.'"

(²⁵Indeed, there never was anyone like Ahab, who committed himself to doing what was displeasing to the LORD, at the instigation of his wife Jezebel. ²⁶He acted most abominably, straying after the fetishes just like the Amorites, whom the LORD had dispossessed before the Israelites.)

²⁷When Ahab heard these words, he rent his clothes and put sackcloth on his body. He fasted and lay in sackcloth and walked about subdued. ²⁸Then the word of the LORD came to Elijah the Tishbite: ²⁹"Have you seen how Ahab has humbled himself before Me? Because he has humbled himself before Me, I will not bring the disaster in his lifetime; I will bring the disaster upon his house in his son's time."

PARAGONS OF EVIL

It is impossible to read this story without feeling overcome by indignation. Ahab's greed and Jezebel's abuse of power are outrageously co-opted to trample the most inalienable of rights. However, hiding between the lines of the narrative is a perverse glee in the retelling of this story, a hand-rubbing, lip-smacking delight in the portrayal of such evil rulers.

In fact, Ahab and Jezebel are the singularly most maligned characters in the Bible, repeatedly trashed by the biblical narrator. Two choice examples: Of Ahab we are told, "there was never anyone like Ahab . . . he acted most abominably" (1 Kings 21:25–26). When Jezebel meets her grisly end and is thrown out the palace window by her eunuchs, we are informed, "The dogs shall devour the flesh of Jezebel in the field of Jezreel; and the carcass of Jezebel shall be like dung on the ground" (2 Kings 9:36–37).

The narrator bent over backward to paint Jezebel as the epitome of evil. Indeed, she's such a perfect villain that some scholars have posited she is no more than a fictional elaboration on an anonymous foreign wife of Ahab. In the Naboth story her innate wickedness reached a pinnacle as she spurned Israel's sacred traditions and made a mockery of the justice system. The elders of Jezreel obediently followed her pernicious directives, indicating she was extremely powerful. She also cleverly operated within the limitations of her role as both a woman and a foreigner by pulling all the right strings from behind her husband's authority.

The queen's devotion to her husband was unshakable; in every story she is right by his side without so much as a hint of tension between them. To Ahab, Jezebel must have been an intriguing creature. She was regal and exotic, yet completely devoted to him. Perhaps he looked to her as a role model for the man-of-the-world he aspired to become. Still, it is difficult to gauge the balance of power in this relationship. If Ahab was a wily, self-confident despot, he would have found Jezebel to be a sexy, alluring, intellectual equal and a superb partner in running a kingdom as complicated as northern Israel. If he was exceptionally shrewd, he may have even skillfully manipulated his wife into taking morally reprehensible action in his name by playing the sulking child. However, it is also possible that Ahab was weak and malleable, easily overpowered, and manipulated by a dominatrix such as Jezebel.

THE YOKEL KING

There was, nonetheless, one issue that appears to have been unresolved between them: who was the ruling deity in Israel? On one hand, it seems that Ahab deferred to Jezebel. He constructed a temple to Baal, allowed her to engage in intensive missionary activity, and stood idly by while she persecuted and murdered the prophets of the Lord. Yet the narrative is scattered with subtle hints indicating that Ahab had by no means severed links to his native faith. For starters his children with Jezebel all had classic, Yahwistic names—Athaliah, Ahaziah, and Jehoram. In modern translation their kids were Rachel and Jonathan, not Shannon and Christopher.

Ahab's chief steward and right-hand man was Obadiah, a deeply God-fearing individual who risked his own life to protect a group of prophets from Jezebel (1 Kings 18:13). His identity could not have been unknown in the royal circles, and Obadiah may have even served as a counterweight to the queen in palace politics.

Ahab was also present at the contest on Mount Carmel when Elijah defeated the prophets of Baal (1 Kings 18:20). Ahab made no attempt to intervene as Elijah mocked Jezebel's prophets and dragged them down the mountainside to slaughter them. He then went home and announced the news of the tournament to Jezebel (1 Kings 19:1), probably with great excitement over the awe-inspiring pyrotechnics of his own Israelite God.

And so an image of Ahab gradually emerges as a striving, up-and-coming Israelite king with a sophisticated foreign wife who devotedly influenced him from behind the scenes. He respected and admired her but superstitiously clung to his native religion, a point of contention in their relationship.

This picture is cemented by their bedroom dialogue following Naboth's refusal to part with his family plot. Ahab's foul mood was the result of his resignation. The laws of Leviticus state that all the land belongs to the Lord and is held in trust by the Israelites; therefore it cannot be sold (Lev. 25:23). Although the people of Israel served only as the caretakers of the land, the concept of stewardship was a radical departure from ancient Middle Eastern culture, where land was typically the private property of kings and temples. The biblical system of inherited family plots divested the wealthy and powerful of their landholdings and ensured that people would always have a source of livelihood.

In relating the conversation with Naboth to Jezebel, Ahab presented a version with artful but significant differences. The deference with which he approached Naboth was erased, and his request was presented to Jezebel as a demand. While Ahab first offered Naboth a better vineyard and then monetary compensation, in the revised version he told Jezebel he had offered the money first (knowing what was most important to her) and only afterward "another vineyard" of no identifiable value. Even though Ahab coveted Naboth's vineyard, he knew and respected the Israelite laws of land inheritance that protected his subject's rights. However, he concealed this tacit acceptance from his wife by omitting the key words of Naboth's claim. Naboth said, "The Lord forbid that I should give up to you what I have inherited from my fathers" (1 Kings 21:3). When Ahab repeated the conversation to Jezebel, he only quoted Naboth saying, "I will not give my vineyard to you," slyly removing the reference to Israelite law.

Ahab knew that in Jezebel's world the king could take whatever he liked from any of his subjects and that she would despise him for his weakness in the face of the laws of the Israelite God. Torn between his commitment to the Israelite legal system and his foreign wife's approval, he took refuge in passivity. Their unspoken understanding meant that Jezebel would take whatever action was necessary to obtain the vineyard, and Ahab would turn a blind eye to her nefarious scheme.

A LITERARY MYSTERY

Numerous scholars have grappled with the questionable historicity of the Naboth story—it doesn't quite flow with the rest of the narrative. In addition to its designer antagonist Jezebel, it has no outside supporting sources and raises issues of chronology within the broader narrative of the Omride dynasty. Also, in this story Elijah plays the role of Ahab's moral conscience, a significant departure from the narrative pattern of the Elijah cycle, which is concerned primarily with Baal worship.

In fact, astute readers will find an extremely condensed version of the same events at a later point in the text:

> Jehu thereupon ordered his officer Bidkar, "Pick him up and throw him into the field of Naboth the Jezreelite. Remember how you and I were riding side by side behind his father Ahab, when the LORD made this pronouncement about him: 'I swear, I have taken note of the blood of Naboth and the blood of his sons yesterday—declares the LORD. And I will requite you in this plot—declares the LORD.' So pick him up and throw him unto the plot in accordance with the word of the LORD." (2 Kings 9:25-26)

It seems that the author of 1 Kings 21 used his poetic license to expand and elaborate the condensed version of the story toward an important objective. A linguistic analysis of the Naboth story reveals a broad familiarity with the laws and language of the Torah, most notably the laws of land inheritance. The centrality of the Pentateuchal laws and the idea of Torah as a moral obligation are not characteristic of the writings from the period of the

Israelite kingdom. Rather, they are far more typical of the literature written and recorded following the return of the Jewish exiles from Babylon over three hundred years after Ahab's time. If this story was parachuted into the text at a later date by the biblical redactors, then they must have harbored an agenda.

Scholars suggest that the longer version of the Naboth story reflects the quest during the postexilic period to understand the reasons for the destruction of the temple and the obliteration of the kingdom of Judah. The prophets writing at this time identified the rampant social immorality during the time of the Israelite kings as the root cause of Judah's terrible fate. In the Naboth story they emphasized the prophet's role as social critic by placing Elijah in a face-to-face confrontation with Ahab, where he minced no words in calling the king to task. More importantly, they underscored the king's obligation to serve as a moral example. While the narrator took great pains to present Jezebel as the true villain and Ahab as passive and uninvolved in Naboth's murder, the moral of the story is that ignorance is no excuse. Ahab could play dumb and claim that he had no idea how poor Naboth's vineyard wound up in his possession, but as king he bore responsibility for the crime committed in his name. This imperative is masterfully articulated by God when he instructed Elijah to ask Ahab, "Would you murder and take possession?" (1 Kings 21:19). (Accentuate "and" for the full effect.)

Ahab appears to have deeply internalized the gravity of his transgressions. After hearing Elijah's pronouncement, he plunged himself into anguished mourning for a prolonged period, a sincere expression of remorse. Recognizing the humility of his reflection, God ultimately pardoned Ahab by postponing his dynasty's demise to the next generation.

In an interesting echo of biblical land ownership, today 93 percent of the land in the state of Israel is held in stewardship for the Jewish people by the state, the Jewish National Fund, and the Development Authority. Land ownership is managed by the Israel Lands Authority, which is prohibited by law from selling state-owned lands. Homes purchased in Israel come with leasing rights on the land for forty-nine or ninety-eight years. This system ensures that the land will always belong to the Jewish people.

When the land came back under Jewish ownership in the Zionist enterprise, the biblical laws governing agriculture were reactivated, most notably the observance of *shmitta*, the sabbatical year. Under this law every seventh year the land owned by Jews must be left to lie fallow. All agricultural work beyond basic maintenance is prohibited, and fruits grown during this year may not be sold and may be picked by anyone.

A creative interpretation of this law was developed in the *shmitta* year of 1888–89, when Jewish farmers in pre-state Palestine found themselves on the brink of destitution. Rabbis devised the *heter mechira* (leniency of sale), a permit to sell the land to non-Jews (usually Arab neighbors) for the duration of the sabbatical year so that they could continue to farm it without violating the biblical law. This temporary interpretation eventually became permanent, although in recent years some hard-line religious authorities have nullified it and prohibited the consumption of locally grown produce during the sabbatical year.

Today the laws of *shmitta* are observed voluntarily by farmers who wish to follow them. During the *shmitta* year observant Jews in Israel may eat fruits and vegetables distributed under rabbinic supervision, grown in the sixth year, and grown in greenhouses and on land owned by non-Jews or land outside Israel. For the Arab farmers in Israel, Gaza, and the West Bank, the *shmitta* year is always a prosperous one.

17

Elisha and the Wealthy Woman at Shunem

2 Kings 4:8–37

A prophet intervenes for a wealthy woman with no sons

See page 327 for visitor information.

WHERE ARE WE?

Our lookout point is the Hill of Moreh (Givat HaMoreh in Hebrew), which could mean "the hill seen from afar" or "the hill from which one sees." At a height of 515 meters (1,540 feet) above sea level, we may assume it offered a strategic location on the northern side of the Jezreel Valley. The plain at the foot of the Hill of Moreh served as the campsite of the Midianite army (Judg. 7:1), and the Philistine host assembled on its slopes at Shunem before going to war against King Saul (1 Sam. 28:4). To the south is the Gilboa range, southwest are the Samarian hills, and Afula lies nearby to the west. In the distance to the west you can see Mount Carmel. Just below you is the Arab village of Sulam, known in biblical times as Shunem. The current village was established in the eighteenth century by members of the Zoabi clan from A-Dahi and currently numbers about 2,300 inhabitants. Tel Shunem, the site of the ancient settlement, sits at the northeastern edge of the village. Salvage excavations in recent years have uncovered remains going back as far as the fifteenth century

Fig. 17. Sulam village (Shunem)

BCE. Today the slopes and the summit of the tel serve as the village's cemetery.

SETTING THE SCENE

The spring or water source lay at the heart of many ancient villages; as they developed often churches, synagogues, and mosques were built near the water, at the center of the community. According to local legend, the wealthy woman of Shunem's home was located behind the mosque on the hill, next to a cave. The cave's entrance is now blocked but marked by a semicircular wall faced in white stone with an adjacent prayer area. It is a place of quiet meditation for women praying for fertility and hoping to give birth to a baby boy.

THE CONTEXT

Elisha son of Shaphat was a mild-mannered farmer out plowing his field one day in Abel-mehola when he was approached by the prophet Elijah and informed he would be his successor (1 Kings 19:19–21). Almost without saying good-bye to his family, Elisha left his fields and became Elijah's devoted disciple, although he remained behind the scenes until the prophet's dramatic death by the Jordan River seven or eight years later (2 Kings 1:1–15). He subsequently served as the main prophet in Israel for sixty years, from the days of King Jehoram, son of Ahab (851–842 BCE), until the time of King Jehoash, son of Ahaziah (800–784 BCE).

Elisha's style differed from that of Elijah, who remained aloof from the folk. Elisha was hands-on, a people person. He worked slowly and methodically to restore the faith of the Israelites by traveling around the kingdom and ministering to the commoners. He addressed the concerns of the weakest members of the population such as peasants and women, and by using his prophetic powers he enabled them to empower themselves. For example, in Jericho he purified the poisoned waters of the local spring (2 Kings 2:19–22), and a short while later he provided a bottomless cruse of oil to a destitute widow (2 Kings 4:1–7).

Elisha also intervened in foreign affairs and with kings. When the armies of Israel and Judah found themselves stranded in the desert with no water, he led them to a wadi full of pools (2 Kings 3:9–20). In another example, later on we will read how the prophet cured the commander of the Aramean army of leprosy (2 Kings 5:1–14).

Elisha also assumed leadership of the prophetic bands (*bnai nevi'im*). The first time these groups are mentioned is in the days of the prophet Samuel. They traveled throughout the land and attempted to root out idolatry by prophesying while accompanying themselves on musical instruments. Elisha made the rounds of these bands, eating with them, helping them, supporting them, teaching them, and performing miracles for them (e.g., 2 Kings 4:38–41; 6:1–7).

When we meet Elisha in this story, he has arrived in the town of Shunem, one of the regular stops on his pastoral circuit.

- -

2 Kings 4

⁸One day Elisha visited Shunem. A wealthy woman lived there, and she urged him to have a meal; and whenever he passed by, he would stop there for a meal. ⁹Once she said to her husband, "I am sure it is a holy man of God who comes this way regularly. ¹⁰Let us make a small enclosed upper chamber and place a bed, a table, a chair, and a lampstand there for him, so that he can stop there whenever he comes to us." ¹¹One day he came there; he retired to the upper chamber and lay down there. ¹²He said to his servant Gehazi, "Call that Shunammite woman." He called her, and she stood before him. ¹³He said to him, "Tell her, 'You have gone to all this trouble for us. What can we do for you? Can we speak in your behalf to the king or to the army commander?'" She replied, "I live among my own people." ¹⁴"What then can be done for her?" he asked. "The fact is," said Gehazi, "she has no son, and her husband is old." ¹⁵"Call her," he said. He called her, and she stood in the doorway. ¹⁶And Elisha said, "At this season next year, you will be embracing a son." She replied, "Please, my lord, man of God, do not delude your maidservant."

¹⁷The woman conceived and bore a son at the same season the following year, as Elisha had assured her. ¹⁸The child grew up. One day, he went out to his father among the reapers. ¹⁹[Suddenly] he cried to his father, "Oh, my head, my head!" He said to a servant, "Carry him to his mother." ²⁰He picked him up and brought him to his mother. And the child sat on her lap until noon; and he died. ²¹She took him up and laid him on the bed of the man

of God, and left him and closed the door. ²²Then she called to her husband: "Please, send me one of the servants and one of the she-asses, so I can hurry to the man of God and back." ²³But he said, "Why are you going to him today? It is neither new moon nor sabbath." She answered, "It's all right."

²⁴She had the ass saddled, and said to her servant, "Urge [the beast] on; see that I don't slow down unless I tell you." ²⁵She went on until she came to the man of God on Mount Carmel. When the man of God saw her from afar, he said to his servant Gehazi, "There is that Shunammite woman. ²⁶Go, hurry toward her and ask her, 'How are you? How is your husband? How is the child?'" "We are well," she replied. ²⁷But when she came up to the man of God on the mountain, she clasped his feet. Gehazi stepped forward to push her away; but the man of God said, "Let her alone, for she is in bitter distress; and the LORD has hidden it from me and has not told me." ²⁸Then she said, "Did I ask my lord for a son? Didn't I say: 'Don't mislead me'?"

²⁹He said to Gehazi, "Tie up your skirts, take my staff in your hand, and go. If you meet anyone, do not greet him; and if anyone greets you, do not answer him. And place my staff on the face of the boy." ³⁰But the boy's mother said, "As the LORD lives and as you live, I will not leave you!" So he arose and followed her.

³¹Gehazi had gone on before them and had placed the staff on the boy's face; but there was no sound or response. He turned back to meet him and told him, "The boy has not awakened." ³²Elisha came into the house, and there was the boy, laid out dead on his couch. ³³He went in, shut the door behind the two of them, and prayed to the LORD. ³⁴Then he mounted [the bed] and placed himself over the child. He put his mouth on its mouth, his eyes on its eyes, and his hands on its hands, as he bent over it. And the body of the child

became warm. ³⁵He stepped down, walked once up and down the room, then mounted and bent over him. Thereupon, the boy sneezed seven times, and the boy opened his eyes. ³⁶[Elisha] called Gehazi and said, "Call the Shunammite woman," and he called her. When she came to him, he said, "Pick up your son." ³⁷She came and fell at his feet and bowed low to the ground; then she picked up her son and left.

- -

THE SHUNEM CONNECTION

What is the meaning of this story? In ancient times rabbis and sages used midrash, a method of creative exegesis, to explain biblical passages that were difficult to understand or to draw ancient readers closer to scripture. In order to fill in missing information that would illuminate the Scriptures, the sages expanded on hints, spellings that appeared to be typos, simultaneous events, and possible connections to other stories in the Bible. While classical midrash is always in written form, modern midrash continues the tradition of biblical interpretation using literature, artwork, dance, theater, and music.

Below is a modern midrash that attempts to shed light on the story of Elisha and the Shunammite woman. It grew from a search for hints about the village of Shunem in other Bible stories, which turned up this passage in 1 Kings 1:1:

- -

¹When King David was old and well advanced in years, he could not keep warm even when they put covers over him. ²So his servants said to him, "Let us look for a young virgin to attend the king and take care of him. She can lie beside him so that our lord the king may keep warm." ³Then they searched throughout Israel for a beautiful girl and found Abishag, a Shunammite, and brought her to the king.

- -

The road to everywhere passes through Shunem. Whether you're traveling locally or moving between empires, everyone stops here. The town offers the usual basic amenities for wayfarers but most men could care less about their accommodations—they're too busy loitering at the spring, hoping to catch a glimpse of some Shunem girls. Rare is the visitor who lowers his eyes and keeps to himself.

The women of our town are renowned for their exquisite beauty, a curiosity our men had managed to keep discreet until Abishag. They refused to share us with anyone, but when the king's men came in search of a beautiful girl to serve him, it was not possible to turn them away. The poor girl was enchanting, cursed with perfection. One could barely behold her without being blinded by her radiance. When they took her away to serve David, she behaved stoically, knowing she represented all of us in Shunem, but inside she was torn apart. No one leaves their clan willingly, especially a tightly knit, protective family such as ours. Once the rest of the world laid eyes on Abishag, the secret of Shunem was out.

I possess the classic features of a Shunem girl: heart-shaped face, honey-colored complexion, emerald eyes, and sumptuous round breasts. Like all my sisters and girl cousins, I was betrothed at a young age and married as soon as I became a woman. My husband was a relative many years older than I. My parents, who were very wealthy, wanted me to marry him. Thanks to the inheritance I received from them, I have been spared the backbreaking daily efforts required to care for my family. I have servants to cook, wash, and toil, enabling me to preserve my beauty. My sole task over the years has been to produce children, but our house bore the terrible curse that so many families in every generation are marked by in Shunem. Nine little ones I brought into the world, but only the girls survived. Six baby boys were snatched from me before they were old enough to take their first steps. I tried hard not to grow attached to them in their first months, but my efforts were to no avail. Each child's passing brought me deeper and deeper into a private desolation from which no soul could rescue me. My husband continued to demand an heir, but eventually he too became so broken that we agreed to put an end to our efforts. Although our three daughters brought us great joy and all were married off to kind, upstanding men, our empty house was filled with echoes of the lost little boys that only seemed to grow louder by the day.

It was perhaps with the intent of disturbing the deafening silence in our home that I invited the holy man for a meal. It was known that he had been with the great prophet Elijah when he miraculously ascended to the heavens, and stories had reached us from the prophetic bands in the valley regarding miracles he had performed in such places as Jericho and the Jordan River. He passed through Shunem frequently on his rounds between the mystical groups and what impressed me most about him was his modest demeanor. While the other men were gaping and leering at our girls, he avoided any interaction with them. In the privacy of our home, he succeeded in expressing his gracious appreciation for our nourishment without ever actually speaking to me directly, yet without giving offense. On the contrary—his calming presence filled the room the moment he entered it, even though we never made eye contact with each other. I found myself looking forward to his visits and ensured he would always feel comfortable with us.

I was so grateful for the solace he brought that it never occurred to me to ask him for something in return—certainly not a son. I had come full circle in that I no longer desired a baby boy, knowing full well the agony that would accompany him, and in retrospect the prophet should have known this. Yet he was intent on rewarding us somehow, and it was his servant, Gehazi the meddler, who raised the idea of a son. He always seemed to be snooping around, gossiping with the servants about how much this cost and how much that cost. It was he who poked and prodded, until the source of our agony was revealed to him.

At first I resisted, but then I acquiesced. I feared a scandal, but the holy man assured me that the miracle would be received with great joy by everyone. His essence penetrated to the deepest recesses of my being, and I had complete faith in his power. Just as he predicted, it was not long before I was with child. Miraculously, he was born healthy. Our joy was indescribable.

The day they brought my son to me, pale and barely breathing, I was sure I could heal him through my embrace. This child did not bear the curse of the others, and it seemed unfathomable that he, too, could be taken from us. When he ceased to exhale, I could not bear to tell my husband that our son was dead—I knew he would not survive the telling. I hid the boy's body in the prophet's room and left in a panic. I arrived at Mount Carmel in great distress, demanding to see the prophet. The cad Gehazi attempted to restrain me by wrapping his arms around me very inappropriately, but my shrieks brought the holy man out immediately.

Yet when the prophet realized that the Lord had hidden my son's death from him, he still did not understand our transgression. He attempted to transfer his power to his staff and invest it in his servant. I knew it was a grave error on his part, and I begged him to take personal responsibility for all that had gone wrong. It was only when he arrived at the upstairs room and saw the boy laid out, lifeless, on his very own bed, that he understood the limitations of his power.

Looking back on those extraordinary days, I now understand where we erred. I was convinced that my healthy son's birth was the prophet's gift to me. I was so captivated by him that I very nearly worshipped him, instead of the Lord. I forgot that he was merely the conduit for the Lord's power, and not the very source of it. He was even more at fault for not redirecting my misguided adoration. As a result we were punished.

But thank heaven, the Lord is a merciful God. It was he who gave the prophet the strength to revive my son. Together we prayed with greater intention than ever before, he inside the upstairs room where my son lay and I outside the door, as the color returned to the child's ashen skin, as his body warmed and his eyelashes fluttered. With each convulsive sneeze we begged for him to remain with us, and the Lord answered our prayers. It is the Lord who takes away, and the Lord who gives.

POSTSCRIPT: MODERN MEDICAL MIRACLES FOR MOTHERS IN ISRAEL

The Shunammite woman was exceptional in her resignation over her lack of sons, perhaps because she was wealthy and her future was economically secure. However, the concern of Gehazi and Elisha raised by the absence of boys in her family hints at one of the broader themes woven through the biblical narrative—the tremendous importance of having children. While sons were the ones to carry on the family name, inherit property, and take care of their parents in old age, families were considered blessed if they had children, both boys and girls. A woman who could not conceive was a tragic figure.

Modern Israeli society has been similarly preoccupied with having babies since its inception. In the state's early years families were encouraged to bring lots of children into the world in order to strengthen the burgeoning country and recover the losses of the Holocaust. David Ben Gurion, Israel's first prime minister, even established a special award to recognize women who had given birth to ten children.

While the average Israeli family today is considerably smaller, having children is still a priority. In fact, the state views the right of a woman to bear children as inalienable. Therefore, it fully underwrites the cost of in vitro fertilization for two live births for Israeli female citizens of all faiths, whether they are married, single, or lesbian couples. Not surprisingly, Israel leads the world in IVF procedures per capita; about 4 percent of babies born in Israel were conceived through IVF, as opposed to about 1 percent in the United States, and thanks to the high success rate many women from abroad with fertility issues come to Israel for treatment. Israeli scientists and doctors are at the forefront of research and technologies that will enable all women who wish to conceive to bring a child into the world.

In a newly developing trend, Israel has recently emerged as the world capital for babies born by surrogacy to gay male couples. It seems that parenthood may be a key to mainstream acceptance for Israeli homosexuals, probably because Israel is a deeply family-oriented society. The unique combination of ancient tradition, existential anxiety, and passion for children has placed the family squarely at the center of modern Israeli culture.

18

Hezekiah Prepares
Jerusalem for War

2 Kings 18:13–19:19, 35–36 (cf. Isa. 36–39)

The King of Judaea builds a wall and digs a tunnel

See pages 301 and 307 for visitor information.

This chapter cites Kings for the Hezekiah story. An additional abbreviated account of this story appears in 2 Chron. 32:1–24, but the Chronicler is generally considered by scholars to be a less historically reliable source. This story involves two different sites. See the appendix for details on accessibility.

WHERE ARE WE?
Hezekiah's Tunnel

Welcome to Hezekiah's Tunnel, one of the most exciting engineering projects in biblical Israel!

You are about to enter a series of ancient water systems all designed to enable residents of the City of David to access the Gihon spring. The quintessential problem of ancient hilltop cities was the location of their water sources outside the city walls, usually at the foot of their fortifications. Residents had to leave the confines of the walls in order to reach the water, which was impossible in times of war when enemies surrounded the city. One thousand years before Hezekiah, the prebiblical Canaanites dug a long tunnel, which you will now walk through, that allowed them to reach the spring by passing beneath the city, underground.

18

Hezekiah Prepares Jerusalem for War

2 Kings 18:13–19:19, 35–36 (cf. Isa. 36–39)

The King of Judaea builds a wall and digs a tunnel

See pages 301 and 307 for visitor information.

This chapter cites Kings for the Hezekiah story. An additional abbreviated account of this story appears in 2 Chron. 32:1–24, but the Chronicler is generally considered by scholars to be a less historically reliable source. This story involves two different sites. See the appendix for details on accessibility.

WHERE ARE WE?
Hezekiah's Tunnel

Welcome to Hezekiah's Tunnel, one of the most exciting engineering projects in biblical Israel!

You are about to enter a series of ancient water systems all designed to enable residents of the City of David to access the Gihon spring. The quintessential problem of ancient hilltop cities was the location of their water sources outside the city walls, usually at the foot of their fortifications. Residents had to leave the confines of the walls in order to reach the water, which was impossible in times of war when enemies surrounded the city. One thousand years before Hezekiah, the prebiblical Canaanites dug a long tunnel, which you will now walk through, that allowed them to reach the spring by passing beneath the city, underground.

245

Hezekiah's innovation was the transport of the spring's water via a man-made tunnel into a pool located inside the city walls. No more schlepping! It seems that in preparation for the Assyrian onslaught, he dug the tunnel and hid the spring's source, ensuring that the enemy would have no access to it. This plan is spelled out in 2 Chronicles 32:2–4. Scholars have guessed that the concealment of the spring significantly contributed to the Assyrian retreat (more on that later). Although the tunnel was discovered in 1838, the spring water has continued to flow through it for 2,700 years. Today the tunnel empties into a pool dated to the Byzantine period (fourth–seventh centuries CE). Remains of the newly excavated Second Temple period pool of Siloam may be seen on the way out.

SETTING THE SCENE
The Broad Wall

Up in the Jewish Quarter, before you lies a small section of an enormous fortification known as the Broad Wall, built by Hezekiah in his attempt to reinforce Jerusalem's defenses in the face of an Assyrian attack. The wall, dated by archaeologists to the late eighth century BCE, is referred to both in Isaiah 22:9–11 and later on in Nehemiah 3:8. It significantly expanded the boundaries of Jerusalem at the time and provided protection for hundreds of refugees from the other towns in Judah who had fled their homes in the wake of the Assyrian destruction and had sought refuge behind the defense of Jerusalem's walls. Hezekiah's new wall was probably unprecedented in its time both in breadth and height (see scale on the wall of the adjacent apartment building). Notice how the outside course of the wall is built right over the remains of earlier buildings, a superb example of archaeology illuminating the biblical

Fig. 18.1. The Broad Wall in the Jewish Quarter of Jerusalem

text. The passage from Isaiah 22:10 notes, "And you . . . pulled houses down to fortify the wall."

The wall was discovered during the excavations of the Jewish Quarter following the Six-Day War in 1967, when the quarter came back into Israeli hands after nineteen years of Jordanian occupation. Extensively excavated and then completely rebuilt, the Jewish Quarter artfully mingles ancient remains with modern life by attempting to accommodate everyone. While a large section of the wall was left exposed, its continuation through the quarter was covered by new construction. Sections of the Broad Wall not visible above ground have been marked on the pavement by large rectangular red flagstones like the ones you can see here.

THE CONTEXT

King Hezekiah came to the throne of Judah in the late eighth century BCE, when Assyria was the great superpower

Fig. 18.2. The entrance to Hezekiah's Tunnel, Jerusalem

of the ancient Middle East. The Assyrians maintained a standing professional army equipped with state-of-the-art military technology such as siege wall warfare, war machinery, supply lines, chariots, and mounted horsemen. One of their particularly creative innovations was mass deportation.

Hezekiah's father, King Ahaz, submitted to the Assyrians and chose to accept the role of vassal state. The biblical authors were critical of Ahaz's capitulation, but it seems his choice was based on the realpolitik of the day. However, the northern kingdom of Israel and Aram threatened to attack Ahaz's kingdom of Judah if he did not join their anti-Assyrian coalition. The prophet Isaiah urged Ahaz to stand independent, but he preferred to compromise and not to risk destruction. Rather than joining the rebels, he called in the Assyrians to rescue him (2 Kings 16:5–9). As they moved westward from northern Mesopotamia, they conquered both Aram and northern Israel.

The devastation in Israel was shocking. Between 732 and 722 BCE thousands of northern Israelites, mostly the elites, were forced into exile in the far reaches of the Assyrian empire (2 Kings 17:5–6). Foreign peoples were transferred and settled in Samaria and other Israelite territories (2 Kings 17:24), and the independent kingdom of Israel became a mere Assyrian province.

The smaller, poorer, and less important kingdom of Judah remained. At first King Hezekiah continued his father Ahaz's alliance with the Assyrians. However, in 705 BCE the invincible Assyrian king Sargon II was slain in battle, creating the impression that Assyria was on the down-and-out. Revolts broke out all over the empire. When Hezekiah's Phoenician neighbors rebelled against Assyria with Egyptian backing, he decided to transfer his allegiance as well and even forced some of the Philistine cities to join him, hoping that the weight of those combined eggs in one basket would tip the balance of power in favor of Egypt (2 Kings 18:7–8), his preferred master.

Yet Hezekiah was well aware that Egyptian support alone would not beat back the Assyrians. According to the text he executed a religious reform that sought to restore both national pride and the glory of the Davidic line, of which he was a descendant. Scholars are divided over the actual extent of his reform, but most agree that he purified the temple in Jerusalem. However, according to only two verses in the book of Kings he abolished the pagan practices that had taken deep root and destroyed all shrines and temples in the countryside, effectively centralizing worship completely in Jerusalem (2 Kings 18:4, 22).

In the end the Egyptians never came through, and Judah found itself overrun by the Assyrian army. Despite Hezekiah's meticulous preparations and the tailwind of his religious devotion, the brave Judaeans were no match for the invaders. As the Assyrian king Sennacherib, the son of Sargon, moved northward from his battle with the Egyptians, he captured all the fortified cities in Judah (2 Kings 18:13); according to Assyrian documents, forty-six walled cities and numerous smaller villages were laid waste, and 200,150 prisoners of war were taken. In order to save Jerusalem Hezekiah sent word to Sennacherib as he was besieging the city of Lachish that he had been mistaken in challenging him. He was forced to pay a huge tribute, not only bankrupting the treasury but also stripping the temple of its gold and silver decorations in order to come up with the money (2 Kings 18:13–16). The Assyrians destroyed Lachish, exiled its population, and marched on Jerusalem nonetheless.

- -

2 Kings 18

¹³In the fourteenth year of King Hezekiah, King Sennacherib of Assyria marched against all the fortified towns of Judah and seized them. ¹⁴King Hezekiah sent this message to the king of Assyria at Lachish: "I have done wrong; withdraw from me; and I shall bear whatever you impose on me." So the king of Assyria imposed upon King Hezekiah of Judah a payment of three hundred talents of silver and thirty talents of gold. ¹⁵Hezekiah gave him all the silver that was on hand in the House of the LORD and in the treasuries of the palace. ¹⁶At that time Hezekiah cut down the doors and the doorposts of the Temple of the LORD, which King Hezekiah had overlaid [with gold], and gave them to the king of Assyria.

¹⁷But the king of Assyria sent the Tartan, the Rabsaris, and the Rabshakeh from Lachish with a large force to King Hezekiah in Jerusalem. They marched up to Jerusalem; and when they arrived, they took up a position near the conduit of the Upper Pool, by the road of the Fuller's Field. ¹⁸They summoned the king; and Eliakim son of Hilkiah, who was in

charge of the palace, Shebna the scribe, and Joah son of Asaph the recorder went out to them.

¹⁹The Rabshakeh said to them, "You tell Hezekiah: Thus said the Great King, the King of Assyria: What makes you so confident? ²⁰You must think that mere talk is counsel and valor for war! Look, on whom are you relying, that you have rebelled against me? ²¹You rely, of all things, on Egypt, that splintered reed of a staff, which enters and punctures the palm of anyone who leans on it! That's what Pharaoh king of Egypt is like to all who rely on him. ²²And if you tell me that you are relying on the LORD your God, He is the very one whose shrines and altars Hezekiah did away with, telling Judah and Jerusalem, 'You must worship only at this altar in Jerusalem.' ²³Come now, make this wager with my master, the king of Assyria: I'll give you two thousand horses if you can produce riders to mount them. ²⁴So how could you refuse anything even to the deputy of one of my master's lesser servants, relying on Egypt for chariots and horsemen? ²⁵And do you think I have marched against this land to destroy it without the LORD? The LORD Himself told me: Go up against that land and destroy it."

²⁶Eliakim son of Hilkiah, Shebna, and Joah replied to the Rabshakeh, "Please, speak to your servants in Aramaic, for we understand it; do not speak to us in Judean in the hearing of the people on the wall." ²⁷But the Rabshakeh answered them, "Was it to your master and to you that my master sent me to speak those words? It was precisely to the men who are sitting on the wall—who will have to eat their dung and drink their urine with you." ²⁸And the Rabshakeh stood and called out in a loud voice in Judean: "Hear the words of the Great King, the King of Assyria. ²⁹Thus said the king: Don't let Hezekiah deceive you, for he will not be able to deliver you from my hands. ³⁰Don't let Hezekiah make you rely on the LORD, saying:

The LORD will surely save us: this city will not fall into the hands of the king of Assyria. ³¹Don't listen to Hezekiah. For thus said the king of Assyria: Make your peace with me and come out to me, so that you may all eat from your vines and your fig trees and drink water from your cisterns, ³²until I come and take you away to a land like your own, a land of grain [fields] and vineyards, of bread and wine, of olive oil and honey, so that you may live and not die. Don't listen to Hezekiah, who misleads you by saying, 'The LORD will save us.' ³³Did any of the gods of other nations save his land from the king of Assyria? ³⁴Where were the gods of Hamath and Arpad? Where were the gods of Sepharvaim, Hena, and Ivvah? [And] did they save Samaria from me? ³⁵Which among all the gods of [those] countries saved their countries from me, that the LORD should save Jerusalem from me?" ³⁶But the people were silent and did not say a word in reply; for the king's order was: "Do not answer him." ³⁷And so Eliakim son of Hilkiah, who was in charge of the palace, Shebna the scribe, and Joah son of Asaph the recorder came to Hezekiah with their clothes rent, and they reported to him what the Rabshakeh had said.

19

¹When King Hezekiah heard this, he rent his clothes, and covered himself with sackcloth, and went into the House of the LORD. ²He also sent Eliakim, who was in charge of the palace, Shebna the scribe, and the senior priests, covered with sackcloth, to the prophet Isaiah son of Amoz. ³They said to him, "Thus said Hezekiah: This day is a day of distress, of chastisement, and of disgrace. The babes have reached the birthstool, but the strength to give birth is lacking. ⁴Perhaps the LORD your God will take note of all the words of the Rabshakeh, whom his master the king of

Assyria has sent to blaspheme the living God, and will mete out judgment for the words that the LORD your God has heard—if you will offer up prayer for the surviving remnant."

5When King Hezekiah's ministers came to Isaiah, 6Isaiah said to them, "Tell your master as follows: Thus said the LORD: Do not be frightened by the words of blasphemy against Me that you have heard from the minions of the king of Assyria. 7I will delude him; he will hear a rumor and return to his land, and I will make him fall by the sword in his land."

8The Rabshakeh, meanwhile, heard that [the king] had left Lachish; he turned back and found the king of Assyria attacking Libnah. 9But [the king of Assyria] learned that King Tirhakah of Nubia had come out to fight him; so he again sent messengers to Hezekiah, saying, 10"Tell this to King Hezekiah of Judah: Do not let your God, on whom you are relying, mislead you into thinking that Jerusalem will not be delivered into the hands of the king of Assyria. 11You yourself have heard what the kings of Assyria have done to all the lands, how they have annihilated them; and can you escape? 12Were the nations that my predecessors destroyed—Gozan, Haran, Rezeph, and the Beth-edenites in Telassar—saved by their gods? 13Where is the king of Hamath? And the king of Arpad? And the kings of Lair, Sepharvaim, Hena, and Ivvah?"

14Hezekiah took the letter from the messengers and read it. Hezekiah then went up to the House of the LORD and spread it out before the LORD. 15And Hezekiah prayed to the LORD and said, "O LORD of Hosts, Enthroned on the Cherubim! You alone are God of all the kingdoms of the earth. You made the heavens and the earth. 16O LORD, incline Your ear and hear; open Your eyes and see. Hear the words that Sennacherib has sent to blaspheme the living God! 17True, O LORD, the kings of Assyria have annihilated the nations and their lands, [18]and have committed their gods to the flames and have destroyed them; for they are not gods, but man's handiwork of wood and stone. [19]But now, O LORD our God, deliver us from his hands, and let all the kingdoms of the earth know that You alone, O LORD, are God." ...

[35]That night an angel of the LORD went out and struck down one hundred and eighty-five thousand in the Assyrian camp, and the following morning they were all dead corpses.

[36]So King Sennacherib of Assyria broke camp and retreated, and stayed in Nineveh.

HE SAID, HE SAID

The Assyrian blockade of Jerusalem in 701 BCE is one of the more richly documented episodes of biblical history. The story is related in the Bible on three separate occasions, in 2 Kings 18:13–19:3; Isaiah 36–37; and 2 Chronicles 32:1–24. Rare corroboration is also provided by clay prisms inscribed with the annals of the Assyrian king Sennacherib and a huge relief discovered in the excavations of the ruins of his palace at Nineveh (now Iraq). The king's various military campaigns are described in Akkadian cuneiform script and specifically mention the siege of Jerusalem. Both texts, Assyrian and biblical, concur remarkably on the Assyrian attack, the submission of all the Judaean cities, Hezekiah's capitulation, and the details of the tribute. However, not surprisingly, Sennacherib's version of the siege of Jerusalem is somewhat different from the biblical account. In contrast to the mysterious rescue of Jerusalem and the decimated Assyrian army recounted in all three biblical texts, Sennacherib writes of the Judaean king, "I imprisoned Hezekiah in Jerusalem like a bird in a cage" (Sennacherib Prism III.20–40). Whom should we believe?

Actually, both Hezekiah and Sennacherib seem to be telling the same story, each with the gloss of the winner. No archaeological evidence shows that the city of Jerusalem at this time was surrounded by a siege wall, nor that the Assyrian army camped outside the city fortifications. In fact, the closest remains of the Assyrian army were found only at Ramat Rachel, about 2.4 kilometers (a mile and a half) south of Jerusalem. The city was "shut up" by blocking off all communication routes and effectively isolating it in the wake of the rest of the kingdom's devastation, but at the end of the day Jerusalem was not destroyed.

So what really happened to the Assyrian army? Sennacherib had proven his point by erasing many Judaean cities and transferring others to the Philistines. He put Hezekiah in his place by destroying Judah economically and demographically. Jerusalem was worth far more to him as a tribute-paying vassal state than as a nonentity. When pressing matters arose elsewhere he broke camp, leaving the city humiliated but intact.

The Judaeans, from their perspective, had proven their point by emphasizing God's intervention and his devotion to Jerusalem. We will never know what truly happened there, but explanations abound.

THE ANGEL OF DEATH

Biblical purists will read the account of the deaths of 185,000 Assyrian soldiers literally, as an act of the angel of death on a mission from God. However, a scientific examination of the circumstances poses a possible explanation for the annihilation of the enemy camp. The Greek historian Herodotus relates that prior to arriving in Judah, the Assyrian army fought a battle in Egypt, where they were overrun by leather-eating mice (Herodotus, Persian

Wars, 2.141). Scholars have hypothesized that these mice infected the troops with bubonic plague and that the epidemic peaked during the blockade of Jerusalem, neatly explaining the sudden deaths of so many Assyrian soldiers.

Despite the successful psychological warfare waged by Sennacherib's crafty Hebrew-speaking generals, it seems that the excavation of the water tunnel and the refortification and expansion of the city's walls by Hezekiah played a critical role in enabling the city to withstand the Assyrian blockade until Hezekiah made the decision to capitulate rather than fight to the end. Although the kingdom lay in shambles after the folly of his disobedience to Assyria, it seems Hezekiah finally came to his senses. Thanks to him, the last remnants of the kingdom of Judah were saved, an accomplishment with enormous implications. Based on the well-documented conquests of the Assyrian army and its ruthless destruction of the northern kingdom of Israel, we can fairly assume that had Sennacherib succeeded in conquering Jerusalem, the kingdom of Judah would have suffered the same fate as the northern tribes—obliteration. Jerusalem, the Davidic line, the tribe of Judah, and the Jewish people would have been erased from the face of the earth. Judaism, Christianity, Islam, the state of Israel, and the world as we know it today would not exist. Ironically, although Hezekiah led Judah to the brink of destruction, by ultimately choosing to submit to Sennacherib he may be counted among a handful of individuals whose actions influenced human civilization for thousands of years to come.

GREAT EXPECTATIONS

The prophet Isaiah counseled both Hezekiah and his father Ahaz before him, warning them that their political machinations with Assyria and Egypt would only bring disaster upon them. Like most prophets he told them what they didn't want to hear: that their salvation depended on their faith and confidence in the one true God, who would protect them from all their enemies if they would only believe. Isaiah spoke like a well-studied op-ed columnist, analyzing the regional political situation and the actions of the neighboring leaders and drawing attention to important facts that had been forgotten. His prophecies are rich in imagery and metaphor, and his promises of peace in the days to come, when the wolf will lie down with the lamb (Isa. 11:6) and when people will beat their swords into plowshares (Isa. 2:4), are among the most enduring messages of the biblical text.

In his plea to Ahaz to stand strong before his enemies, Isaiah painted a hypothetical picture of the great situation that would unfold if Ahaz would only heed him: "Look, the young woman is with child and about to give birth to a son; Let her name him Immanuel [God is with us]. . . . For before the lad knows to reject the bad and choose the good, the ground whose two kings you dread will be abandoned" (Isa. 7:14, 16).

Isaiah implored Ahaz to be careful and calm because the forces he was fighting against had no power to harm him. Hang on, Sloopy—just a short time and your enemies will be toast. Not surprisingly, Ahaz didn't listen to Isaiah and preferred to be a vassal of the Assyrians.

In that prophecy Isaiah may have been speaking of an anonymous woman. Some scholars have understood his words to be a pointed reference to Ahaz's wife, who would give birth to a son, others—to the prophet's wife. Later the prophet goes on to hail the newborn boy who will grow up to succeed his politically disappointing father and usher in a new age of wisdom, faith, and peace (Isa. 9:5–6). In other words, a messiah.

Was Isaiah suggesting that Hezekiah was the Messiah, the man who would save the world? It depends on whom you ask.

Some readers were convinced that this prophecy reflected the elation in Judah following the rescue of Jerusalem from the Assyrians and alluded to Hezekiah or a future, as yet unknown messianic king.

Christian theologians understood Isaiah's words as a foretelling of the birth of Jesus, and not as a reference to Hezekiah.

Jewish authorities are divided, but the fourth-century rabbi Hillel II went so far as to say, "There will be no messiah for Israel because they have already enjoyed him in the days of Hezekiah" (*b. Sanhedrin* 99a). The Jewish sages were not terribly bothered by the Assyrian knockout of Judah under Hezekiah. They were very favorable toward him, more so than any other king apart from Saul, David, and Solomon. He was the best Messiah option among everyone who came after them. Unlike his predecessors he was deeply faithful and attempted a religious reform to bring the people of Israel back to their God. In the eyes of the biblical redactors his favor was proven by two significant miracles performed for him: the Assyrian army was destroyed before him in a single night (2 Kings 19:35), and after his death was foretold he was given an extra fifteen years to live (2 Kings 20:4-6). The wings of God's protection over Hezekiah made him the obvious candidate for a messiah-king.

WAS HE OR WASN'T HE?

What are the qualifications of the Messiah? Jewish sources don't always concur on the special powers with which he will be endowed, but they do agree on a few basic prerequisites. He must be personal and human—check for Hezekiah. He must be a descendant of King David—check. He must be a king—check.

Well then, how are we to know when he arrives? The great first-century sage Rabbi Yochanon ben Zakkai, in a searing comment on messianic expectation, said, "If you are planting a tree and you hear that the messiah has come, finish planting the tree, then go home and inquire" (*Avot de-Rabbi Natan* 31b).

So, was Hezekiah the Messiah? Your call.

POSTSCRIPT: THE SILOAM INSCRIPTION

In 1838 early archaeologists discovered Hezekiah's Tunnel, an underground waterway hewn from the rock beneath First Temple period Jerusalem in order to bring water into the city and enable its residents to withstand the Assyrian siege. Somehow, however, those fearless explorers completely missed the icing on the cake when they failed to discern a dedicatory plaque on the wall of the tunnel not far from its exit. The plaque was discovered many years later in 1891 by a Jewish boy playing hooky from school who had come to explore the tunnel. Written in ancient Hebrew in the late eighth century BCE, it was probably ordered by the chief engineer and tells the story of the tunnel's extraordinary excavation: (the first line is illegible)

The tunnel . . . and this is the history of the tunnel while . . . the axes were against each other and while three cubits were left to cut ? . . . the voice of a man . . . called to his counterpart. (For) there was zada in the rock, on the right . . . and on the day of the tunnel (being finished) the stonecutters struck each man toward his counterpart, ax against ax and flowed water from the source to the pool for 1200 cubits and 100? Cubits was the height over the head of the stonecutters.

It seems that two teams started from either end and dug their way through the rock until they heard each other's axes and met in the middle. A walk through the tunnel reveals a sharp right angle seam where the two sides meet, with the centers off-kilter. Scientists have proposed that when Hezekiah's workers heard each other digging, they understood that they were slightly offtrack and used their voices to readjust course until they broke through at the same place.

Whoever removed the inscription from the tunnel broke it into pieces. It eventually ended up in the Istanbul Archaeological Museum, where it remains until today.

Zedekiah Flees Jerusalem

2 Kings 24:18–25:30

The King of Judah ignores the prophet Jeremiah's advice with disastrous consequences

See page 309 for visitor information.

WHERE ARE WE?

We are standing inside an enormous cavern beneath the Muslim Quarter of the Old City of Jerusalem. Caves are an integral part of the limestone landscape in Israel. Subtly tucked away within mountains and beneath cities, for millennia caves have been used as hideaways, secret storage caches, and clandestine getaway corridors. Some scholars have suggested that this cave served King Solomon as far back as the tenth century BCE as a stone source for his building projects in Jerusalem (hence the name "King Solomon's Quarries"). Hundreds of years later this cave was identified as the escape route of King Zedekiah as he fled Jerusalem. 2 Kings 25:4 relates that the king and his army were able to sneak out by night even though the city was surrounded by Babylonian soldiers. The legend says that Zedekiah and his men used this cave, an underground passageway unknown to the enemy, to reach the eastern desert.

This tradition can also be found in Rashi's commentary on Ezekiel 12:13. He explains in his exegesis of the text of Zedekiah's escape that as the king fled through the cave, a deer accompanied him above ground. The Chaldean sol-

Fig. 19. Zedekiah's Cave, Jerusalem

diers chased the deer all the way to Jericho and thus inter-
cepted Zedekiah as he emerged from the cave's opening.

Although no unequivocal evidence exists to link this
cave to Zedekiah, the ancients were captivated by the
sheer magnitude of this invisible space and its irresist-
ible link to Zedekiah. The tradition lives on until today.

SETTING THE SCENE

Zedekiah's Cave is the largest man-made cave in Israel.
It covers an area underneath the Muslim Quarter of nine
thousand square meters (over two acres) and rises to a
height of five meters, or forty-eight feet (the same as a
four-story building). The roof of the cave, up to the buildings of the Old City, is about ten meters (thirty-two feet)
thick. The cave was an ancient quarry used for centuries
by the builders of Jerusalem, who gradually enlarged it
as they removed more and more rock. Its underground

location away from the elements, the fine quality of its stone, and the cave's proximity to the major construction sites of the Old City made it an ideal source for raw building materials.

However, it seems likely that Jerusalemites began quarrying here only in the late Second Temple period, first century BCE–70 CE. The quarry was used, on and off, until the early twentieth century, although it was probably sealed off by the Turks in the mid-sixteenth century against invaders. The cave was rediscovered entirely by accident in 1854 by the American Bible scholar James Barkley while he was walking his dog outside the Old City walls.

THE CONTEXT

Two parallel dramas have been unfolding since the last time Jerusalem was attacked under Hezekiah in 701 BCE. On the international scene a major upheaval had been under way. The Assyrians, who ruled the ancient Middle East with an iron fist from the mid-ninth century BCE, were finally vanquished in 609 BCE by the Babylonians. Subsequently, a struggle ensued between the Babylonians and the Egyptians over control of the lands north of Egypt, including the kingdom of Judah and the eastern Mediterranean seaboard. Little Judah was caught between the two warring powers.

But in 605 the Egyptians were defeated by the Babylonians at Carchemish, and King Nebuchadnezzar (aka Nebuchadrezzar) took control of Judah. He arrived in the region and forced King Jehoiakim to submit to him. Jehoiakim probably hoped that Egypt would regain control. At subsequent key moments of Babylonian weakness, when revolts broke out in other areas of the empire, the Egyptians encouraged Judah to break free, although they ultimately did not provide the necessary support. In

Babylon Jerusalem earned notoriety as a hotbed of resistance, and the king of Judah was branded a troublemaker. In 597 Nebuchadnezzar marched on Jerusalem to crush a revolt led by King Jehoiakim, who died or was murdered just as they arrived. Jehoiachin, his son and successor, immediately surrendered, but the Babylonians decided to teach the Judaeans a lesson. They took the young king prisoner and rounded up the strongest elements of the population—nobility, army, craftsmen, and the educated—and deported them all to Babylon, where they couldn't cause any trouble. They then appointed Zedekiah, Jehoiachin's uncle, king over the economically and militarily hobbled Judah, assuming he would be loyal to them (2 Kings 24:8–17).

From a covenantal perspective, all was not well in Judah. Although in Hezekiah's day, the late eighth century, the Israelite God was worshipped and he instituted some religious reforms, according to the Deuteronomist (2 Kings 21:1–18) his son Manasseh, who ruled for fifty-five years, turned the wheel back to one of the darkest ages Israel had ever known. He worshipped pagan gods and raised altars to them in the temple of the Lord. He practiced black magic and consulted spirits and witches. He massacred innocent citizens and instituted child sacrifice, offering his own son in the cultic fire (v. 6). He and his subjects broke virtually every covenantal rule. Following a two-year reign by Amon, he was succeeded by Josiah, one of the most righteous of the Judaean kings. Josiah attempted to clean up the mess and institute major reforms, but the damage was done. In following Manasseh and his ilk the Judaeans had proven over and over again their complete disregard for the code of behavior to which they had committed. God was furious and vowed to destroy them, thundering, "I am going to bring such a disaster on Jerusalem and Judah that both ears of everyone who hears about it will tingle. . . . I will wipe Jerusalem clean as one wipes a dish and turns it upside down. And I will cast off the remnant of My own people and deliver them into the hands of their enemies" (vv. 12–14).

Amid the downward spiral of depravity and the impending doom, one voice rose above the chaos and urged a change of direction in Jerusalem. The prophet Jeremiah instructed the people that the only way to ensure their survival was to change their evil ways and to accept the inevitability of Babylonian subjugation. He repeated this message over and over, to kings Jehoiakim, Jehoiachin, and Zedekiah. Not surprisingly, no one listened.

- -

2 Kings 24

[18]Zedekiah was twenty-one years old when he became king, and he reigned eleven years in Jerusalem; his mother's name was Hamutal daughter of Jeremiah of Libnah. [19]He did what was displeasing to the LORD, just as Jehoiakim had done. [20]Indeed, Jerusalem and Judah were a cause of anger for the LORD, so that He cast them out of His presence.

25

Zedekiah rebelled against the king of Babylon. [1]And in the ninth year of his reign, on the tenth day of the tenth month, Nebuchadnezzar moved against Jerusalem with his whole army. He besieged it; and they built towers against it all around. [2]The city continued in a state of siege until the eleventh year of King Zedekiah. [3]By the ninth day [of the fourth month] the famine had become acute in the city; there was no food left for the common people.

⁴Then [the wall of] the city was breached. All the soldiers [left the city] by night through the gate between the double walls, which is near the king's garden—the Chaldeans were all around the city; and [the king] set out for the Arabah. ⁵But the Chaldean troops pursued the king, and they overtook him in the steppes of Jericho as his entire force left him and scattered. ⁶They captured the king and brought him before the king of Babylon at Riblah; and they put him on trial. ⁷They slaughtered Zedekiah's sons before his eyes; then Zedekiah's eyes were put out. He was chained in bronze fetters and he was brought to Babylon.

⁸On the seventh day of the fifth month—that was the nineteenth year of King Nebuchadnezzar of Babylon—Nebuzaradan, the chief of the guards, an officer of the king of Babylon, came to Jerusalem. ⁹He burned the House of the LORD, the king's palace, and all the houses of Jerusalem; he burned down the house of every notable person. ¹⁰The entire Chaldean force that was with the chief of the guard tore down the walls of Jerusalem on every side. ¹¹The remnant of the people that was left in the city, the defectors who had gone over to the king of Babylon—and the remnant of the population—were taken into exile by Nebuzaradan, the chief of the guards. ¹²But some of the poorest in the land were left by the chief of the guards, to be vinedressers and field hands.

¹³The Chaldeans broke up the bronze columns of the House of the LORD, the stands, and the bronze tank that was in the House of the LORD; and they carried the bronze away to Babylon. ¹⁴They also took all the pails, scrapers, snuffers, ladles, and all the other bronze vessels used in the service. ¹⁵The chief of the guards took whatever was of gold and whatever was of silver: firepans and sprinkling bowls. ¹⁶The two columns, the one tank, and the stands that Solomon provided for the House of the LORD—all these

objects contained bronze beyond weighing. [17]The one column was eighteen cubits high. It had a bronze capital above it; the height of the capital was three cubits, and there was a meshwork [decorated] with pomegranates about the capital, all made of bronze. And the like was true of the other column with its meshwork.

[18]The chief of the guards also took Seraiah, the chief priest, Zephaniah, the deputy priest, and the three guardians of the threshold. [19]And from the city he took a eunuch who was in command of the soldiers; five royal privy councillors who were present in the city; the scribe of the army commander, who was in charge of mustering the people of the land; and sixty of the common people who were inside the city. [20]Nebuzaradan, the chief of the guards, took them and brought them to the king of Babylon at Riblah. [21]The king of Babylon had them struck down and put to death at Riblah, in the region of Hamath.

THE KING'S TRUE COLORS

The account from 2 Kings 25 doesn't reveal much about Zedekiah the man, other than that he (and his army) fled the city in a panic and was corralled not far from Jerusalem by the Babylonians. A king on the run is not an encouraging sight. Suspicions about his character raised by this compromising behavior are confirmed by reading about him in the book of Jeremiah, where a more three-dimensional portrait of him emerges, and it's not pretty. In a series of encounters between the king and the prophet, Zedekiah shows his true colors, and he's a wimp.

In the first encounter Zedekiah had recently been crowned king and was surrounded by a second-rate cadre of belligerent advisors. Jeremiah was a salty old prophet well known around Jerusalem for saying what no one wanted to hear. On the counsel of his officials, the new king publically treated Jeremiah as persona non grata and ignored all his advice. But when no one was looking, Zedekiah sent an emissary with a message to the prophet, asking him, nonetheless, to put in a good word for him with the Lord (Jer. 21:1–2). It seems the king was either extremely wishy-washy or simply too weak to publicly articulate his admiration of the prophet.

Shortly afterward Jeremiah was arrested by the king's officials as he attempted to leave the city. Fed up with being harassed by the prophet, they accused him of treason, beat the living daylights out of him, and tossed him into the dungeon, hoping to silence him once and for all. But after a time Zedekiah sent for him, unbeknown to anyone. He queried the prophet, "Is there any word from the Lord?" (Jer. 37:12–17). Although still incapable of standing behind Jeremiah's predictions, Zedekiah ordered an improvement in his conditions and moved him to a prominent location where he could continue to petition people (Jer. 37:20–21).

When the king's officials heard Jeremiah's same old broken record playing, they were incensed. They charged him with demoralizing the soldiers and the populace. They sentenced him to death and threw him into a muddy pit to die. Although Zedekiah respected and admired the prophet, he made no motion to intervene. Instead, he told the angry cohort, "He is in your hands, the king cannot oppose you in anything." Luckily for Jeremiah, a servant in the palace came to his aid and asked the king to rescue him—and he did (Jer. 38:1–13).

In each of these encounters Zedekiah stands out as a weak, indecisive man, a puppet easily manipulated by his powerful advisors. In truth he's pathetic. Yet his spinelessness is almost treated with understanding by the biblical author. In this drama the king isn't the principle villain—he's just part of the scenery. Instead, the main protagonist is the entire people of the Judaean kingdom, together with their kings, who are all guilty of terrible sins and wickedness. The hero is Jeremiah, but despised and rejected, he failed miserably in his undying attempts to convince people to change.

The Babylonians, who had inherited the Assyrian empire, had proven that their wrath was harsh. They invaded Jerusalem, tortured the king, deported most of the population of Judah, and razed the city to the ground. The biblical text is rife with powerful images of wanton destruction: the twenty-seven-feet-high pillars of the temple dismantled and pillaged for the king by hoards of soldiers; the murder of Zedekiah's children before his eyes and his blinding; the wholesale execution of the remaining leadership. The Babylonians were clear—they would not tolerate any more rebellious kings. Before returning home they appointed the pro-Babylon, capable, but non-Davidic Gedaliah son of Ahikam to remain in Benjamin, north of Jerusalem and govern the last remnants of the population wisely. Almost predictably a faction led by a Davidic descendent revolted against Babylonian interference by assassinating him, a move that cost them their last remaining semblance of national identity (2 Kings 25:22–26).

Why did the tiny, insignificant kingdom of Judah insist on confronting the monster head on, again and again, when all the odds were against it?

This stubborn refusal to acknowledge an imminent catastrophe can perhaps be explained by the iconic Israeli expression "imprisoned in the conception." This turn of phrase comes to us from the most traumatic of all modern Israel's military conflicts, the Yom Kippur War of 1973. Six years earlier in 1967, Israel had brilliantly defeated three very well-equipped Arab armies in a mere six days, capturing vast territories from each of them. The enemies that at first appeared to pose an existential threat to the young state turned out to be fumbling, inept armies that quickly capitulated to what turned out to be mighty Israel. Riding the wave of victory and awash in hubris, in the years following the 1967 war the Israeli military establishment was arrogantly confident that it had nothing to worry about. It was so "imprisoned in the conception" that when signs began to appear that Egypt and Syria were planning to attack it was blind to them. When the war broke out on Yom Kippur in 1973, the Israeli army was painfully unprepared thanks to the shocking inability of the military and the elected leadership to think outside the box. The result was over 2,600 casualties and a deep crisis of trust between the Israelis and their leadership that has yet to pass.

The Judaeans of 586 BCE were also imprisoned in a conception formulated on a previous military victory. One hundred fifteen years earlier the kingdom of Judah was devastated and the city of Jerusalem besieged by the Assyrians in what looked to be inevitable annihilation. However, against all odds, one morning the Assyrian army packed up and retreated back to Nineveh, and Jerusalem was saved. Years later this deliverance was understood as uncontestable evidence of God's power and his promise to safeguard the city forever. The Judaeans facing the Babylonian menace were convinced that Jerusalem could never, ever be vanquished by an enemy. This belief was bolstered by a potent religious-nationalist fanaticism that probably ran very deeply in Jerusalem in the final years of the kingdom. Religious zealotry heavily influenced people's conviction that God would not abandon them, and this zeitgeist ultimately overrode more pragmatic considerations.

Jeremiah understood this skewed perception and spoke out in no uncertain terms. "Don't put your trust in illusions and say, "The Temple of the Lord, The Temple of the Lord, The Temple of the Lord are these [buildings]" (Jer. 7:4). In fact, Jeremiah had a dual message for the people of Jerusalem. The first point was the absolute futility of challenging the Babylonians. Jeremiah is sometimes referred to as the first pacifist, but more than an antiwar activist he was a pragmatist. His outlook was based not on the surprising delivery of Jerusalem in 701BCE but rather on the obliteration of Samaria twenty years earlier when the northern tribes of Israel attempted to overcome the Assyrians. The Samaritan rebellion of 722 marked the demise of the northern kingdom of Israel. With this painful precedent in mind, Jeremiah posited that the Judaeans hadn't a ghost of a chance to defeat the Babylonians. As detestable as they were, it was infinitely wiser to submit to them and to live, rather than to die in vain. No gimmick was too over-the-top to challenge the palace prophets who predicted far rosier scenarios. To drive his exhaustingly argued point home, when a conclave of six nations was conferring in Jerusalem about a cooperative rebellion against Babylon, Jeremiah showed up at Zedekiah's court with a wooden yoke affixed to his neck, pronouncing, "Put your necks under the yoke of the king of Babylon; serve him and his people, and live!" (Jer. 27:12).

Jeremiah's second message aimed straight for the heart of Judaean society. He continually castigated his contemporaries for their utter abandonment of the covenant that they had entered into at Mount Sinai. This betrayal was twofold; not only were they guilty of worshipping other deities, but they had turned their backs on the revolutionary moral code articulated in the Ten Commandments. In God's name Jeremiah asked them, "Will you steal and murder and commit adultery and swear falsely, and sacrifice to Baal, and follow other gods whom you have not experienced, and then come and stand before Me in this House which bears My name and say, 'We are safe?'" (Jer. 7:9–10).

In a letter he wrote to the Judaeans who had been deported to Babylon, Jeremiah fostered no illusions of hope for an imminent return. He beseeched people to settle in for a long spell of exile: "Build houses and live in them, plant gardens and eat their fruit. Take wives and beget sons and daughters; and take wives for your sons, and give your daughters to husbands, that they may bear sons and daughters. Multiply there, do not decrease" (Jer. 29:5–6).

Jeremiah was a relentless, hounding critic, despised and rejected. One of his few friends was the scribe Baruch son of Neriah, who faithfully recorded his messages. In the forty-five years he was active as a prophet, few came over to his side. Ultimately, his terrible predictions came true. Egypt was defeated, and Nebuchadnezzar destroyed the temple and the city of Jerusalem. The people of Judah were banished from their homeland and sent to Babylon. Jeremiah himself was forced into exile following the murder of Gedaliah, abducted to Egypt by fleeing refugees. He continued to preach his message and eventually died there, far from Jerusalem. Yet despite the horrors he had witnessed throughout his life, Jeremiah remained a man of faith, believing that God's punishment was an act of justice on a sinful nation. He trusted that better days would return, even though he never lived to see them.

In recounting their calamities, the exiles in Babylon acknowledged that all Jeremiah had foretold had come to pass, a realization that prompted some serious soul searching. The destruction of the temple and Jerusalem was a powerful object lesson to the Judaeans, who finally sat up and took stock of their errors. They noted that while Jeremiah prophesied violent ruin, he also revealed a light at the end of the tunnel. Inherent in his message was the possibility of change. No one is a hopeless case—everyone gets a second chance.

> The days are coming, says the LORD, when I will make a new covenant with the house of Israel and the house of Judah. It will not be like the covenant that I made with their fathers when I took them by the hand to lead them out of the land of Egypt—they broke that covenant, so I rejected them, says the LORD. But such is the covenant that I will make with the house of Israel after that time, says the LORD: I will put my torah inside them, I will write it on their very hearts: I will be their God, and they will be My people. No longer will they need to teach one another or say to one the other, "Be obedient to the LORD," for they shall all be obedient to Me, from the least of them to the greatest, says the LORD; then I will forgive their iniquity, and remember their sin no more. (Jer. 31:31–34)

Jeremiah's message was, in our terms: Jews, get cracking. Each morning when you wake up in exile, look in the mirror and ask yourselves: "How did we get here? Were we faithful to the agreement we signed? Is this where we want to be?" Then sit down at your desks and start studying the Torah. Read, memorize, analyze, deconstruct, and debate those laws from every possible angle. Internalize them so deeply that the Jewish people will never stray from the path again. Then one day soon, we will return to Jerusalem.

Fascinating evidence for the Babylonian destruction of Judah has been unearthed in a number of places in Israel. At Tel Lachish, a sizable city from the sixth century BCE southwest of Jerusalem, a cachet of missives known as the Lachish letters was found among the burned layer corresponding to the Babylonian invasion. Written on broken pieces of pottery, the letters record the correspondence of a Judaean military officer and his subordinate in the city of Azekah, another important stronghold not far away. They were probably written shortly before Lachish fell around 588/586 BCE, during the reign of Zedekiah (Jer. 34:7). The most intriguing letter mentions the daily search for a signal fire from Azekah, indicating the city was still holding out against the enemy. When the fire at Azekah was no longer visible, the soldiers at Lachish understood that the city had fallen and the Babylonians were closing in.

Archaeological excavations at Area G in the City of David have revealed some additional fascinating evidence dating to the time of the Babylonian destruction of Jerusalem. In a building that seems to have served as a public archive, a collection of close to fifty clay stamps, or bullae, were found. When Nebuchadnezzar burned the city, the documents written on papyrus and stored in the archive were incinerated, but the bullae that sealed them were baked at high temperatures and preserved for posterity. Many of the inscriptions on the bullae were beautifully legible and included individuals' names. Archaeologists were thrilled to discover that among those names was someone mentioned specifically in the book of Jeremiah: the scribe Gemaryahu ben Shafan (Jer. 36:10). Subsequent excavations in the City of David yielded three more bullae with biblical signatures: Jucal ben Shelamiah and Gedaliah

Pashtur, two of the ministers responsible for Jeremiah's arrest (Jer. 38:1), and Azaryahu ben Hilkiyahu, a member of a priestly family mentioned in 1 Chronicles 9:10.

Also, a small annex off one of the homes in Area G contained a square-cut block of stone with a round hole in its middle, resting over a lime-covered cesspit—in other words, a 2,700-year-old toilet. Utilizing fascinating new disciplines that combine archaeology with the study of ancient pollen and parasites (both of which are extremely durable), scientists analyzed the fecal matter excavated from the cesspit in an attempt to discover what was going on in the intestines of sixth-century BCE Jerusalemites during the twenty months of the Babylonian siege.

Based on the kinds of pollen present, it appears that their diet was hopelessly meager—mostly salad greens and herbs, with virtually no grains or legumes, which means the besieged residents were probably gathering wild plants from the hillsides within the city walls. An abundance of tapeworm eggs and whipworms means that the little meat they ate was not properly cooked and that sanitary conditions were poor—there probably wasn't much water to clean their hands with, and they may have eaten unwashed produce from gardens fertilized with human waste. 2 Kings 25:3 tells us that "by the ninth day (of the fourth month) the famine had become acute in the city; there was no food left for the common people." Judging from the remains beneath a fancy toilet that hearkened back to better days, on the eve of the Babylonian destruction of Jerusalem its residents were clearly on the brink of starvation.

20

Ezra and Nehemiah Rehabilitate Jerusalem

Ezra 8:31–10:17; Nehemiah 2:11–20; 4:1–16

*The renewal of Jerusalem and the
Jewish people by Ezra and Nehemiah*

See page 302 for visitor information.

WHERE ARE WE?

This secluded overlook provides a bird's-eye view of the entire expanse of the modern-day Western Wall plaza and the rising domes of the Muslim buildings above it on the Temple Mount.

SETTING THE SCENE

A pilgrim returning to Jerusalem in 520 BCE to see the miracle of the newly rebuilt temple would have gazed upon a very different sight from this vantage point high up in the Jewish Quarter. The great esplanade of the current Temple Mount and its western retaining wall, the Kotel, were constructed by King Herod almost five hundred years later. The Dome of the Rock and the Al-Aqsa Mosque on the platform were built an additional seven hundred years into the future, in 691 and 720 CE. The buildings up against the northern side of the Kotel are medieval.

Instead, try to imagine an abandoned war zone. The city walls, to the south of the temple area, lay in ruins. Haphazard mounds of stone ashlars were all that remained of

Fig. 20. The Western Wall Plaza beneath the Temple Mount, Jerusalem

most of the earlier buildings. Many streets were impassable, with makeshift alleys wending through the rubble. Amid this desolation rose the new tabernacle, a modest, rebuilt temple somewhere close to the golden dome today, on the peak of a lone hilltop. No other structures abutted the hill, and a small plaza surrounded the tabernacle. The Mount of Olives was clearly visible to the east. The temple stood alone, the new sacred building in resettled Jerusalem.

THE CONTEXT

The Babylonian destruction of Jerusalem in 586 BCE was an almost unfathomable catastrophe for the people of Judah. In one fell swoop they lost their temple, their land, and their independence. The king who governed Judah was led away, Jerusalem lay in ruins, and the majority of the population was deported to Babylon and forbidden to return. Those who stayed behind resettled at Mizpah in Benjamin under Gedaliah son of Ahikam (2 Kings 25:22-26) and accompanied by the prophet Jeremiah (Jer. 39:11-40:6), but following the murder of Gedaliah most fled to Egypt, and they forced Jeremiah to go with them (Jer. 40:7-43:7).

The Babylonians were ruthless conquerors but tolerant masters. The exiled Judaeans were not persecuted in captivity but absorbed into Babylonian territories. They were permitted to establish communities together. A short time after the destruction and exile, the people of Judah found peace, prosperity, and influence in Babylon. Moreover, the book of Kings tells us that King Jehoiachin, Josiah's son, who was exiled in 597 BCE, was released from prison in 560, his status was changed ,and the new Babylonian king "gave him a throne above those of other kings who were with him in Babylon" (2 Kings 25:28, but see also 27-30). We can imagine that the elevated status of the Judaean king changed the situation of all Judaean exiles. All in all, life was actually pretty good in Babylon, under the circumstances.

Ironically, however, the glorious Babylonian empire lasted only until 538 BCE, less than seventy years. Embroiled from within, it was toppled by the Persians, who favored rehabilitating countries of strategic importance and restoring their native populations. The Persian king Cyrus invited the Judaeans to return and rebuild Jerusalem (Ezra 1:1-4). To the exiles this astonishing change of circumstances was an undeniable fulfillment of the words of the prophets. Nonetheless, the majority chose to remain in Babylon. Only the most fervent ran home, packed their suitcases, and set off for Jerusalem.

This first group of returnees in 536 BCE was led by Sheshbazzar , the prince of Judah and apparently Jehoiachin's son, and by Zerubbabel, Jehoiachin's grandson, who followed him. Both were scions of the Davidic dynasty (Ezra 1:8; 2:2; Hag. 1:1; Zech. 4, and more). Despite hostility from foreign elements that had penetrated the land in the exiles' absence, the returnees managed to settle in and rebuild the temple in Jerusalem. It was consecrated in 520 BCE, almost seventy years after the destruction of the first temple, echoing Jeremiah's prophecy that the exile would last for seventy years (Jer. 25:11, 29:10). Judaean returnees who had witnessed Solomon's Temple wept to behold this modest house of worship, but it was a beginning (Ezra 3:12).

In the years that followed, the returnees in Jerusalem fell on hard times. They lacked the funds to rebuild the city walls, and they were left undefended and vulnerable. A prolonged drought caused crops to fail, further exacerbating a struggling economy. The returnees were unable to overpower the foreigners living among them, and outsiders like the Samaritans continually meddled in Judaean affairs (Ezra 4).

When the priest and scribe Ezra arrived with a second wave of returnees, possibly in 458 BCE, he found a dismal state of affairs. The priestly oversight of the temple rituals was appalling; sacrificial offerings were made with second-rate animals, even though unblemished ones were available (Mal. 1:6–14), and the priests were corrupt (Mal. 2:8–9). According to some interpretations, non-Judaean priests had commandeered key positions in the temple hierarchy (Neh. 13:4–9). To make matters worse, the Judaeans who arrived in the first wave of immigration had intermarried in significant numbers (Ezra 9:1–2; 10:18). The danger was that foreign wives would bring pagan gods into their homes and educate their children in the ways of idolatry.

Ezra understood that drastic measures were needed. A devoutly religious man, a teacher, and a scholar, Ezra attempted to restore the law according to the teaching of Moses and rebuild the community. However, he lacked the administrative leadership required to rebuild Jerusalem's fortifications, integrate the returnees with the Judaean remnant, and stabilize the economy. The man who fulfilled this role was Nehemiah, a Judaean advisor to the Persian king, who arrived in Jerusalem thirteen years after Ezra.

- -

Ezra 8

[31]We set out for Jerusalem from the Ahava River on the twelfth of the first month. We enjoyed the care of our God, who saved us from enemy ambush on the journey.

[32]We arrived in Jerusalem and stayed there three days. [33]On the fourth day the silver, gold, and vessels were weighed out in the House of our God into the keeping of Meremoth son of Uriah the priest, with whom was Eleazar son of Phinehas. Jozabad son of Jeshua, and Noadiah son of Binnui, the Levites, were with them. [34]Everything accorded as to number and weight, the entire cargo being recorded at that time.

[35]The returning exiles who arrived from captivity made burnt offerings to the God of Israel: twelve bulls for all Israel, ninety-six rams, seventy-seven lambs and twelve he-goats as a purification offering, all this a burnt offering to the LORD. [36]They handed the royal orders to the king's satraps and the governors of the province of Beyond the River who gave support to the people and the House of God.

9

[1]When this was over, the officers approached me, saying, "The people of Israel and the priests and Levites have not

separated themselves from the peoples of the land whose abhorrent practices are like those of the Canaanites, the Hittites, the Perizzites, the Jebusites, the Ammonites, the Moabites, the Egyptians, and the Amorites. ²They have taken their daughters as wives for themselves and for their sons, so that the holy seed has become intermingled with the peoples of the land; and it is the officers and prefects who have taken the lead in this trespass."

³When I heard this, I rent my garment and robe, I tore hair out of my head and beard, and I sat desolate. ⁴Around me gathered all who were concerned over the words of the God of Israel because of the returning exiles' trespass, while I sat desolate until the evening offering. ⁵At the time of the evening offering I ended my self-affliction; still in my torn garment and robe, I got down on my knees and spread out my hands to the LORD my God, ⁶and said, "O my God, I am too ashamed and mortified to lift my face to You, O my God, for our iniquities are overwhelming and our guilt has grown high as heaven. ⁷From the time of our fathers to this very day we have been deep in guilt. Because of our iniquities, we, our kings, and our priests have been handed over to foreign kings, to the sword, to captivity, to pillage, and to humiliation, as is now the case.

⁸"But now, for a short while, there has been a reprieve from the LORD our God, who has granted us a surviving remnant and given us a stake in His holy place; our God has restored the luster to our eyes and furnished us with a little sustenance in our bondage. ⁹For bondsmen we are, though even in our bondage God has not forsaken us, but has disposed the king of Persia favorably toward us, to furnish us with sustenance and to raise again the House of our God, repairing its ruins and giving us a hold in Judah and Jerusalem.

¹⁰"Now, what can we say in the face of this, O our God, for we have forsaken Your commandments, ¹¹which You

gave us through Your servants the prophets when You said, 'The land that you are about to possess is a land unclean through the uncleanness of the peoples of the land, through their abhorrent practices with which they, in their impurity, have filled it from one end to the other. ¹²Now then, do not give your daughters in marriage to their sons or let their daughters marry your sons; do nothing for their well-being or advantage, then you will be strong and enjoy the bounty of the land and bequeath it to your children forever.' ¹³After all that has happened to us because of our evil deeds and our deep guilt—though You, our God, have been forbearing, [punishing us] less than our iniquity [deserves] in that You have granted us such a remnant as this—¹⁴shall we once again violate Your commandments by intermarrying with these peoples who follow such abhorrent practices? Will You not rage against us till we are destroyed without remnant or survivor? ¹⁵O LORD, God of Israel, You are benevolent, for we have survived as a remnant, as is now the case. We stand before You in all our guilt, for we cannot face You on this account."

10

¹While Ezra was praying and making confession, weeping and prostrating himself before the House of God, a very great crowd of Israelites gathered about him, men, women, and children; the people were weeping bitterly. ²Then Shecaniah son of Jehiel of the family of Elam spoke up and said to Ezra, "We have trespassed against our God by bringing into our homes foreign women from the peoples of the land; but there is still hope for Israel despite this. ³Now then, let us make a covenant with our God to expel all these women and those who have been born to them, in accordance with the bidding of the Lord and of all who are

concerned over the commandment of our God, and let the Teaching be obeyed. [4]Take action, for the responsibility is yours and we are with you. Act with resolve!"

[5]So Ezra at once put the officers of the priests and the Levites and all Israel under oath to act accordingly, and they took the oath. [6]Then Ezra rose from his place in front of the House of God and went into the chamber of Jehohanan son of Eliashib; there, he ate no bread and drank no water, for he was in mourning over the trespass of those who had returned from exile. [7]Then a proclamation was issued in Judah and Jerusalem that all who had returned from the exile should assemble in Jerusalem, [8]and that anyone who did not come in three days would, by decision of the officers and elders, have his property confiscated and himself excluded from the congregation of the returning exiles.

[9]All the men of Judah and Benjamin assembled in Jerusalem in three days; it was the ninth month, the twentieth of the month. All the people sat in the square of the House of God, trembling on account of the event and because of the rains. [10]Then Ezra the priest got up and said to them, "You have trespassed by bringing home foreign women, thus aggravating the guilt of Israel. [11]So now, make confession to the LORD, God of your fathers, and do His will, and separate yourselves from the peoples of the land and from the foreign women."

[12]The entire congregation responded in a loud voice, "We must surely do just as you say. [13]However, many people are involved, and it is the rainy season; it is not possible to remain out in the open, nor is this the work of a day or two, because we have transgressed extensively in this matter. [14]Let our officers remain on behalf of the entire congregation, and all our townspeople who have brought

home foreign women shall appear before them at scheduled times, together with the elders and judges of each town, in order to avert the burning anger of our God from us on this account." ¹⁵Only Jonathan son of Asahel and Jahzeiah son of Tikvah remained for this purpose, assisted by Meshullam and Shabbethai, the Levites. ¹⁶The returning exiles did so. Ezra the priest and the men who were the chiefs of the ancestral clans—all listed by name—sequestered themselves on the first day of the tenth month to study the matter. ¹⁷By the first day of the first month they were done with all the men who had brought home foreign women.

- -

Nehemiah 2

¹¹I arrived in Jerusalem. After I was there three days ¹²I got up at night, I and a few men with me, and telling no one what my God had put into my mind to do for Jerusalem, and taking no other beast than the one on which I was riding, ¹³I went out by the Valley Gate, at night, toward the Jackals' Spring and the Dung Gate; and I surveyed the walls of Jerusalem that were breached, and its gates, consumed by fire. ¹⁴I proceeded to the Fountain Gate and to the King's Pool, where there was no room for the beast under me to continue. ¹⁵So I went up the wadi by night, surveying the wall, and, entering again by the Valley Gate, I returned. ¹⁶The prefects knew nothing of where I had gone or what I had done, since I had not yet divulged it to the Jews—the priests, the nobles, the prefects, or the rest of the officials.

¹⁷Then I said to them, "You see the bad state we are in—Jerusalem lying in ruins and its gates destroyed by fire. Come, let us rebuild the wall of Jerusalem and suffer no more disgrace." ¹⁸I told them of my God's benevolent care for me, also of the things that the king had said to me, and

they said, "Let us start building!" They were encouraged by [His] benevolence.

[19] When Sanballat the Horonite and Tobiah the Ammonite servant and Geshem the Arab heard, they mocked us and held us in contempt and said, "What is this that you are doing? Are you rebelling against the king?" [20] I said to them in reply, "The God of Heaven will grant us success, and we, His servants, will start building. But you have no share or claim or stake in Jerusalem!"

4

[1] When Sanballat and Tobiah, and the Arabs, the Ammonites, and the Ashdodites heard that healing had come to the walls of Jerusalem, that the breached parts had begun to be filled, it angered them very much, [2] and they all conspired together to come and fight against Jerusalem and to throw it into confusion. [3] Because of them we prayed to our God, and set up a watch over them day and night.

[4] Judah was saying,

"The strength of the basket-carrier has failed,
And there is so much rubble;
We are not able ourselves
To rebuild the wall."

[5] And our foes were saying, "Before they know or see it, we shall be in among them and kill them, and put a stop to the work." [6] When the Jews living near them would arrive, they would tell us time and again ". . . from all the places where . . . you shall come back to us . . ." [7] I stationed, on the lower levels of the place, behind the walls, on the bare rock—I stationed the people by families with their swords, their lances, and their bows. [8] Then I decided to exhort the nobles, the prefects, and the rest of the people, "Do not be afraid of them! Think of the great and awesome Lord,

and fight for your brothers, your sons and daughters, your wives and homes!"

⁹When our enemies learned that it had become known to us, since God had thus frustrated their plan, we could all return to the wall, each to his work. ¹⁰From that day on, half my servants did work and half held lances and shields, bows and armor. And the officers stood behind the whole house of Judah ¹¹who were rebuilding the wall. The basket-carriers were burdened, doing work with one hand while the other held a weapon. ¹²As for the builders, each had his sword girded at his side as he was building. The trumpeter stood beside me. ¹³I said to the nobles, the prefects, and the rest of the people, "There is much work and it is spread out; we are scattered over the wall, far from one another. ¹⁴When you hear a trumpet call, gather yourselves to me at that place; our God will fight for us!" ¹⁵And so we worked on, while half were holding lances, from the break of day until the stars appeared.

¹⁶I further said to the people at that time, "Let every man with his servant lodge in Jerusalem, that we may use the night to stand guard and the day to work."

PICKING UP THE PIECES

The accounts given by Ezra and Nehemiah, presumably the first-person narrators in the books of Ezra and Nehemiah, are problematic in numerous areas from a historical point of view. For example, the chronology of the Persian kings doesn't always match the events as they're retold, there is no supporting evidence of a mass migration of Judaeans under Cyrus, the order of the arrival of Ezra and Nehemiah may be reversed, and there are virtually no archaeological remains that support the account of the rebuilding of Jerusalem's walls.

And yet the Jewish people are alive and well, despite the Babylonian destruction. The Judaeans returned to the land of Israel, rebuilt the temple, and continued to evolve and grow over many centuries. The period of the exile and the restoration were replete with existential challenges. The ultimate stability that followed the horrendous catastrophe of the demise of the state of Judah was largely the result of major changes in the Judaean worldview instituted by the leadership during the exile and after the return.

To many Judaeans it seemed that the Israelite God had been defeated by the more powerful Babylonian deities on his home turf and had abandoned his people. Why continue to worship him, especially since the temple was no more? Despite the profound spiritual questions raised by the disaster, the Judaeans deported to Babylon landed on their feet and rapidly integrated into the most cosmopolitan locale in the ancient realm. Economically, culturally, and politically Babylon was a great place to find oneself in the sixth century BCE. How tempting it must have been to put the old homeland out of mind and to simply choose to be a citizen of the world. In Babylonian captivity the most burning issue for Judaeans was undoubtedly assimilation.

It seems that the architect of the new Judaean identity in the exilic period was the prophet Ezekiel. He emphasized that the Israelite God on the heavenly throne was the only God in the world, a universal God, who would follow the people of Israel wherever they went (Ezek. 1:26–28). Ezekiel, among others, redefined faith, to be understood no longer as a physical association between a person and a place but rather as an everlasting personal bond between each individual and God.

He also taught the exiles that God judged each of them on the basis of their own personal deeds, and not as a collective, effectively refocusing the Israelite faith on the individual's relationship to God. The basis of this relationship was justice and mercy: do the right thing, but if you recognize your sins, God will always forgive you (Ezek. 33:10–20).

Without knowing what would come to be in the distant future, Ezekiel emphasized the unique role that the exiles were to play in the upcoming chapters of Jewish history. Although they were uprooted and displaced, ultimately they would return to their homeland (Ezek. 37:11–12). He beseeched them to withstand the temptations of assimilation; he forged their identity by nurturing feelings of distinctiveness and urged them to preserve their faith in the Israelite God and their traditions, such as Sabbath observance (Ezek. 20).

Since the Babylonians had allowed the Judaeans to settle in their own communities and to organize their own affairs as an ethnic minority, it was fairly easy for them to maintain a separate identity. The exiles kept meticulous genealogical records that documented every member of the community according to associations of families in order to ascertain exactly who was a Judaean (Ezra 2:1–67).

HOMEWARD BOUND

About eighty years after Sheshbazzar, Zerubbabel, and the first group of exiles arrived in Jerusalem and rebuilt the temple, Ezra and his assemblage set out in their footsteps with a great sense of mission. Upon their arrival, however, their enthusiasm was dampened when they witnessed the abysmal state of the earlier returnees and the Judaean farmers who had remained behind. Helpless in the face of stronger neighboring nations who greedily eyed the desolate Israelite land, the Judaeans had no choice but to accept the Samaritans, Ammonites, Edomites, and others who had encroached on their territory and dwelled among them. Intermarriage was rampant (Ezra 9:1–2). When later

Ezra read from the scroll of the Teaching of Moses in the public square, it seemed that most of the people needed explanations (Neh. 8:1-8).

To complicate matters, the Judaeans who had not been exiled claimed to be the true heirs of the land (Ezek. 11:14-16; 33:23-24). Arguments broke out over land ownership, which had been transferred from the wealthy exiles to the remnant by the Babylonians (Jer. 39:10). The socio-economic gaps were widened even more dramatically thanks to the heavy taxation burden imposed by the Persian Empire. The poor were forced to take out loans from the wealthy, and when they could not pay the exorbitant (illegal) interest, they were often forced to sell their children into slavery (Neh. 5:1-5). Also, the remnant and the earlier returnees took issue with the strict religious standards advocated by Ezra. In short, Ezra found the situation in the early period of the return to Zion a mess.

Amid the constant tension between the exiles and the veterans, Ezra adopted a hard-line, no-nonsense approach in his religious reforms. He insisted that the Judaeans completely separate themselves from the foreign women in order to eradicate their pagan influences and to maintain strict standards of purity (Ezra 9-10). Ezra also restored the Teaching of Moses to its place at the center of Judaean daily existence. Ezra's role in painstakingly disseminating the Teaching of Moses was so pivotal that in Jewish tradition he is referred to as the second Moses. (At a later point this teaching would be compiled and edited into the compendium known as the Torah.)

But ultimately Ezra was not successful in enforcing the law, probably because he lacked the temperament of a charismatic, go-getting administrator. He was unable to overcome the hostility of the adversaries of the returnees, who attempted to interfere in the construction of the temple.

The Judaeans, feeling threatened, launched a campaign to rebuild the walls of Jerusalem to protect themselves, but their neighbors reported their efforts to the Persians as an attempted rebellion. The Persians, convinced, destroyed the walls, and Ezra lost his status and power as a leader (Ezra 4; Neh. 1:3). At this time it seems he disappeared from public life.

The pieces were picked up by Nehemiah, a Judaean advisor to the Persian king who took a leave of absence from his job to journey to Jerusalem (Neh. 1–2:9), arriving about thirteen years after Ezra. Although not a scholar and man of letters like Ezra, Nehemiah quickly understood the dire need for strong, organized leadership.

He recruited Judaean forces for construction of the wall and protection of the laborers so that finally, the city and its inhabitants were well secured (Neh. 3), despite the attempted sabotage by non-Judaeans (Neh. 4:1–3). He urged the wealthy to release their debtors from economic bondage and set a personal example by canceling all outstanding debts owed to him (Neh. 5:6–13). Nehemiah also introduced socioeconomic reforms by using the Teaching of Moses as the constitution. He restored all property to its original owners, prohibited shopping on the Sabbath, and forbade the consumption of produce reaped in the sabbatical year (Neh. 10:32). He put the temple in order, reforming its administration, regulating a tax to ensure it would always be supported, and establishing a work roster for priestly and Levitical shifts (Neh. 10:33–40). In order to strengthen Jerusalem and expose the peasantry to the new reforms. he ordered 10 percent of the Judaean population from the countryside to take up residence in the city (Neh. 11:1).

After twelve years (Neh. 5:14) Nehemiah returned to Persia to serve his king. However, it wasn't long before people in Jerusalem reverted back to their old ways. Only when Nehemiah returned for the second time and laid down the law did the new order finally take root. Backed by the authority of his Persian commission, he evicted Tobiah the Ammonite from the temple (Neh. 13:4–9), reorganized the tithes, and assigned the temple treasury to honest priests (Neh. 13:10–13). He chastised Judaeans for continuing to work on the Sabbath and once and for all locked the gates of Jerusalem to foreign merchants on the day of rest (Neh. 13:15–22). He issued yet another decree against intermarriage (Neh. 13:23–28).

THE NEW DEAL

The reestablishment of the temple and Mosaic law and the successful settlement of the returnees were two critical steps taken by Ezra and Nehemiah to restore the Judaeans in their homeland. The third and no less important step was accepting that the Persian invitation to resettle Judah and rebuild the temple was limited to just that. The Persians would not suffer national aspirations, and the Judaeans understood that the new world order would not permit the reestablishment of an independent Judaean state. Sheshbazzar and Zerubbabel, the Davidic descendants who led the first group of exiles, disappear mysteriously from the narrative, perhaps because their political ambitions did not receive support from the Persian authorities. The Davidic dynasty, the longest ruling monarchy in Jerusalem, was not to rise again. Pragmatically, its resurgence was relegated to the vague future of the messianic era. It was from this time that the Judaeans, a people formerly linked to a specific place, became known wherever they settled as people of the Jewish faith, or Jews.

The new system set up by the Persians allowed the Judaeans to organize under the authority of the Persian king and his provincial administration. After the disappearance of Sheshbazzar and Zerubbabel, the priests and the lay leaders were delighted—they received power that they never could have enjoyed under the Davidic monarchy, and they reciprocated by pledging their loyalty to Persia. The establishment of a Jewish theocracy in Jerusalem under Persian auspices also served to strengthen the burgeoning Jewish diaspora. Since Jews had officially relinquished their dream of an independent state, they could pledge their loyalty unreservedly to the Persian king. This, in turn, meant that wherever they lived in the Persian empire, they could reach influential roles and ensure safety and security for the Jewish communities there.

Ezekiel, Ezra, Nehemiah, and others (such as Deutero-Isaiah) effectively contributed to the transformation of the people of Judaea from a shattered political entity into tightly knit religious communities centered around the house of God on earth, the temple in Jerusalem. Their redefinition of the Jewish relationship to an all-powerful, universal Creator would take on new meaning when the temple was destroyed for a second and final time in 70 CE by the Romans. Broken and scattered to the ends of the earth, Jews took their God and their law with them everywhere they went for the two thousand years that Jerusalem was ruled by foreign conquerors. The Jewish faith in exile survived, even without Jerusalem, but was always nourished by the dream of return and rebuilding (the service for Yom Kippur and the Passover seder both conclude with the words, "Next Year in (rebuilt) Jerusalem").

The modern Jewish people, however, could not hope to survive without the existence of the political entity forgone by the returnees from exile. Centuries of persecution culminating in the Holocaust made the creation of a sovereign Jewish state an imperative. The troubled course of Jewish history and the ingathering of the exiles in the ancestral homeland of Israel echo presciently in the prophecy of Ezekiel:

Thus said the Lord God: I am going to open your graves and lift you out of the graves, O My people, and bring you to the land of Israel. . . . I will put My breath into you and you shall live again, and I will set you upon your own soil. . . . I am going to take the Israelite people from among the nations they have gone to, and gather them from every quarter, and bring them to their own land. (Ezek. 37:12–21)

The establishment of the state of Israel in 1948 marked the completion of the circle. Following a three-thousand-year journey, we're right back where we started . . . almost. The Davidic monarchy has no place in a democracy (do you know anyone related to King David?), but where does the temple fit in? Do we truly wish to return to the Judaism of priests and animal sacrifice? Yet can we live comfortably with foreign hegemony over what we perceive to be the holiest place on earth? The meaning and the relevance of the temple and its hilltop domain will continue to be discussed and debated by Jews in Israel and the diaspora for years to come. The Book is written, but the story continues.

POSTSCRIPT: THE TEMPLE MOUNT—TO ASCEND, OR NOT?

Rabbis and sages have discussed the issue of Jewish access to the Temple Mount platform for centuries. From the time of the second caliph Omar, in the mid-seventh century CE, for a period of four hundred years a synagogue stood on the temple esplanade, by then the home of two mosques. However, today the prevailing view states that Jews are forbidden to ascend the mount for two reasons: since the ashes of the red heifer necessary for ritual purification are not available, all Jews remain impure, a condition that prevents access to the holy precinct. Also, since the exact location of the temple and the Holy of Holies is unknown, Jews who ascend the mount run the risk of violating the sacred boundaries, which would be a terrible desecration.

Yet some rabbinic scholars maintain that ascending the Temple Mount is a deeply spiritual experience and may be permitted to Jewish pilgrims who have undergone ritual purification in the mikveh, who are not wearing leather shoes, and who restrict their visit to the periphery of the platform (i.e., those areas that have been unanimously declared to be outside the temple limits by scholars).

Since 1967 the chief rabbinate of Israel has consistently prohibited Jewish access, issuing a warning on the radio not to go up within hours of the IDF's capture of the Temple Mount on the second day of the Six-Day War. A sign in place at the entrance to the Mugrabi Gate until today reads:

ANNOUNCEMENT AND WARNING

According to the Torah it is forbidden for any person to enter the area of the Temple Mount due to its sacredness.—The Chief Rabbinate of Israel

21

Megiddo

The Untold Story

See page 329 for visitor information.

 Megiddo was one of the most important cities in ancient Israel; the tel is an archaeological layer cake comprising twenty-six strata, each from a different civilization. Although Megiddo does not figure prominently in any full Bible story, it is a showcase of biblical archaeology and has been recognized by UNESCO as a World Heritage Site.

Megiddo's claim to fame was its strategic position overlooking one of the most important intersections of the ancient Middle Eastern trade routes. The Great Trunk Road connected Egypt in the west to Mesopotamia in the east by a main highway with many divergent branches. The road came up from Egypt along the Mediterranean coast and then turned eastward via Canaan, wending through a narrow bottleneck pass that emerged at the western corner of the Jezreel Valley and the junction of two other highways. This major intersection was controlled by the hilltop city of Megiddo. In real-estate parlance, it was location, location, location.

In prebiblical times Megiddo was a Canaanite city-state under Egyptian aegis and served as an important Egyptian stronghold. It was, in fact, so strong that the Israelites were unable to overcome it until the days of the united monarchy. Although it is not mentioned explicitly, Megiddo appar-

Fig. 21. Tel Megiddo

ently came under Israelite control when it was conquered by King David; King Solomon then refortified it and rebuilt it as one of his main citadels. After a brief reappearance of the Egyptians at Megiddo, it was again rebuilt, probably by the Israelite kings Omri and Ahab in the ninth century BCE during the time of the divided monarchy; many of the finds on view at the tel date to this period, such as the walls, the four-chambered gate, the stable complexes, and the water system.

Megiddo was conquered in 732 BCE by the Assyrian king Tiglath Pileser III, who built a new gate and public buildings in the Assyrian style and made it the capital of the Assyrian province of the Galilee. After the fall of the Assyrian empire, the Judaean king Josiah probably ruled here for a while. The city was eventually conquered and settled by the Persians in the sixth century BCE and then abandoned.

At Megiddo National Park you will find:

· a small museum with maps, a 3-D model of the tel, exhibits of the tel's highlights, and an audiovisual presentation.

- fabulous examples of ancient structures that appear over and over in the biblical text, such as city fortifications, gates, high places, palaces, stables, and a grain silo. Not to be missed is the ancient water system consisting of a shaft and tunnel deep in the belly of the tel that you can walk through.

So, grab your Bible, your hat and water bottle, and a brochure from the national park cashier explaining the finds at the site and conquer Tel Megiddo yourself.

BIBLICAL REFERENCES TO MEGIDDO

Joshua 12:7, 21; 17:11
Judges 1:27; 5:19–20
1 Kings 4:12; 9:15
2 Kings 9:27; 23:29–30
1 Chronicles 7:29
2 Chronicles 35:20–24

IN CHRISTIAN SCRIPTURE

Revelation 16:16

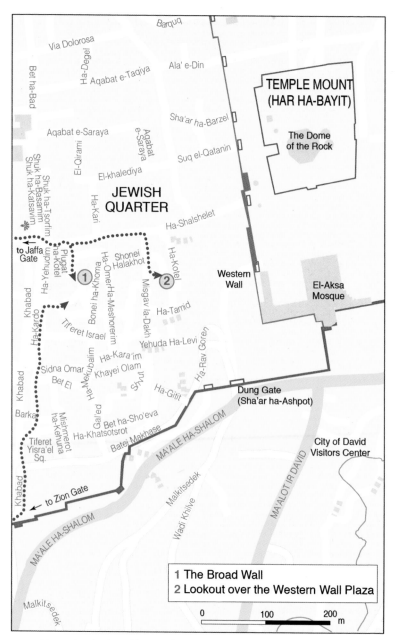

Map 2. Inside the Old City of Jerusalem

How to Find the Biblical Sites

DESTINATION 1: THE BROAD WALL

For the narrative behind this destination, see chapter 18, "Hezekiah Prepares Jerusalem for War."

Getting There

From Jaffa Gate: walk through the gate and continue straight onto David Street, which goes downhill through the market. When you reach the end at the bottom, turn right. Walk down about one block until you reach the second street on your left, Plugat Ha-Kotel Street (see signs pointing to public restrooms). Turn left, pass the restrooms, and when you come out into a small plaza the Broad Wall will be right in front of you.

From Zion Gate: walk through the gate, cross the street onto the sidewalk on the left, and follow the road leading into the Jewish Quarter, staying on the sidewalk as it skirts the parking lot on your right. At the parking lot's edge turn right down a paved ramp and left at the bottom onto Jewish Quarter Road. Continue straight for a distance of about two blocks, passing the Cardo on your left and the Hurva synagogue on your right. Keep going until you reach Plugat Ha-Kotel Street on your right (see signs pointing to public restrooms). Turn right, pass the restrooms, and when you come out into a small plaza the Broad Wall will be right in front of you.

24/7

- Start your day with a walk on the Old City walls, ascending at Jaffa Gate and descending at Zion Gate.
- Visit the Dormition Abbey, King David's tomb, and the Upper Room, all on Mount Zion.
- Then either enter the Old City via Zion Gate, or walk down along the wall to the City of David.

DESTINATION 2: LOOKOUT OVER THE WESTERN WALL PLAZA

For the narrative behind this destination, see chapter 20, "Ezra and Nehemiah Rehabilitate Jerusalem."

Getting There

From Jaffa Gate: Walk through the gate and continue straight to David Street, the main market street. Follow it all the way down until the street ends at a T intersection (see restrooms). Turn right and make an immediate left onto the Street of the Chain, continuing downhill. About one block down, turn right onto Misgav la-Dakh Street (if you reach the turnoff for the Western Wall on the right, you've gone too far). Pass a few shops and you will find yourself in a large, open plaza on the left. Cross over diagonally to the other side, approaching a low wall. Turn right, up the steps, onto Ha-Tamid Street. Follow the lane across and down the steps and turn left. Approach the railing and you will find an outstanding view, as well as some benches to sit quietly and read.

From the Jewish Quarter: Find your way to the top of the steps that lead down to the Western Wall Plaza and turn left there onto Misgav la-Dakh Street. Follow the street all the way down. When you walk beneath a covered area and reach Shonei Halakhot Street on your left, turn right into a large, open plaza. Cross over to the other side and turn right, up the steps, onto Ha-Tamid Street. Follow the lane across and down the steps and turn left. Approach the railing and you will find an outstanding view, as well as some benches to sit quietly and read.

Opening Hours

24/7

Make It a Day

- Take a tour of the Western Wall Tunnel.
- Visit the Temple Mount.

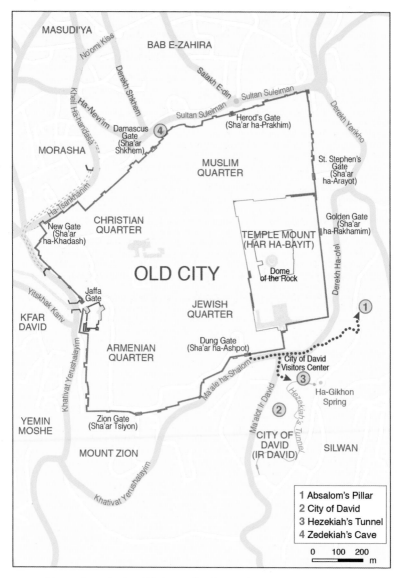

Map 3. Outside the Old City walls of Jerusalem

For the narrative behind this destination, see chapter 13, "Absalom's Rebellion in the Kidron Valley."

Getting There

On foot from the Old City: Exit the Old City via the Dung Gate. Cross the street and turn left, walking down the hill and keeping the Old City wall on your left. Pass the street leading to the City of David on your right and continue around the bend in the road, where you will see a brown sign pointing to Absalom's Pillar. (You might want to stop and enjoy the view of the Kidron Valley and the Mount of Olives from the observation point a few meters/feet further down.) Return to the brown sign and follow the stairs leading down into the Kidron Valley. Descend 172 steps to reach the bottom of the path. The monument is right in front of you.

By taxi: Ask the driver to let you off in front of the church at the Garden of Gethsemane. The facade of the church has a huge triangular mosaic over three arches. Walk south, with the church on your left and the Old City wall on your right (a Christian cemetery is down below in the Kidron Valley). Continue about 140 paces until you reach a small booth with the sign Mount of Olives Information Center, Absalom's Pillar. (If you would like to expand your tour to include other ancient graves and monuments in the area, purchase a map here.) Descend the stairs on the right and continue down the path into the Kidron Valley. Walk about one block's distance until you reach the monument on your left.

Opening Hours

24/7. Restrooms one flight down from the information booth by Gethsemane are open summer, 7 a.m.–6 p.m.; winter, 6 a.m.–5 p.m.

Make It a Day

- Start your day at the lookout point from the top of the Mount of Olives, walk down the Palm Sunday walk to Gethsemane, and continue to Absalom's tomb.
- Explore the other tombs in the Kidron Valley.
- Continue hiking on the Jerusalem trail via the Kidron Valley to the Valley of Hinom as far as the Cinemateque and grab a coffee at its restaurant.

DESTINATION 2: CITY OF DAVID

For the narrative behind this destination, see chapter 11, "Bathsheba in the City of David."

Getting There

On foot from the Old City: Exit the Old City walls via the Dung Gate and cross the street. Turn left and walk downhill, keeping the walls on your left. Make the first right turn just down the hill and walk downward a short distance until you see the entrance to the City of David on your left, marked with a large harp.

Follow the signs pointing to the observation deck and climb the stairs to the top. There is no shade there, and the platform is often crowded, so after reading the introductory information and studying the view feel free to climb back down and find a quieter, shady spot to read the story.

Sunday–Thursday, 8 a.m.–5 p.m.; Friday, 8 a.m.–2 p.m. During daylight saving time months the site often stays open longer. The observation deck, the location for this story, is open 24/7. Entrance fee. For more information visit the City of David website at www.cityofdavid.org.il.

Make It a Day

- Continue exploring the City of David archaeological park, including Hezekiah's Tunnel (see chapter 18).
- Continue through the park to the Pool of Siloam. Hike back up to the Old City via the Roman sewer system as far as Robinson's Arch. Tour the Davidson archaeological park just inside Dung Gate.

DESTINATION 3: HEZEKIAH'S TUNNEL

For the narrative behind this destination, see chapter 18, "Hezekiah Prepares Jerusalem for War."

Getting There

From the Dung Gate: walk out the gate and cross the street. Turn left and walk downhill, keeping the Old City wall on your left. Make the first right turn just down the hill and walk downward until you see the entrance for the City of David on your left, marked by a large harp. Enter the gate, purchase an entry ticket for Hezekiah's Tunnel, and ask for a site map, which will direct you to the entrance of the water system. Follow the signs to Warren's Shaft. When you enter, you will walk down a long, dry tunnel that is actually a water system predating Hezekiah's Tunnel (for more information consult the pamphlet you received with your entry ticket). When you reach the bottom of the descent, you will find the entrance to the wet tunnel, as well as a short dry tunnel that will lead you to an exit in case you change your mind about going into the water. At the entrance to Warren's Shaft is a revolving gate and an attendant. Before you enter, find a place to sit quietly and read.

Hezekiah's Tunnel is in the City of David, outside the walls. It is a 533 meter (1,750-feet-long) tunnel carved out of the rock; water flows through it anywhere from mid-calf to high thigh, depending on the season. The walk through the tunnel takes twenty–thirty-five minutes and requires closed water shoes (flip-flops not recommended) and a flashlight. After exiting the tunnel you may climb the long hike back up to the top of the hill (either outdoors or via a first-century sewer) or pay to ride the shuttle van.

Opening Hours

Sunday–Thursday, 8 a.m.–5 p.m.; Friday, 8 a.m.–2 p.m. Entrance fee. On Saturdays the observation deck and Area G are open, but the tunnels are closed. During daylight saving time the park is often open for extended hours; call before visiting. (Note: When you buy your tickets you will be assigned an entrance hour. Remember that you might need some time to change clothes [lockers are available], use restrooms, fill water bottles, tour the rest of the site, and read the Hezekiah story. Make sure your entrance slot allows you enough time to do everything before going into the tunnel.) Entrance to Hezekiah's tunnel only until two hours before closing; tunnels close one hour before closing. No reservation necessary for groups numbering fewer than fourteen people. However, during school vacations the tunnel gets very crowded so it's advisable to call in advance. For more information call 02–6262341 or *6033. Visit their website at www.cityofda-vid.org.il. (Note: In addition to Hezekiah's Tunnel there is much more to see at the City of David at no extra cost. If you wish to tour the site more extensively, be sure to ask for some explanatory literature when you purchase your tickets. Guided tours are also available, reservations required.)

DESTINATION 4: ZEDEKIAH'S CAVE

For the narrative behind this destination, see chapter 19, "Zedekiah Flees Jerusalem."

Getting There

On foot from the Old City: Exit the Old City via the Damascus Gate. At the street level above the gate, walk eastward, keeping the Old City wall on your right. Continue about one hundred paces, or half a block, until you reach the entrance to Solomon's Quarries (Zedekiah's Cave)—a green iron gate fitted into the natural rock under the city wall. Once inside, follow the path deep into the caves. When the path begins to circle back, find a place to sit on the rocks and read.

Opening Hours

Summer, 9 a.m.–5 p.m.; winter, 9 a.m.–4 p.m.; holiday evenings until 2 p.m. Closed Friday, open Saturday. Entrance fee. Restrooms.

Make It a Day

- Climb up the Old City ramparts and walk on top of the walls from the Jaffa Gate to the Damascus Gate.
- Visit the Garden Tomb, the Protestant alternative to the Church of the Holy Sepulchre.
- Enjoy a drink and spectacular views of the Old City from the terrace café at Notre Dame.

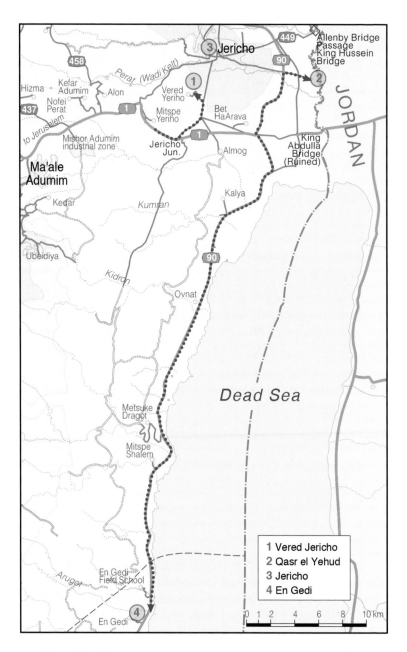

Map 4. Dead Sea vicinity

For the narrative behind this destination, see chapter 1, "Rahab at Jericho."

Getting There

Two sites within a few miles of each other paint the picture of this story. If you have lots of time, start with Vered Yeriho (1). If you're short on time skip directly to Qasr el Yehud (2). Both sites are within the immediate vicinity of the modern city of Jericho (3).

First Stop: Start at the lookout point from Moshav Vered Yeriho. Set your GPS to "Vered Yeriho." If you are using a map, coming down eastward from Jerusalem on Route 1 turn left at the Jericho junction and drive a short distance until you reach a turnoff on the left and sign pointing to Vered Yeriho. Continue up the road until you reach the entrance of the moshav. After passing through the gate turn right and then take another immediate right. Drive along the settlement fence for about 200 meters (650 feet) until you reach a lookout point with two benches in a garden on your right, at the Pninat Vered guesthouse (telephone: 02-9942763). Park on the right and take a seat on the benches.

Second Stop: When you finish reading the Rahab story, proceed to our second stop, Qasr el Yehud (2): Return to the Jericho junction at Route 1 and turn left, driving toward the Dead Sea. Proceed a short distance down the road and turn left onto Route 90 North, the Jericho bypass road (if you reach the Dead Sea, you've gone too far). Drive a few miles up the road until you reach the sign for Qasr el

Yehud on the right. Turn right and drive approximately three kilometers (two miles) eastward until you reach the entrance of the park, which is a Christian pilgrims' baptismal site on the Jordan River.

Although the Jordan River was wider and deeper in biblical times than it is today, standing on its banks gives you a fabulous picture of a barren, unforgiving wilderness festooned with a single green ribbon. Shortly after the two spies returned to camp, the Israelites crossed the river at Jericho, somewhere near here, and set the story of the conquest of the land in motion.

Opening Hours

First Stop: 24/7. Note: no access to restrooms here. Restrooms and snack bar available at the Almog gas station just past the Jericho intersection on Route 1.

Second Stop: April–September: 8 a.m.–5 p.m., Friday and holiday eves 8 a.m.–4 p.m. October–March: 8 a.m.–4 p.m., Fridays and holiday eves 8 a.m.–3 p.m. Telephone: 02-6504844.

Make It a Day

On the drive down from Jerusalem (or on the way back):
- Check out the Wadi Kelt lookout point for a fabulous view of St. George's monastery.
- Visit the nature reserve at Ein Prat.
- Stop in at the Samaritan Museum.

DESTINATION 4: EN GEDI

For the narrative behind this destination, see chapter 9, "David's Flight to En Gedi."

Getting There

Set your GPS to "Ein Gedi Nature Reserve" (it may appear as Nahal David). The En Gedi Field School and En Gedi Youth Hostel/Guesthouse are at the same turnoff, but Kibbutz En Gedi is about one kilometer (0.6 miles) south on Route 90. If you're driving south on 90 and you've reached the kibbutz, you've gone too far.

If you're using a map and coming from Jerusalem, head to the northeastern corner of the city, either via the Begin Highway, or Route 1 from the area of the Old City. Look for the signs to Highway 1 and Maaleh Adumim. Pass through a checkpoint and stay on 1 for about thirty-two kilometers (twenty miles) as you make a steep descent. Continue until you reach the Dead Sea, where Route 1 ends. Turn right at the intersection onto Route 90 and continue approximately thirty minutes to En Gedi Nature Reserve on the right. Take the paved path at the entrance and walk into the reserve until you find a shaded area to stop and read (there are benches along the way).

Opening Hours

April–September, 8 a.m.–5 p.m.; October–March, 8 a.m.–4 p.m. From October to March, last entrance to the David Stream: 3 p.m.; last entrance to the Arugot Stream: 2 p.m. Last exit from the reserve 4 p.m. Telephone: 08-658-4285. Entrance fee. Restrooms, snack bar, souvenir shop.

Note: The En Gedi Nature Reserve includes the short (and most popular) hiking trail at Nahal David, several longer trails for experienced hikers, and the remains of an ancient synagogue with a beautiful mosaic floor. The short trail, which is circular, includes an uphill climb on marked paths to the David Waterfall. It is suitable for families and includes several wading pools fed by the stream on the way up. If you wish to opt for a more challenging hike of several hours, be sure to get an early start to avoid the heat and consult with the rangers at the entrance about maps, routes, and timing. In the warm months the heat at En Gedi is intense, so regardless of the duration of your visit, be sure to have plenty of drinking water when you start your hike. Fill up your water bottles at the cooler by the ticket booths.

Make It a Day

- Hike up to the waterfall at Nahal David.
- Visit the ancient synagogue.
- Go for a dip in the Dead Sea.
- Visit Masada National Park.
- Visit Qumran National Park.

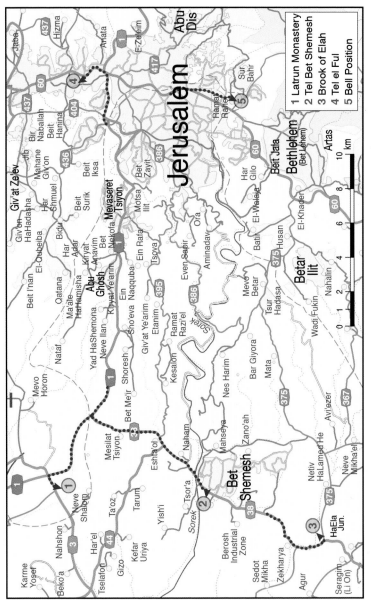

Map 5. Greater Jerusalem and central Israel

1 Latrun Monastery
2 Tel Bet Shemesh
3 Brook of Elah
4 Tel el Ful
5 Bell Position

For the narrative behind this destination, see chapter 2, "Joshua in the Valley of Aijalon."

Getting There

Set your GPS to "Latrun Monastery." If you are using a map, from Highway 1 (the Jerusalem–Tel Aviv Highway) get off at the Latrun Junction and onto Route 3 south (toward Ashkelon). Drive a short distance to the next intersection and turn left at the light to the Latrun Monastery. Follow the road up into the parking lot. Just before the lot a road branches off to the right with a blue and white trail marker. Park your car and return to the trail to begin the walk to the Crusader fortress on the hill. (Note: this uphill walk takes ten–fifteen minutes. Use extreme caution when walking through the ruins, which are full of pits and trenches. Due to tall, thorny weeds long pants are recommended.) Walk along the monastery's fence, following the path up the hill. When the path straightens out, you will be standing beneath an old Jordanian outpost made of stone and concrete. On your left follow the path that cuts sharply through a breach in the fence until you reach the outpost. Sit down in the shade and take in the view.

Opening Hours

Latrun fortress: during daylight hours. **Monastery shop**: 8:00 a.m.–12:00 noon, 1:00–6:00 p.m. Church: 8:00–11:00 a.m., 2:30–4:00 p.m. Closed Sundays.

Make It a Day

- Tour the IDF Armored Corps museum and climb on the tanks.
- Take a walk on one of the hiking trails at Canada Park.

- Visit the monastery at Latrun and stop by the gift shop for local wine and olive oil.

For the narrative behind this destination, see chapter 5, "Samson at Zorah."

Getting There

Set your GPS to "Tel Beit Shemesh." If you are using a map, from Highway 1 (the Jerusalem–Tel Aviv Highway) take the Shaar Hagai exit onto Route 38 south, toward Bet Shemesh. The tel is an archaeological site about 8.5 kilometers (a bit more than five miles) down the road on the right, but it's not well marked. You will be close when you pass a large shopping center on the left and go over railroad tracks. Pass two yellow "slow" signs on either side of the road and then a large green sign that says "Bet Shemesh/Yishi." Pull your car over at the green sign and park it safely. You are now at the entrance to the tel. Climb up the small incline and make yourself comfortable on the round concrete platform at the top of the hill.

Opening Hours

24/7

Make It a Day

- Take a drive through the sculpture path at the President's Forest (Yaar Hanasi).
- Visit the monastery at Bet Jimal.

For the narrative behind this destination, see chapter 8, "David and Goliath in the Valley of Elah."

Getting There

The brook of Elah is a dry creek bed that passes under a country road, and it's easy to miss. Follow the instructions carefully and do not attempt to approach the brook from the wrong side of the road.

Set your GPS to "Haela Paz Service Station" and read further below to get from the gas station to the site.

If you are using a map, from Route 1, the Tel Aviv–Jerusalem Highway, turn off at the sign for Bet Shemesh, just west of Shaar Hagai onto Route 38 south. Follow 38 for 18 kilometers (about eleven miles). When you pass the turnoff to Tsafririm on the left, be ready to look for Haela Junction, where Route 38 bears right and the left turn leads to Route 375. Turn left onto 375, take an immediate right into the gas station parking lot, and make a U-turn, returning to Route 38 north. About seventy meters (two hundred feet) from the intersection, roll your car off the road and onto the shoulder where you can park safely. Walking in the same direction as the road, continue through the field along a beaten path until you reach the edge of the dry bed of the brook of Elah, which passes beneath Route 38.

Make It a Day

- If you're visiting during winter, drive up to Givat HaTurmusin to see the lupines.
- Explore the caves at Bet Guvrin National Park.
- Join a real archaeological dig with Archaeological Seminars (www.archesem.com).

For the narrative behind this destination, see chapter 7, "The Levite and His Concubine at Gibeah."

Getting There

This site is isolated and deserted, so it's best to visit during daylight hours in a small group.

By car: From the French Hill Junction in Jerusalem, get on to Route 60 north, toward Pisgat Zeev. At the Pisgat Zeev exit, turn left at the light onto Yekutiel Adam Street. Take the second right turn (no street name), driving uphill, and make the first right. Drive up to the end of the street and park your car by the school. Walk up to the summit of the hill until you are standing beneath the shell of an unfinished building.

By light rail: Take the Red Line north and get off at the Bet Hanina station. Continue walking in the same direction as the train travels and make the first left turn onto an unnamed street (just by the car wash). Walk uphill and make the first right turn, continuing up the street past the school. Walk up to the summit of the hill until you reach the shell of an unfinished building.

Opening Hours

24/7

Make It a Day

- Continue by car to Nebi Samuel and climb up to the roof of the mosque for a spectacular view.
- Walk or bicycle along the Ramot bike path.

DESTINATION 5: BELL POSITION

For the narrative behind this destination, see chapter 6, "Ruth the Moabitess at Bethlehem."

Getting There

By car: Set your GPS to "Kibbutz Ramat Rahel." As you reach the kibbutz you will come to a T intersection. The kibbutz is to the right, but you will turn left, following the sign to the Bell Position. Take the first right turn and follow the dirt road until you reach the kibbutz cemetery and park your car nearby. Continue walking in the same direction, following along the cemetery fence, passing the sculpture of two olive trees on pillars on your left. Follow the road, going straight, until you reach on old military position on the edge of the hill. Find a comfortable place to sit.

By bus: Take bus 7 from the center of town (King George Street) to Kibbutz Ramat Rahel, the last stop. From the bus stop, walk back toward the intersection and continue straight for a short distance until you reach a turnoff on the right to the Bell Position. Follow the road to its end, continuing straight until you reach the old military position on the edge of the hill.

Opening Hours

24/7

Make It a Day

- Walk back via the olive tree sculpture.
- Explore the archaeological park at Kibbutz Ramat Rahel.

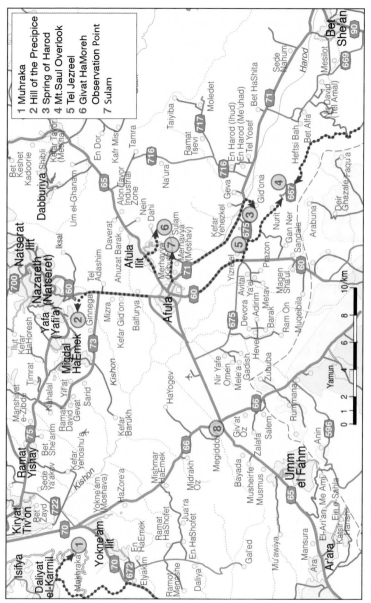

Map 6. Jezreel Valley

1 Muhraka
2 Hill of the Precipice
3 Spring of Harod
4 Mt. Saul Overlook
5 Tel Jezreel
6 Givat HaMoreh
  Observation Point
7 Sulam

321

For the narrative behind this destination, see chapter 15, "Elijah at Mount Carmel."

Getting there

Set your GPS to "Muhraka." If you are using a map: Take the coastal highway (Route 2) to Route 70, the Zichron Yaacov Interchange, and continue until you reach the Elyakim Interchange; an alternative is to take Highway 6 (toll road) to the Elyakim Interchange. At the traffic circle proceed north through a second traffic circle onto Route 672, driving up to the plateau of the Carmel ridge (a gas station is located on the right side of 672 north just after the second circle). Drive eight kilometers (five miles) until you reach a traffic circle; drive straight through it to a second circle, then a third, where you will see a brown sign on the right pointing toward the Carmelite monastery. Turn right from the circle onto a local road and follow it for a few kilometers until it ends at the Mukhraka, a Carmelite church and monastery.

Make your way up to the monastery roof via the stairs in the small shop to view the spectacular panorama. If it's too hot up there, take in the view and read the introductory information. Then come back down to the main yard and find a quiet spot in the shade to read the Elijah story.

Opening Hours

Open daily 8:30 a.m.–6 p.m. Entrance fee. Modest dress required (no shorts or tank tops). Restrooms.

Make It a Day

- Have lunch and tour the market of the Druze village Daliyat el Karmil.

- Drive up to Mount Carmel and Haifa and tour the Bahai gardens.

DESTINATION 2: HILL OF THE PRECIPICE

For the narrative behind this destination, see chapter 3, "Deborah and Jael at Mount Tabor."

Getting There

Set your GPS to "Hill of the Precipice." If you are using a map, coming from Afula drive north on Route 60 toward Nazareth and drive through the tunnel. When you emerge at the intersection, turn left. Drive about 800 meters (260 feet) and turn left at the second traffic light (a brown sign points to the Hill of the Precipice, approximately 2 kilometers [1.6 miles] from here). Follow the road and at the first fork make a left, continuing uphill. At the next intersection, at a pink and orange building, turn right and continue uphill. Pass through a large green gate and go straight until you reach a traffic circle at the summit of the hill. Park here and walk up the paved trail on the right until you reach a circular platform at the edge of the cliff overlooking the Jezreel Valley. Find a comfortable spot to sit and read.

Opening Hours

24/7

Make It a Day

- Wander through downtown Nazareth and visit the Catholic Church of the Annunciation and the Church of St. Joseph; the Greek Catholic Synagogue Church; and the Greek Orthodox Church of St. Gabriel.

For the narrative behind this destination, see chapter 4, "Gideon at En Harod."

Getting There

Set your GPS to "Maayan Harod." If you are using a map, take Route 71 east from Afula. Travel about ten kilometers (six miles) and take the turn off for Gid'ona on the right. Follow the road until you reach a traffic circle and turn right to the entrance of Maayan Harod, a national park. Park your car in the parking lot and follow along the road that continues into the park on foot, passing the gigantic swimming pool on your left. When you reach the public restrooms on the other side of the pool, turn left onto the footpath and follow it to the end, where you will find Gideon's spring, the spring of Harod.

Opening Hours

April–September, 8 a.m.–5 p.m. (entrance until 4 p.m.); October–March: 8 a.m.–4 p.m. (entrance until 3 p.m.). On Fridays and holiday eves the site closes one hour earlier. Entrance fee. Swimming pool. Restrooms. Recently the park has been closed on weekends. Call first for updated visiting hours. 04-653-2211.

Make It a Day

- Tour the stunning mosaic floor of the ancient synagogue at Bet Alfa.
- Take a swim at the natural spring pool at Gan HaShlosha.
- Take a nature walk along the Harod Creek Trail (a sharp right turn before the train tracks as you approach Route 71; see http://www.kkl.org.il/eng/tourism-and-recreation/forests-and-parks/nahal-harod-park.aspx).

For the narrative behind this destination, see chapter 10, "King Saul at Mount Gilboa."

Getting There

GPS reception is unreliable in this area, so use a map. From Afula, take Route 60 south. Turn left at Yizrael junction onto Route 675, then an immediate right onto Route 667, the Mount Gilboa Scenic Route. Travel up the road for 5.5 kilometers (3 ½ miles) and turn left at the entrance for Mount Shaul. Drive 1.3 kilometers (0.8 miles) going straight until you reach a large parking lot. As you face the view (north) two observation platforms with stunning views of the Jezreel Valley are located at either end of the parking lot. The left one looks west toward Givat HaMoreh, and the right one looks east toward Bet She'an. Two paths connect the platforms: an upper, paved path and a lower, unpaved one marked with green and white trail markers.

Alternately, if you are coming from Route 90 in the east, make a left turn onto Route 667 from the east, just after you pass through the West Bank checkpoint. Stay with 667 for almost the whole length until you reach Mount Shaul on the right.

Opening Hours

24/7

Make It a Day

- Visit the Bet She'an National Park.
- Cool off at the Gan Hashlosha swimming hole.

For the narrative behind this destination, see chapter 16, "Naboth's Vineyard at Jezreel."

Getting There

Set your GPS to "Tel Izrael entrance." If you are using a map, from Afula travel eastward on Route 71, toward Bet She'an. A few kilometers out of town turn right at Navot Junction onto Route 675 west. About one kilometer from the intersection turn right at the sign for Kibbutz Yizrael, and then an immediate right on the service road that goes down to Tel Jezreel. Park your car in the parking lot and follow the handicapped-accessible trail along the hillside, passing an obelisk monument to fallen soldiers on the left. Continue down the path until you reach a covered lookout area. Make yourself comfortable.

Opening Hours

24/7

Make It a Day

- Go skiing, bike riding, or play laser tag at the Ski Gilboa site (www.skigilboa.co.il).
- Hike along the Harod Creek Trail (for more information, see http://www.kkl.org.il/eng/tourism-and-recreation /forests-and-parks/nahal-harod-park.aspx).

For the narrative behind this destination, see chapter 17, "Elisha and the Wealthy Woman at Shunem."

Getting There

Two sites paint the picture of this ancient town. The view from Givat HaMoreh enables a pastoral but distant panorama of the modern village of Sulam. A short ride into the village square enables a hands-on visit to the source of the ancient spring and a modern monument to the Shunammite woman. Both are recommended.

For the panoramic view from Givat HaMoreh: Set your GPS to "12 Seyfan St. Afula." If you are using a map, from Afula drive northeast on Route 65. After you pass HaEmek Hospital on the right, turn right at the next light toward Givat HaMoreh onto Jabotinsky Street, which turns into Connecticut Street. Drive 0.75 kilometers (about ½ mile) and make the first right onto HaIrisim Street. Continue driving and make the fourth right turn onto Seyfan Street.

Park your car near no.12 and take in the view of Sulam village, located near the site of the biblical Shunem. The best view is between buildings 12 and 14. The small park at the end of the street has a comfortable bench to sit and read. If you would like to continue to the village, return to your car and head back toward Afula.

For the spring of Sulam village and the monument to the Shunammite woman: Set your GPS to "Kibbutz Merhavia," which will bring you to Route 7155, just east of Afula. Follow the instructions below. If you are using a map, take Route 71 east from Afula and turn left onto Route 7155, just outside of town (see sign for Sulam Village, 3 kms). If you are coming from 71 west, look for the turnoff just before you reach Afula. Continue straight on 7155 through two traffic circles, passing Kibbutz Merhavya and the dairy cow barn on the right. When you reach a T intersection turn left and then make the first right turn. Continue straight, passing through the entrance of the village, until you reach a traffic circle. If it's a quiet day during midweek, turn right at the circle and drive about three hundred meters (nine hundred feet) until you reach the mosque on the left. Park in the small square. On weekends or later in the day the square is full of cars, so park on the road near the traffic circle and walk the three hundred meters to the mosque.

The spring is located down a few steps between the mosque and Bnai Abu El Abed's restaurant.

To reach the monument to the Shunammite woman, from the spring walk back toward the traffic circle and turn right at the mosque, up a steep hill, about one hundred meters (three hundred feet). On the right you will see a semicircular stone monument a few steps down from the road. Enter through green bars, down the steps to the left.

Opening Hours

24/7. Come during daylight.

Make It a Day

- Drive up to the summit of Mount Tabor to visit the Church of the Transfiguration.

For the narrative behind this destination, see chapter 21, "Megiddo—the Untold Story."

Getting There

Set your GPS to "Tel Megido." If you are using a map: From the Tel Aviv area, take Highway 2 or Route 6 north to Route 65 east toward Afula. At the intersection of Route 66 (see prison on right), turn left onto Route 66 and drive a short distance to the entrance to Tel Megiddo on the left. From Jerusalem: take Highway 1 west to Route 6 north and follow above instructions.

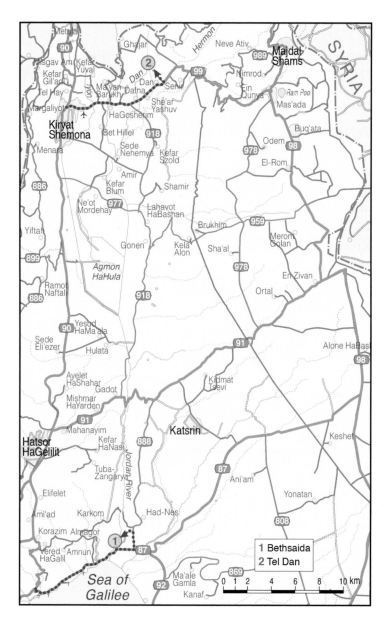

Map 7. Northern Israel

For the narrative behind this destination, see chapter 12, "Absalom's Flight to Geshur."

Getting There

Set your GPS to "Jordan River Park." If you are using a map, coming from Tiberias drive clockwise around Lake Kinneret/the Sea of Galilee, going north along Route 90. When 90 breaks away from the lakeshore at the intersection, turn right and stay with the road as it becomes Route 87 and continues eastward along the lake. Pass Kfar Nahum on the right and then turn left a short distance down the road at Bet Zayda Junction, onto Route 888. Several meters (a few hundred feet) up the road, turn left into the Jordan River Park. After you pass the ticket booth at the entrance, bear left and continue down the road until you reach Tel Bethsaida.

After reading the additional information on the sign at the entrance, turn left (walking away from the restrooms) and proceed up the path that circumvents the tel until you reach the ancient gate. Read the introductory material about the ruins here, then proceed through the gate and follow the path to the left until you reach a lookout point with large, flat stones. Find a spot in the shade here to read the story of Amnon and Tamar.

Opening Hours

April–September, 8 a.m.–6 p.m.; October–March, 8 a.m.–5 p.m. Entrance fee. Restrooms. In addition to the archaeological site, the park offers camping facilities, hiking trails, rafting and fishing on the Jordan, and more. See park rangers at entrance for more information.

Make It a Day

- Go rafting on the Jordan River.
- Visit the Christian holy sites on the western shore of Lake Kinneret: Kfar Nahum, Mensa Christi, Tabgha and the Church of the Beatitudes
- Hike the path between Kfar Nahum and Tabgha.

DESTINATION 2: TEL DAN

For the narrative behind this destination, see chapter 14, "Jereboam in Dan."

Getting There

Set your GPS to "Tel Dan." If you are using a map, from the area of Lake Kinneret drive northward on Route 90 until you reach the town of Kiryat Shemona. Drive straight through the town, and when you reach the other side turn right at the traffic light onto Route 99 (a mall is at the intersection on the right). Continue along 99 about ten kilometers (six miles) until you see a brown sign on the right side of the road pointing to the Tel Dan nature reserve on the left. Turn left and drive down the road into the reserve.

The Tel Dan nature reserve includes hiking paths, archaeological remains, and some of the most beautiful landscapes in Israel. Give yourself plenty of time here to enjoy the reserve and be sure to take a map when you pay your entrance fee. The ideal tour here should cover the high place, the Israelite gate, and the wading pool (if you're up for a cool dip). Any route that takes you to these places is fine; here is one possibility: From the parking lot, walk along the paved trail until the wooden walkway ends at a T. Turn left, following the green arrows on the map and the sign to the Long Trail. You will tiptoe over the stepping-stones in the water, glide through the underbrush, and pass by the main spring of Dan. After the little amphitheater the path climbs slightly uphill and then turns left to the high place. This is where you will read the Jeroboam story. When you reach the high place, find a quiet spot to sit and continue reading.

When you are finished, follow the trail to the Israelite gate, another impressive excavated area of the ancient city. (You will find more information on the gate in the Tel Dan pamphlet.) Exit the ancient gate (not the modern, revolving one that takes you outside the reserve) and turn right, connecting with the ancient Dan trail (the orange arrows on the map). Follow this path back into the reserve until you reach the wading pool. When you're ready to head back. take any of the trails pointing toward the exit.

Opening Hours

April–September, 8 a.m.–5 p.m. (entrance until 4 p.m.); October–March: 8 a.m.–4 p.m. (entrance until 3 p.m.). On Fridays and holiday eves the reserve closes one hour earlier. Telephone: 04-6951579. Entrance fee. Restrooms.

Make It a Day

- Ride the cable car up the Manara Cliff, where you can bike ride, rappel, or hike down.
- Drive up into the Golan Heights to see the Syrian border, pick fruit, visit a chocolate factory, or tour a winery.

BIBLIOGRAPHY

Ahituv, Shmuel. *Joshua with Introduction and Commentary* [in Hebrew]. Tel Aviv: Am Oved, 1995.

Albertz, Ranier. *Israel in Exile: The History and Literature of the Sixth Century BCE*. Atlanta: Society of Biblical Literature, 2003.

Alter, Robert. *The David Story*. New York: W. W. Norton, 1999.

Amit, Yairah. *The Book of Judges: The Art of Editing*. Leiden: Brill, 1999.

———. *In Praise of Editing in the Hebrew Bible: Collected Essays in Retrospect*. Sheffield: Sheffield Phoenix Press, 2012.

———. "A Prophet Tested: Elisha, the Great Woman of Shunem and the Story's Double Message." *Biblical Interpretation* 11, no. 3.4 (2003): 279–94.

———. "The Vineyard of Naboth the Jezreelite." Paper presented at meeting of NAPH, New York, June 24, 2013.

Anderson, Francis I. "The Socio-Juridical Background of the Naboth Incident." *Journal of Biblical Literature* 85, no. 1 (March 1966): 46–57.

Angel, Hayyim. "Hopping between Two Opinions: Understanding the Biblical Portrait of Ahab." *Jewish Bible Quarterly* (January–March 2007): 3–10.

———. "The Literary Significance of the Name Lists in Ezra—Nehemiah." *Jewish Bible Quarterly* 35, no. 3 (2007): 143–52.

Appler, Deborah A. "From Queen to Cuisine: Food Imagery in the Jezebel Narrative." *Semeia* 86 (1999): 55–71.

Arav, Rami, and Richard A. Freud. *Bethsaida: A City by the North Shore of the Sea of Galilee*. Kirksville MO: Truman State University Press, 1995.

Arnow, David. *Creating Lively Passover Seders*. Woodstock VT: Jewish Lights, 2004.

Avioz, Michael. "The Role and Significance of Jebus in Judges 19." *Biblische Zeitschrift* 51, no. 2 (2007): 249–56.

Bach, Alice. "Rereading the Body Politic: Women and Violence in Judges 21." *Biblical Interpretation* 6, no. 1 (1995): 87–107.

Bakon, Shimon. "Elisha the Prophet." *Jewish Bible Quarterly* 29, no. 4 (2001): 242–48.

———. "Zedekiah: Last King of Judah." *Jewish Bible Quarterly* (April–June 2008): 93–101.

Baly, Denis. *A Geographical Companion to the Bible*. New York: McGraw Hill, 1963.

Bar Efrat, Shimon. *Narrative Art in the Bible*. Decatur GA: Almond Press, 1989.

Barker, Margaret. "Hezekiah's Boil." *Journal for the Study of the Old Testament* 95 (2001): 31–42.

Ben Nahum, Yonathan. "What Ailed the Son of Kish?" *Jewish Bible Quarterly* 19, no. 4 (1991): 244–49.

Berlin, Adele, and Marc Zvi Brettler, eds. *The Jewish Study Bible*. Jewish Publication Society Tanakh translation. Oxford: Oxford University Press, 2004.

Berlyn, P. J. "Divided They Stand: The United Monarchy Split in Two." *Jewish Bible Quarterly* (October–December 1999): 211–21.

Bird, Phyllis A. "Prostitution in the Social World and the Religious Rhetoric of Ancient Israel." In *Prostitutes and Courtesans in the Ancient World*, edited by C. Faraone and L. McClure, 40–58. Madison: University of Wisconsin Press, 2006.

Blenkinsopp, Joseph. *Ezra-Nehemiah—A Commentary*. Philadelphia: Westminster Press, 1988.

———. "Miracles: Elisha and Hanina Ben Dosa." In *Miracles in Jewish and Christian Antiquity*, edited by John C. Cavadini, 57–82. Notre Dame IN: Notre Dame University Press, 1999.

Bohmbach, Karla. "Conventions/Contraventions: The Meaning of Public and Private for the Judges 19 Concubine." *Journal for the Study of Old Testament* 83 (1999): 83–98.

Borowski, Oded. "Hezekiah's Reforms and the Revolt against Syria." *Biblical Archaeologist* 58, no. 3 (1995): 148–55.

Bronner, Leah. *The Stories of Elijah and Elisha as Polemics against Baal Worship*. Leiden: Brill, 1968.

Browner, Leah. *Biblical Personalities and Archaeology*. Jerusalem: Keter, 1974.

Bustanai, Oded, and Michael Kaufman, eds. *2 Kings* [in Hebrew]. The World of the Bible. Tel Aviv: Davidson, 1994.

Coggins, R. J. *The Books of Ezra and Nehemiah*. Cambridge Bible Commentary. Edited by P. R Ackroyd, A. R. C. Leaney, and J. W. Parker. Cambridge: Cambridge University Press, 1976.

Cohen, Kenneth I. "King Saul—A Bungler from the Beginning." *Bible Review* (October 1994): 34–39, 56–57.

Cohen, Malcolm. "The Transparency of King Saul." *European Judaism* (Spring 2006): 106–13.

Cohen, Marcia I. *Identifying and Combating Juvenile Prostitution: A Manual for Action*. Washington DC: National Association of Counties Research, 1982.

Cohon, Beryl T. *The Prophets*. New York: Bloch, 1960.

Cross, Frank Moore. *From Epic to Canon*. Baltimore: Johns Hopkins University Press, 1998.

———. "A Response to Zakovitch's 'Successful Failure of Israelite Intelligence.'" In *Text and Tradition*, edited by Susan Niditch, 75–98. Atlanta: Scholars Press, 1990.

Donner, Herbert. "The Separate States of Israel and Judah." In *Israelite and Judaean History*, edited by John H. Hayes and J. Maxwell Miller, Old Testament Library, 399–408. London: SCM Press; Philadelphia: Westminster Press, 1977.

Erlich, Carl S. "Joshua, Judaism and Genocide." Vol. 1 of *Jewish Studies at the Turn of the 20th Century*, edited by Judit Borras and Angel Saenz-Badillas, 117–24. Leiden: Brill, 1999.

Exum, Cheryl. *Fragmented Women: Feminist (Sub)Versions of Biblical Narratives*. Journal for the Study of the Old Testament, Supplement Series, 163. The Library of Hebrew Bible/Old Testament Studies. London: Continuum, 1997.

Feldman, Louis H. "Josephus's Portrait of Hezekiah." *Journal of Biblical Literature* 111, no. 4 (1992): 597–610.

Finklestein, Israel. "Jerusalem in the Persian (and Early Hellenistic) Period and the Wall of Nehemiah." *Journal for the Study of the Old Testament* 32, no. 4 (2008): 501–20

Finklestein, Israel, and Neil Asher Silberman. *The Bible Unearthed: Archaeology's New Vision of Ancient Israel and the Origin of Israel's Sacred Texts*. New York: Free Press, 2001.

———. "Temple and Dynasty: Hezekiah, the Remaking of Judah and the Rise of the Pan-Israelite Ideology." *Journal for the Study of the Old Testament* 30, no. 3 (2006): 259–85.

Fokkelman, Jan P. "Saul and David—Crossed Fates." *Bible Review* (June 1989): 20–32.

Friedman, Richard Elliot. *Who Wrote the Bible?* New York: Harper Collins, 1997.

Frymer-Kensky, Tikva. "Reading Rahab." In *Tehillah L'Moshe: Biblical and Judaic Studies in Honor of Moshe Greenberg*, edited by M. Greenberg, M. Cogan, B. Eichler, and J. Tigay, 57–67. Winona Lake IN: Eisenbrauns, 1997.

———. *Reading the Women of the Bible.* New York: Schocken Books, 2002.

Gaines, Janet Howe "How Bad Was Jezebel?" *Bible Review* (October 2000): 13–23.

Gale, General Sir Richard. *Great Battles of Biblical History.* New York: John Day, 1970.

Garsiel, Moshe. "The Valley of Elah Battle and the Duel of David with Goliath: Between History and Artistic Theological Historiography. In *Homeland and Exile*, edited by Gershon Galil, Mark Geller, and Alan Millard, 391–426. Leiden: Brill, 2009.

Ginsbury, Philip, and Raphael Cutler. *The Phases of Jewish History.* Jerusalem: Devora, 2005.

Ginzberg, Louis. *The Legends of the Jews.* Philadelphia: Jewish Publication Society of America, 1968.

Goldenberg, Robert. *The Origins of Judaism from Canaan to the Rise of Islam.* Cambridge: Cambridge University Press, 2007.

Goodman, Hannah Grad. *The Story of Prophecy.* New York: Behrman House, 1965.

Gordon, Cyrus H. *The World of the Old Testament.* Garden City NY: Doubleday, 1958.

Grabbe, Lester, ed. Introduction to *"Like a Bird in a Cage": The Invasion of Sennacherib in 701 BCE.* JSOT Supplement Series 363. London: Sheffield Academic Press, 2003.

Gravett, Sandie. "Regarding 'Rape' in the Hebrew Bible: A Consideration in Language." *Journal for the Study of the Old Testament* (March 2004): 279–99.

Grayzel, Solomon. *A History of the Jews*. Philadelphia: Jewish Publication Society of America, 1968.

Grossman, David. *Lion's Honey: The Myth of Samson*. Edinburgh: Canongate Books, 2006.

Hadas-Lebel, Mireille. "Hezekiah as King Messiah: Traces of an Early Jewish-Christian Polemic in Tannaitic Tradition." In *Jewish Studies at the Turn of the 20th Century*, edited by Judit Targarona Borras and Angel Saenz-Badillos, 1:275–81. Leiden: Brill, 1999.

Hamilton, Edith. *Spokesmen for God: The Great Teachers of the Old Testament*. New York: W. W. Norton, 1949.

Harel, Menashe. *Journeys and Battles in the Land of Israel in Ancient Times* [in Hebrew]. Reut: Effie Meltzer, 2002.

———. "Sun, Stand Still over Gibeon, and You, Moon, over the Valley of Aijalon" [in Hebrew]. *Land and Nature* 8, no. 2 (May 1960): 408–11 (in Hebrew).

HaReuveni, Noga. *Desert and Shepherd in Our Biblical Heritage*. Kiryat Ono: Neot Kedumim, 1991.

———. *Nature in Our Biblical Heritage*. Kiryat Ono: Neot Kedumim, 1980.

Hauser, Alan T., and Russell Gregory. *From Carmel to Horeb—Elijah in Crisis*. Sheffield: Almond Press, 1990.

Hepner, Gershon. "Three's a Crowd in Shunem: Elisha's Misconduct with the Shunammite Reflects a Polemic against Prophetism." *Zeitschrift für die alttestamentliche Wissenschaft* 122, no. 4 (2010): 387–400.

Herzog, Chaim, and Mordechai Gichon. *Battles of the Bible*. Jerusalem: Edanim, Yediot Aharonot, 1981.

Hoffman, Yair, ed. *The Israeli Encyclopedia of the Bible*. Givatayim: Masada, 1988.

Holt, Elise K. ". . . Urged on by His Wife Jezebel: A Literary Reading of I Kings 18 in Context." *Scandinavian Journal of the Old Testament* (1995): 83–96

Hudson, Don Michael. "Living in a Land of Epithets: Anonymity in Judges 19–21." *Journal for the Study of Old Testament* 62 (1994): 49–66.

Karmon, Yehuda. "Sun, Stand Still over Gibeon: A Geographic and Historic Journey" [in Hebrew]. *Ariel* (July 1985): 69–76.

King, Philip. "David Defeats Goliath." In *Up to the Gates of Ekron: Essays on the Archaeology and History of the Eastern Mediterranean in Honor of Seymour Gitin*, edited by S. W. Crawford, A. Ben-tor, J. P. Dessel, W. G. Dever, A. Mazar, and J. Aviram, 350–57. Jerusalem: Albright Institute of Research and Israel Exploration Society, 2007.

Klein, Lillian R. *The Triumph of Irony in the Book of Judges*. Sheffield: Almond Press, 1988.

Knohl, Israel. *The Divine Symphony: The Bible's Many Voices*. Philadelphia: Jewish Publication Society, 2003.

Koch, Klaus, *The Prophets*. Vol. 2, *The Babylonian and Persian Periods*. Philadelphia: Fortress Press, 1984.

Kruger, Hennie. "Sun and Moon Marking Time: A Cursory Survey of Exegetical Possibilities in Joshua 10:9–14." *Journal of Northwest Semitic Languages* 26, no. 1 (2000):137–52.

Kruger, Paul. "Ahab's 'Slowly' Walking About: Another Look at I Kings 21:27." *Journal of Northwest Semitic Languages* 29, no. 2 (2003): 133–42.

Kugel, James. *How to Read the Bible*. New York: Free Press, 2007.

Levine, Lee I. *The Ancient Synagogue: The First Thousand Years*. New Haven CT: Yale University Press, 2005.

———. *The Synagogue of Late Antiquity*. Philadelphia: American School of Oriental Research, 1987.

Levine, Nachman. "Twice as Much of Your Spirit: Pattern, Parallel and Paronomasia in the Miracles of Elijah and Elisha." *Journal for the Study of Old Testament* 85 (1999): 25–46.

Lipschits, Oded. *The Fall and Rise of Jerusalem*. Winona Lake IN: Eisenbrauns, 2005.

Long, Burke O. "The Shunammite Woman—In the Shadow of the Prophet?" *Bible Review* (February 1991): 12–19.

Ludwig, Dean C., and Clinton O. Longenecker. "The Bathsheba Syndrome: The Ethical Failure of Successful Leaders." *Journal of Business Ethics* 12 (1993): 265–73.

Luria, D. Z. "For the Statutes of Omri Are Kept . . . (Micah 6:16)." *Jewish Bible Quarterly* 18, no. 2 (1989–90): 69–73.

Macalister, R. A. S. *The Philistines: Their History and Civilization*. London: Humphrey, 1913.

Maier, Paul L. *Josephus: The Essential Writings*. Grand Rapids MI: Kregel, 1988.

Malamat, Abraham. *History of Biblical Israel: Major Problems and Minor Issues*. Leiden: Brill, 2001.

McKenzie, John L. *The World of the Judges*. London: Geoffrey Chapman, 1967.

McKenzie, Steven L. *King David: A Biography*. New York: Oxford University Press, 2000.

———. "Saul in the Deuteronomistic History." In *Saul in Story and Tradition*, edited by Carl S. Erlich and Marsha C. White, 59-70. Tubingen: Mohr Siebeck, 2006.

Mehlman, Bernard. "Rahab as a Model of Human Redemption." In *Open Thou Mine Eyes: Essays on Aggadah and Judaica*, 193-207. Hoboken NJ: KTAV, 1992.

Merecz, Robert T. "Jezebel's Oath." *Biblica* 90, no. 2 (2009): 257-59.

"Messiah." In *The Encyclopedia of Judaism*. New York: Macmillan; London: Collier Macmillan, 1989.

Miller, J. M. "The Fall of the House of Ahab." *Vetus Testamentum* 17 (1967): 307-24.

Miller, J. Maxwell, and John H. Hayes. *A History of Ancient Israel and Judah*. Louisville: Westminster John Knox Press, 1986.

Mills, Mary E. *Joshua to Kings: History, Story, Theology*. London: T&T Clark, 2006.

Mitchell, Gordon. *Together in the Land: A Reading of the Book of Joshua*. Sheffield: Sheffield Academic Press, 1993.

Mobley, Gregory. "Glimpses of the Heroic Saul." In *Saul in Story and Tradition*, edited by Carl S. Erlich and Marsha C. White, 80-87. Tubingen: Mohr Siebeck, 2006.

Naaman, Nadav. "Naboth's Vineyard and the Foundation of Jezreel." *Journal for the Study of Old Testament* 33, no. 2 (2008): 197-218.

Nehorai, Michael. "Sun, Stand Still over Gibeon, and You, Moon, over the Valley of Aijalon" [in Hebrew]. *Da'at* 32-33, (1994): 97-101.

Newman, Murray L. "Rahab and the Conquest." In *Understanding the Word: Essays in Honor of Bernhard W. Anderson*, edited by James T. Britter, Edward W. Conrad, and Ben C. Ollenburger, 167–81. Sheffield: JSOT Press, 1985.

Niditch, Susan. "The 'Sodomite' Theme in Judges 19–21: Family, Community and Social Disintegration." *Catholic Bible Quarterly* 44, no. 3 (1982): 365–78.

Parmiter, Geoffrey de C. *King David*. London: Arthur Barker, 1960.

Polzin, Robert. *Samuel and the Deuteronomist: A Literary Study of the Deuteronomic History; part 2, 1 Samuel*. San Francisco: Harper and Row, 1989.

"Prostitution." In *Dictionary of Biblical Imagery*. Downers Grove IL: InterVarsity, 1998.

Prouser, Ora Horn. "Suited to the Throne: The Symbolic Use of Clothing in the David and Saul Narratives." *Journal for the Study of Old Testament* 71 (1996): 27–37.

Pruin, Dagmar. "What Is in a Text? Searching for Jezebel." In *Ahab Agonistes: The Rise and Fall of the Omride Dynasty*, edited by Lester L. Grabbe, 208–35. London: T&T Clark, 2007.

Pruzansky, Rabbi Steven. *A Prophet for Today: Contemporary Lessons from the Book of Yehoshua*. Jerusalem: Gefen, 2006.

Raban, Avner, and Robert R. Stieglitz. "The Sea Peoples and Their Contributions to Civilization." *Biblical Archaeological Review* (November/December 1991): 34–41.

Reis, Pamela Tumarkin. "The Levite's Concubine: New Light on a Dark Story." *Scandinavian Journal of the Old Testament* 20, no.1 (2006): 125–46.

Reiss, Moshe. "Elijah the Zealot: A Foil to Moses." *Jewish Bible Quarterly* (July–Sept 2004): 174–80.

Rendsburg, Gary A. "The Mock of Baal in I Kings 18:27." *Catholic Bible Quarterly* 50, no. 3 (July 1988): 414–17.

Renteria, Tamis Hoover. "The Elijah/Elisha Stories: A Sociocultural Analysis of Prophets and People in Ninth-Century BCE Israel." In *Elijah and Elisha in Socioliterary Perspective,* edited by Robert B. Coole, 75–126. Atlanta: Scholars Press, 1992.

Robinson, Bernard P. "Rahav of Canaan and Israel." *Scandinavian Journal of the Old Testament* 23, no. 2 (2009): 257–73.

Rofe, Alexander. "The Vineyard and Naboth: the Origin and Message of the Story." *Vetus Testamentum* 38, no. 1 (1988): 89–104.

Roman, Yadin. *The Bethsaida Pilgrim's Companion*. Tel Aviv: ERETZ Magazine, 1999.

Roncace, Mark. "Elisha and the Woman of Shunem: 2 Kings 4:8–37 and 8:1–6 Read in Conjunction." *Journal for the Study of Old Testament* 91 (2000): 109–127.

Sawyer, John F. A. "Joshua 10:12–14 and the Solar Eclipse of 30 Sept 1131 BC." *Palestine Exploration Quarterly* 104 (1972): 139–46.

Schniedewind, William. "History and Interpretation: The Religion of Ahab and Manasseh in the Book of Kings." *Catholic Bible Quarterly* 1993: 649–61.

Schwartz, Regina. "Adultery in the House of David." In *Women in the Hebrew Bible*, edited by Alice Bach, 343–47. London: Routledge, 1999.

Shields, Mary E. "Subverting a Man of God, Elevating a Woman: Role and Power Reversals in 2 Kings 4." *Journal for the Study of Old Testament* 58 (1993): 59–69.

Sisson, Jonathan Paige. "Jeremiah and the Jerusalem Concept of Peace." *Journal of Biblical Literature* 105, no. 3 (1986): 429–42.

Soggin, J. Alberto. *An Introduction to the History of Israel and Judah*. London: SCM Press, 1993.

Sparks, Kenton L. *Ethnicity and Identity in Ancient Israel*. Winona Lake IN: Eisenbrauns, 1998.

Stipp, Herman-Josef. "Zedekiah in the Book of Jeremiah: On the Formation of a Biblical Character." *Catholic Bible Quarterly* (October 1996): 627–48.

Stone, Ken. "Gender and Homosexuality in Judges 19: Subject-Honor, Object-Shame?" *Journal for the Study of Old Testament* 67 (1995): 87–107.

Toews, Wesley I. *Monarchy and Religious Institution in Israel under Jeroboam I*. Atlanta: Scholars Press, 1993.

Tracy, Steven R. *Mending the Soul: Understanding and Healing Abuse*. Grand Rapids MI: Zondervan, 2005.

Trible, Phyllis. "Exegesis for Storytellers and Other Strangers." *Journal of Biblical Literature* 114, no. 1 (1995): 3–19.

Van der Kooij, A. "The Story of Hezekiah and Sennacherib (2 Kings 18–19)." In *Past, Present, Future: The Deuteronomic History and the Prophets*, edited by Johannes C. De Moor and Harry F. Van Rooy, 107–19. Leiden: Brill, 2000.

Vermaak, P. A. "The Prowess of the Benjaminites." *Jewish Bible Quarterly* (April 1994): 73–84.

Walton, John H. "Joshua 10:12–15 and Mesopotamian Celestial Omen Texts." In *Faith, Tradition and History*, edited by A. R. Millard, J. K. Hoffmeier, and D. W. Baker, 181–90. Winona Lake IN: Eisenbrauns, 1994.

Webb, Barry G. *The Book of the Judges: An Integrated Reading.* Worcester, England: Sheffield Academic Press, 1987.

Weiner, Aharon. *The Prophet Elijah in the Development of Judaism: A Depth-Psychological Study.* Littman Library of Jewish Civilization. London: Routledge and K. Paul, 1984.

Whitley, Charles Francis. *The Exilic Age.* London: Longmans, Green, 1957.

Wong, Gregory T. K. "Gideon: A New Moses?" In *Reflection and Refraction*, edited by R. Rezetko, Timothy H. Lim, and W. Brian Aucker, 529–45. Leiden: Brill, 2007.

Yadin, Yigael. *The Art of Warfare in Biblical Lands* [in Hebrew]. Vol. 2. Jerusalem-Ramat Gan: International, 1963.

Zakovitch, Yair. *David: From Shepherd to Messiah* [in Hebrew]. Jerusalem: Yad Yitzhak Ben Zvi, 1995.

———. "Humor and Theology or the Successful Failure of Israelite Intelligence: A Literary-Folkloric Approach to Joshua 2." In *Text and Tradition*, edited by Susan Niditch, 75–98. Atlanta: Scholars Press, 1990.

———. "The Tale of Naboth's Vineyard (I Kings 21)." In *The Bible from Within*, by Meir Weiss, 379–405. Jerusalem: Magnes Press of the Hebrew University, 1984.

Zlotnick, Helena. "From Jezebel to Esther: Fashioning Images of Queenship in the Hebrew Bible." *Biblica* 82, no. 4 (2001): 477–95.